Degrowth, Depth and Hope in Sustainable Business

This book takes degrowth theorising in the direction of honouring collaboration, creating new dialogues and emphasising growth and human capacities.

Traditionally, degrowth theorising has focussed on reduction and non-growth. While the ecological concerns of degrowth scholarship are felt acutely by many, the suggestion of "less" can be experienced as undesirable, going against who we are as humans, and even be false in some industries and spaces. Indeed, for a degrowth society to come into being, unprecedented (though not materialistic) growth is needed. This book unpicks the business and sustainability framework rooted in degrowth scholarship and proposes a gentler approach to business for a sustainable society living harmoniously with nature. Drawing on case studies from Finland, Sweden and Denmark, Iana Nesterova reflects on how degrowth manifests in imperfect and nuanced ways and examines the ways in which businesses navigate creatively and cautiously challenging socio-economic landscapes, and why they do this. She puts forward a new framework for growth within degrowth, centred around humanism and hope, which celebrates empathy, care, solidarity and connectedness with human and non-human others and nature.

Presenting an empowering and liberating view on sustainable business, this book will be of great interest to students and scholars of business ethics, ecological economics, business organisation and management.

Iana Nesterova is a researcher at Roskilde University, Denmark, and a long-term practitioner of voluntary simplicity. Her research on business and degrowth transformations has been published in the leading journals in the field of sustainable organisations, including *Ecological Economics* and *Journal of Cleaner Production and Futures*.

Routledge Research in Sustainability and Business

The Role of Business in Global Sustainability Transformations
Edited by Dalia D'Amato, Anne Toppinen and Robert Kozak

Understanding Sustainability Performance *in* Business Organizations
Implications for the Sustainability Service Industry
Jean-Pierre Imbrogiano

Comparative CSR and Sustainability
New Accounting for Social Consequences
Edited by Gabriel Donleavy and Carlos Noronha

Environmental Disclosure
Critical Issues and New Trends
Luigi Lepore and Sabrina Pisano

Sustainable Football
Environmental Management in Practice
Luca Marrucci, Tiberio Daddi and Fabio Iraldo

Circular Economy in the European Union
Organisational Practice and Future Directions in Germany, Poland and Spain
Dagmara Lewicka, Joanna Zarębska, Roman Batko, Maciej Woźniak, Dariusz Cichoń, Beata Tarczydło, Monika Pec

Degrowth, Depth and Hope in Sustainable Business
Reflections from Denmark, Finland and Sweden
Iana Nesterova

For more information about this series, please visit: www.routledge.com/Routledge-Research-in-Sustainability-and-Business/book-series/RRSB

Degrowth, Depth and Hope in Sustainable Business

Reflections from Denmark, Finland and Sweden

Iana Nesterova

Routledge
Taylor & Francis Group
LONDON AND NEW YORK

earthscan
from Routledge

Designed cover image: © Getty Images

First published 2025
by Routledge
4 Park Square, Milton Park, Abingdon, Oxon OX14 4RN

and by Routledge
605 Third Avenue, New York, NY 10158

Routledge is an imprint of the Taylor & Francis Group, an informa business

British Library Cataloguing-in-Publication Data
A catalogue record for this book is available from the British Library

ISBN: 978-1-032-58957-2 (hbk)
ISBN: 978-1-032-58958-9 (pbk)
ISBN: 978-1-003-45230-0 (ebk)

DOI: 10.4324/ 9781003452300

Typeset in Times New Roman
by codeMantra

Dedication: to Mother Nature

Contents

Tables

Acknowledgements

I want to express my gratitude to non-human beings who were with me on this journey, especially the stone from northern Sweden that lived with me in Sweden, Finland and Denmark. I am also grateful to my fellow humans from Routledge, Annabelle and Jyotsna, to the businesspersons in Denmark, Finland and Sweden from whom I learned a lot, and to my partner HBH.

1 Introduction

This book has been crystallising in my mind for many years. It is a space where I gather all my thoughts, ideas and contemplations on the link between degrowth and business that I have been reflecting on and writing about since 2016 when I started my PhD on this topic. My PhD thesis was not part of any research project, so it was my own space to think freely. In my PhD, I tried to answer the question of what business should be like for a degrowth society to be possible. This question has been on my mind for many years, so this topic is genuinely close to my heart. Oftentimes my fellow humans ask me why I decided to write about degrowth and business. I want to explain it in more detail here, because when I write an academic article, unfortunately the most acceptable format is still impersonal. And the mode of communication is impersonal too. Unlike an academic article, this book is a very personal project. In fact, it became increasingly more personal as I was writing it.

I always wanted to be in academia, in a space where I could read freely and contemplate a lot as part of my job. When I was younger, I somewhat naively thought that academia was a space outside capitalism, that by going into academia I would be in a space guided by a different, alternative set of values such as curiosity, care, collegiality and creativity. At universities, I studied mainstream economics and business. Studying these subjects was not something I chose myself. Rather, my family chose it for me when I was still at school, in my early teenage years. Personally, I wanted to study psychology, and psychoanalysis in particular, as I have always been interested in individual humans, their journeys, experiences and stories rather than in social systems. My mother and stepfather, both of whom worked closely with fellow humans, thought that studying economics is a safer option than studying something that would lead me to work with different humans, their paths, challenges and struggles, too. At the first university where I studied, mainstream economics and business were supplemented by a plurality of other subjects such as sociology, psychology, philosophy and ecology. That large constellation of sciences and fields of knowledge was meant to turn young persons into so-called highly educated individuals. Yet, the links between mainstream economics and other subjects were never discussed. It felt strange to study mainstream microeconomics alongside psychology, as the presentation of who we, humans, are, were so different. During the same course I heard that humans are selfish, greedy, detached from their life's journeys, childhood experiences, emotions and feelings, and that

DOI: 10.4324/ 9781003452300-1

our past shapes at least to some extent our mode of relating with the world. There were lectures and seminars on microeconomics, humans maximising utility and firms maximising their profits. At the same time, there were lectures on Kant, Freud and Jung. The first few years of the university were so overwhelming in terms of quantity and fragmentation of information that was given to the students, that I do not remember much of what was taught. But being exposed to this enormous constellation of knowledges made me think that the same events, entities and phenomena can be seen from so many different perspectives. Somehow, that education, based on the quantity of information and memorising, contributed to thinking critically and freely.

I was born in a large city, but due to my stepfather's job, I lived in a remote, rural area most of my childhood, where I developed close connection with nature, non-humans and the cosmos. It feels that when one is surrounded by magical nature, objects created by human beings pale in comparison. By surrounded I do not mean that nature is close enough or reachable by bike or public transport. What I mean is nature being immediately there, at one's doorstep. Our garden merged with fields and bodies of water. To be with nature, I did not need to travel anywhere. I could simply walk outside. At the same time, to be with fellow humans, in a very small town, I would have to take a long walk or cycle. When I was growing up, I was not interested in plastic toys, or toys made from sustainable materials for that matter. Where I was growing up, there were many other things and beings that were infinitely more interesting. At times, I would play with my grandmother's jewellery or my mother's clothes, but more often I played in fields, with my dog and with my cat. I was not brought up, convinced or educated to love nature or explained why and how nature should be loved, what it means in practice. This love arose and manifested naturally, spontaneously and organically. Growing up in a remote rural area meant that I could observe around me where things that we used daily came from. Around me I saw how long it takes for corn, hemp and potatoes to grow. I saw how a tree becomes a table or a chair. I saw how honey is made, how chicks hatch from eggs and how their life unfolds. I always felt the need to live my life in a way that aligned with nature. While I never felt bad or felt shame about taking from nature what it provided readily and nearly, such as herbs, nuts, roots, mushrooms, berries, sap or flowers, I did not feel comfortable with consuming many human-made objects. Eventually I became conscious of my practice of voluntary simplicity. I learned this term only much later in my life. In my childhood and teenage years, I did not have an appropriate vocabulary to describe my feelings towards nature or my practice.

At some point, my education in economics and business studies and my worldview, manifested in the practices of voluntary simplicity, clashed. As I was progressing on my academic journey, unfortunately far away from the magical rural area where I lived for many years, I was contemplating how I could live even more ecologically, how I could manifest love towards nature in my everyday life. I started to experiment with different modes of practising consumption and relating with beings and objects, such as veganism, extreme minimalism and zero-waste.

During my master's studies, I realised that apart from mainstream economics, there are many other schools of thought within economics. Initially, behavioural economics caught my attention. In comparison to mainstream economics, it felt new, interdisciplinary and liberating. Later, I saw various issues with this school of thought, but it was an academic space where at least human feelings and emotions were acknowledged. Then I started to read ecological economics literature. This is where I felt more at home, especially within the space of social ecological economics (Spash, 2011, 2012). Ecological economics eventually led me to degrowth. At around the same time, an opportunity arose to do a PhD on a topic related broadly to sustainability and business. So, I stepped on that path. I was based in a business school. In 2016, there was very little about degrowth and business, or degrowth and the microeconomic level in general. There was much discussion of a general vision of a degrowth society and why degrowth is necessary, but not so much discussion of practices and what degrowth actually meant for different spaces and social entities. Being based in a business school and having studied economics and business for some years prior to my PhD, I began to wonder what business should be like for a degrowth society to be possible. I dedicated my PhD and the years after that to contemplating this question. And this is where I am as I am writing these words. I am still contemplating this question, though I feel that I've come a long way since I first had an internal dialogue, a dialogue with myself, on this topic. I am glad that I decided to write this book a few years after I finished my PhD. I feel that my thoughts matured, and I can offer to my fellow humans something that is a result of a longer and deeper contemplation. I also feel that as I am maturing as an academic, I am feeling much more comfortable with expressing myself more authentically and with being vulnerable. I feel comfortable with talking about loose ends, new and difficult questions, returning to old questions and revisiting contentious topics again and again. I feel comfortable with saying that I do not know something, that I do not understand something yet or that I am in two minds about something. I feel more comfortable with saying that I have changed my mind or was wrong at some point in the past. At the very beginning of my PhD journey, I thought that it was important to provide concrete or even final answers. But now I believe that other things are more important. They are, for example, asking better questions, coming up with better ideas, embracing own vulnerability, honouring the vulnerability of fellow beings, manifesting one's worldview in one's everyday practices and being honest about how one's imperfect practice unfolds.

At times, my fellow humans ask me what it felt like to do a PhD on degrowth in a business school in England. I have conflicting feelings about it. Once a fellow human in academia said that doing a PhD about degrowth was not science, it was activism and that my work would never be published in academic journals. I had an inner feeling that it would be published, and I decided to trust that feeling. What helped me at that point, as in so many other situations in academia, was my political position. I come from an anarchist perspective. The viewpoint of that fellow human was just a viewpoint of one human being amongst many. I listened to my intuition and felt that continuing on the path of researching degrowth was important for my authenticity, for others who could benefit from living in a genuinely sustainable society and for nature and non-human beings. Despite some negative and discouraging comments, I enjoyed those years of contemplation. It was an intense period of deep inner growth for me, as finally my research and my ecological practice in my everyday life aligned. I dedicated my PhD thesis, as well as my whole life's work, to Mother Nature. To me, there is no separation between research and activism, between my life and research. At some points in my life, it felt vulnerable to say this, but it is no more so.

Writing simply

Something that has always been very important to me is writing simply. This is not to say that I've always been good at it, but I try. There is absolutely no need to mystify science and philosophy. Using obscure language that excludes many fellow humans from understanding a book or an article feels narcissistic and hierarchical. If we want a degrowth society to come into being, i.e., to be brought into being collectively by many humans from all walks of life, surely it is essential to make our so-called scientific writing as clear as possible for everyone. Anything in science and philosophy can be explained in a simple manner. This is not to say that issues we are dealing with and trying to understand are simple, trivial and easy to resolve. In reality, they are the opposite of this. But adding to already complex and messy issues the issue of deciphering someone's writing is not helpful. Talking about complex issues in a simple way increases participation. And if anyone can understand the issue, they can dive deeper into contemplating this issue. The main and general issue I am talking about is severe and heartbreaking unsustainability. Together with it come other issues of understanding the causes and solutions in different domains of society. At times, I caught myself working on an academic article and at the same time responding to a text message or an email from a friend, a student, a businessperson or a colleague. It was so interesting to see the difference between the forms my expressions assumed. I contemplate it often, and it makes very little sense to me to write my academic contributions differently to how I write a text message or an email to a fellow human being. If I wrote my text message in a pretentious academic way, it would feel detached, unnecessarily complicated, perhaps even convoluted, obscure and unkind. It would not feel gentle, caring and humane. Why should I pursue that in my academic writing? Perhaps to provide a sense of our knowledge being final and an illusion of us being absolutely confident in what we discover in our research. But in the social sciences, it is not this way. At least not from a critical realist perspective that I feel at home with. Our knowledge is always subject to critique. It is messy. The way academic articles are structured (introduction, literature review, materials and methods, findings discussion, conclusions) provides a false sense of security. At the very least I would like to see a section about emotions and feelings that accompany the writing of every academic article. I would like to see a section about doubts, mistakes, nuances and loose ends.

Since the start of my PhD, I have been working with businesses who were and still are on various sustainability paths. Much of what I learned is from talking to them rather than from academic books and papers, though naturally I also learned from books and papers and found inspiration in them. With those businesspersons who came from all kinds of walks of life, we would often engage in long discussions on sustainability, degrowth, personal practices of consumers, social systems and what businesses could do or are doing currently. Those businesspersons were genuinely curious. I want to write in a way that all those businesspersons can understand. I want this book to be easy to read, something I would want to read myself, even if I came from a different discipline and even if English was not my primary language.

Position

The philosophical position one adopts is, unfortunately, not always explicitly stated. Here I refer to both one's worldview and philosophy of science perspective. But these positions are always implied. So, the reader often needs to read between the lines and look for specific language to understand the author's position. In fact, both myself and fellow academics who teach philosophy of science offer the following exercise to our students. We ask them to read a paper of their choice or some paper we select. And then we ask them to discuss the authors' philosophy of science perspective. It feels important to outline explicitly the constellation of positions I come from, so my readers, including students, do not have to decipher my writing. It is important because these positions guide my thinking, my writing, how I relate with various literatures and my own different roles in society and in nature. Perhaps if another fellow human wanted to contemplate the same topic I am discussing in this book, they would approach it completely differently. Some could survey the businesses. Others would approach the subject theoretically. Perhaps many would not write in a personal way that I am adopting in this book and my other works. Perhaps many would not talk about their own experiences and life. But every human being is unique, and the way we relate with the world and its different aspects also manifests in the way we relate with science.

In terms of philosophy of science, I adopt a critical realist perspective. Critical realism (see Buch-Hansen and Nielsen, 2020) was initiated and originally developed by Roy Bhaskar and then many other thinkers such as Margaret Archer and Tony Lawson. Critical realism combines a realist ontology (theory of being), relativist epistemology (theory of knowledge) and explicit axiology (theory of value). Realist ontology means that critical realists believe that objective reality exists, though it is stratified and emergent. For example, biological systems, processes, phenomena and events arise from the chemical level of reality. But they cannot be reduced to it. The social and psychological systems, processes, phenomena, events and so on arise from the biological level of reality but cannot be reduced to biology. Not everything that exists can be observed readily or immediately. Another important critical realist insight into ontology is that the physical and social realities are different. This has implications for how we study them. Critical realism is a philosophy of science specifically underlabouring for the social sciences, which study social reality. Social reality is seen as open, ever unfolding, and characterised by tendencies rather than laws of nature. For example, capitalism is not seen as a law of nature. Relativist epistemology means that there exist different knowledges about the same reality, and knowledge is always socially constructed. It is always subject to critique. It is never perfect or final. This epistemological position is very humble. It acknowledges diverse knowledges such as indigenous and lay knowledges (Spash, 2012). At times, when philosophy of science is taught, axiology is overlooked. Perhaps this is because for a long time social sciences have tried to rid themselves of values rather than embrace and explicate them. But critical realist approach to axiology is different and liberating and valuable, in my view. Critical realism does not claim that the knowledge we produce is perfectly objective, value-free and detached from ourselves. It claims that scientific efforts should in fact be normative. They should have human emancipation at their core. In other words, we do science for something. We do it to make the world a better place.

I met critical realism for the first time when I was contemplating my doctoral research and philosophy of science in relation to it. Critical realism as a philosophy of science perspective felt as liberating to me as did ecological economics as a science when I first met it. When I was studying mainstream economics and business, positivism was suggested as *the* acceptable philosophy of science perspective. Positivism felt naïve and constraining, just like mainstream economics. There was no space within positivist research for feelings, emotions, bodily experiences, activism, normativity and creative methods such as autoethnography, stories, diaries, art and poetry. Critical realism, in my view and experience, is a beautiful alternative to positivism. My favourite moment in critical realism is the least popular one within this philosophy of science. It is referred to as the spiritual turn. This is when Bhaskar developed his philosophy of metareality (Bhaskar, 2012). This philosophy postulates oneness, i.e., it proposes that everything is interrelated with everything else. While for my more formal research purposes basic critical realism was useful, my heart and mind connected to the philosophy of metareality on some deeper, intuitive level.

However, I never felt the need to commit to only one perspective or only one representation of some perspective religiously, especially considering that critical realism is living and ever developing. That is to say, critical realism is constantly evolving and is being advanced by many fellow humans. While critical realism is a philosophy of science perspective, it is also more generally a philosophy. It is especially so when it comes to the philosophy of metareality. I supplement my contemplations and inquiry with many other philosophical traditions, such as existentialism, humanism and new materialism. One of the strongest influences for me has been deep ecology (Naess, 1995; Nesterova, 2023b; Sessions, 1995). In my reading, there is much in common between deep ecology and the philosophy of metareality. Both discuss self-transcendence, recognition that there is an inherently meaningful world beyond the self. Both invite us, humans, to recognise oneness, or interconnectedness of everything with everything else, to expand the narrow sense of self to embrace the world.

Something that I feel is implied but not explicitly or at length discussed in the philosophy of metareality is non-human beings. Deep ecology considers them more explicitly. I want to spend some time contemplating this in what follows.

Non-human beings have not received enough attention within the degrowth discourse. I have found it problematic. There is no particular vocabulary to refer to non-humans either. There exist words such as fellow beings, more-than-human others, kin. When my colleagues and I were working on an article about non-humans and organisations in the context of sustainability transformation, we found that it was such an underexplored field with various concepts that referred to the same entities. I grew up with non-human beings such as animals, plants, fungi and trees. To me, animals have always been family members. Since my childhood, I would talk to trees and ascribe emotions to them. Somehow in our society this anthropomorphism has a bad reputation and is seen as something naïve, something that children do. My family members and teachers were probably hoping that I would give up on this habit when I grow up. Years have gone by, and very little has changed about my attitude towards fellow beings. Animals and trees, as well as rivers, mountains, stones and lakes, are still my kin. My academic work is at least partly shaped by this worldview. Deep ecology is a philosophy that embraces this perspective.

I reflect so much on how non-human beings and their presence have helped me with writing this book. I started writing this book when I was living in southern Finland. That time of my life was perhaps the most challenging. I missed Sweden where I lived before I moved to Finland. My now-partner and I were trying to figure out our relationship. I was dealing with health issues. And then I realised that I had to exit the Finnish university I was working for as an act of activism. In southern Finland, I lived on an island and went for a walk around it every day. On the island, there were many rocks, coniferous trees, birches, lichen, wild raspberries and red currants, nettles, mushrooms, squirrels, deer, ducks, geese, insects and so many other beings. I spent much time with the sea that surrounded the island, with the trees that were growing on it, with the stones. Somehow those beings provided a safe space for me to contemplate this book, my other works, life in general and its meaning(s). These beings helped me put my life and various projects into perspective. I learned a lot from various non-human beings. Oftentimes, I would stand on the edge of the island and look at the sea or the stars. I was thinking that none of the negative unfoldings in my life mattered much in comparison to the scale of the sea and the cosmos. None of the managers, their viewpoints and ambitions mattered as much as the sea and the cosmos. My career, citations, the number of publications, the length of my curriculum vitae – all of those paled in comparison to the sea and the cosmos. All of those indicators of so-called success paled even in comparison to the smallest flower or a piece of granite. I was sketching many notes for this book in the presence of non-humans. It is while walking barefoot on the moss, sitting on the rocks, looking at the sun that many ideas and reflections manifested and crystallised in my mind. I do not think I could have written this book in a different setting. I would struggle to write it in an office, in a sterile environment with an air conditioner. Perhaps this book would have looked and felt very different if I wrote it entirely at home too.

As I am writing these words, I am living in Copenhagen. Copenhagen feels more built than the city in northern Sweden where I used to live or the area in southern Finland where I lived more recently, right before I moved to Copenhagen. I live in a green neighbourhood in Copenhagen, close to Søndermarken. But the green spaces around me are parks and cemeteries. Here, non-humans like trees and flowers are instrumentalised and consumed as decorations. They are here for fellow humans' pleasure and entertainment and not so much for their own sake, to pursue their own unfolding in natural communities of fellow beings. Too many trees are trimmed and cut into shapes. One of my windows faces a cemetery, Solbjerg Parkkirkegård. I learned much from the trees growing there. For example, one of the main themes of this work is change. There is time for intense growth and there is time for a steady state. I observe change in the trees outside as the seasons change. I observe these trees being lit up differently as days are getting shorter and then longer again.

While I was writing this book, a magpie started to visit my balcony. I began to share oats with her and then made a cake for her from organic coconut oil, peanut butter, seeds and oats. Initially it felt like a manifestation of a fellow feeling in practice. Then I realised that such an act is somewhat tokenistic. The food I prepared for this fellow being came from a supermarket, part of the capitalist system. It was bought in the city. Perhaps to truly manifest love and care towards non-humans, I had to move away from the city and work with the land, grow my own food and share it with fellow humans and non-humans.

Literatures

Something that I knew even before I began to write this book was that I would not be using a systematic literature review. This book is not a summary or an analysis of the literatures that explore the link between degrowth and business. Every now and then, such reviews appear in academic spaces (see e.g., Hankammer et al., 2021). While at times I read them with interest and certainly recommend them to my students and fellow academics, I have never felt drawn to doing them myself. What I felt drawn to is diving deep into some topic, reading widely outside one's area of expertise, learning from non-academic spaces, from nature and especially from local nature, from non-human beings, engaging dreams, intuition, hopes, feelings, emotions and experiences into one's exploration. Literature in general is only one part of my exploration. The social sciences are different to the natural sciences. Perhaps I would not want to take medication developed solely on the grounds of a fellow human's intuition or dreams. Perhaps I would not want to take a train journey over the Øresund Bridge if it was developed in this manner too. If I were an engineer or a chemist, most likely I would be approaching science differently. But social sciences are so often about softer things such as love, care, hopes and dreams of different futures.

After many years of contemplating degrowth and business, I feel that there is no lack of knowledge in terms of practices and policies that need to be in place for a genuinely sustainable society to come into being. Even in the beginning of my PhD I realised that practices are well known, though they were scattered across different literatures and were called different names in different spaces. At times I think that the same practices that I included in my degrowth business framework (Nesterova, 2020a) could be sketched if I sat down with a piece of paper, or even better, with a piece of paper and with a group of fellow humans coming from different backgrounds and walks of life. Something that remains important to understand is why these practices manifest in businesses. And I felt that I could begin to understand it via engaging in deep conversations with businesspersons and other practitioners, as well as understanding my own practice, rather than merely via reading academic literatures. As for degrowth itself, I connected even more deeply with degrowth and its key messages and ideas when I was reading deep ecology, humanism and philosophy of metareality than degrowth literatures.

Something that I was missing in the field of degrowth were emotional and personal accounts of the thinking process and the process of creating knowledge. Throughout this book, there are multiple references to the thinking processes that were unfolding while I was researching and writing. This is for transparency reasons. I want to show that so much is unfolding behind and in parallel with scientific and philosophical efforts. This is something that readers often do not see when they are reading the finished product. Perhaps some fellow humans only want to see the finished product, but my goal is to have a holistic and raw one. Finality and perfection are something I have tried to avoid intentionally. The processes of thinking, writing, conceptualising are emotional, discontinuous, imperfect and nuanced. They are deeply personal and intimate.

I will outline the fields that influence my thinking. The most recent field that inspired me is new materialism (e.g., Page, 2020). New materialist writings felt refreshing, honouring our emotions, our embodiment and materiality. Engaging with new materialism and scholars who are inspired by new materialisms brought into my consciousness more clearly various reasons why places felt so important to me. I often contemplate dwelling in places. It is problematic to study anything in a detached manner when in reality everything exists and unfolds within certain constellations of natural and social structures, in places. One of the reviewers of the book proposal that I wrote for this book posed an interesting question which concerned exclusion of Norway from this book that is about businesses in the Nordics. I thought about this a lot after I read this comment. I am very curious about businesses everywhere and would like to study Norwegian cases too. But my own life path unfolded in such a way that in the Nordics I dwelled in Denmark, Finland and Sweden – though in reverse, rather than alphabetical, order. That is to say, after living in England, I moved to Sweden, then to Finland and then to Denmark. As I am writing these words, I can say that I have never even visited Norway. Writing about Norwegian cases without having stepped on the Norwegian soil would feel shallow to me. I would not want to study businesses if I went to Norway for just a few days either. I cannot talk about depth while engaging in what I would experience as shallow research, considering how I prefer to do my own research. Reflections from Denmark, Finland and Sweden are not only the places where the businesses I research are located. These are also the places where I lived, where I had different experiences, where I felt different things and that in various ways have significance to me. I will say more about it below.

New materialism, in my view, has a close affinity with geography, and especially those strands thereof that are philosophically inclined. Humanistic geography (Tuan, 1976) has influenced my thinking a lot too. I was very lucky to be based in a geography department in Sweden for a year and some months after being in a business school for many years. During my time in the geography department, and especially during a long, cold and dark northern Swedish winter I was reading humanistic geography and sketching thoughts that came to my mind about degrowth, business and places. I believe I read all the works by Yi-Fu Tuan at that time, and they left a lasting impression on me.

Humanism is a field that is close to my heart, too. It assumes general human goodness. Humanistic writings make intuitive sense to me and present humanity in a way that is very close to how I see and experience the world. Humanism gives hope. To say that humans are generally good does not mean that we are perfect or holy, or that all humans are equally good. Certainly, there are examples of violent and abusive individuals. There is a chapter dedicated to humanism in this book. I wrote much of this book in 2023, which so far has been the worst year in my life. Much disappointment, sadness and sorrow came from experiences with my fellow humans. Throughout the year, as it was unfolding, I was often asking myself if I still believed in humanistic perspective on fellow humans. My perspective never changed despite all the negative experiences. In fact, at the very same time I was still seeing much beauty in humans. I was seeing kindness, helpfulness, gentleness, care, authenticity, empathy, love, solidarity and so much more.

As I mentioned above, critical realism influenced my thinking. Some models from critical realism that I find useful are, for example, the dialectic between agents and structures and the four planes of being. As for the interactions between agency and structures, critical realism assumes that agents transform or reproduce social structures, while social structures constrain and empower agents (Buch-Hansen and Nielsen, 2020; Collier, 1994). Critical realism is a philosophy of science for the social sciences, so it pays particular attention to the social structures. When I contemplate the relationship between agents and structures, natural structures (e.g., ecosystems) often come to mind. This is something that geography makes us more mindful of. We, humans, interact with natural structures that constrain, shape and empower us. Yet, when contemplating natural structures, it feels important to avoid reducing nature to something abstract, as nature is *home* to many non-human beings. Talking about nature while recognising individual (and interconnected) beings such as trees, rocks, rivers and lakes is something that I am struggling with as I am writing this book. I do not feel that the language is helpful. Perhaps when the dialogues between new materialisms and organisation studies unfold, there will be better vocabularies that recognise both structures and agency within nature and non-human spaces.

Critical realism assumes that everything that happens in the social reality happens at the same time on the four planes of being: (1) material transactions with nature, (2) social relations, (3) social structures and (4) inner being (Bhaskar, 2008). This model I found incredibly useful to contemplate degrowth and transformations (Buch-Hansen and Nesterova, 2021). I will use it much in this book too.

Apart from the literatures I mentioned above, there are always new knowledges and ideas, and old knowledges and ideas, that I constantly become acquainted with. I see this as a path of learning. Something that I am aware of is that much knowledge is captured in other languages, and in various forms such as tales and personal journals. While in Denmark, I learned about a Danish scholar who writes beautifully. They write important, interesting things, but they choose to write most of their works in Danish. Perhaps from the perspective of getting more citations and attention from English-speaking academia, it would be better for this person to write in English. But they still chose to write in Danish. I found it very inspiring, as via writing in Danish they could connect more deeply with the Danish audience and facilitate change in proximity. Unfortunately, none of the other languages that I speak I can use so well as to write a book in them. I am also thinking about wonderful conversations I had with fellow academics while I was working on this book. So often I found these conversations more honest, more thought-provoking, raw, deep and nuanced in comparison to academic articles, even the articles written by those academics themselves. In conversations, we felt that feelings and emotions such as hopelessness, hope, sorrow, frustration, disappointment, joy and gratitude could accompany our contemplations of theories, practices and research findings.

To think about knowledges being scattered, fragmented or even hidden from the public eye is humbling. What is expressed in academic papers is just a very small part of humanity's knowledge. While I was writing this chapter, a Danish man visited my home. This man was an intellectual who implemented many sustainability practices in his life. For example, he always wore a uniform voluntarily, repaired objects, kept objects for a long time. He came across as a humble person, not someone seeking attention, following and fame. He used to be a teacher of the German language here in Denmark. There is something about his worldview that constellated beautiful morality and anarchism. He never wrote academic papers and did not own a business. I don't know if he even had a personal journal where he would express his thoughts on being in the world. But it felt to me that he knew something about being that I was only learning. And it was not something that I could learn from academic papers, conferences and books.

Degrowth and its definition

Degrowth as an idea is a response to ecological and social degradation. The main assumptions of degrowth are simple and intuitive. Our economies cannot grow forever because they use finite resources, we are failing to honour nature and her limits, and our economic systems which use ever more resources fail to satisfy basic needs of all humans (see Buch-Hansen et al., 2024). Degrowth proposes that our use of materials and energy needs to reduce. We must focus on production for genuine humans needs, and the outcomes of production need to be distributed more equally so that everyone's needs are sufficiently satisfied. For this to happen, the way we collectively and individually relate with the world (the self, human and non-human others and nature) needs to change. Currently, we live in the world where, to a large extent, "wealth and money seem to be the only measures for success". This is not a profound quote from a famous and well-cited professor. This is a text message from the Danish elderly man I just mentioned above. This man did not read this anywhere, but it is something he has seen so clearly as he walked his long life path. I believe that many fellow humans notice the same. And while for us, without doing studies or reading scientific contributions, it is hard to tell how exactly we fail to respect nature's limits, it is not as difficult to see social degradation all around us. The Danish man I just mentioned in our exchange said that "it is giving us [his wife and him] some hope to hear how your generation can also feel about things and the way they are going!" It was humbling to hear these words, especially from an elderly man who perhaps will not live to see where things are going.

Degrowth is at once a political project, a social movement and a research field (Buch-Hansen, 2021). As a political project, degrowth is both anti- and post capitalist. The nature of anti- and post capitalism is diverse. Though probably most would agree on the points of critique of capitalism, whether a degrowth society should be based on anarchist or socialist principles (or some combination of those) is subject to discussion. Oftentimes it is a matter of preference and personal convictions of different degrowth theorists. Personally, I come from an anarchist perspective. I am concerned about hierarchies, power and distance between governments and those humans whose lives they are affecting. At the same time, I do not have any clear image of how a small-scale, highly localised, profoundly caring and profoundly loving society will unfold in the near future from what currently exists. This is something my co-author Hubert Buch-Hansen and I discuss often. This is one of the loose ends I want to emphasise as I do not have an answer. I do not think that a society that I and many other fellow anarchists would like to see is immediately possible. As an anarchist, I certainly feel sorrow and sadness about it. Perhaps eco-social policies are needed to help us transition towards a society that is more localised and based on anarchist principles (Buch-Hansen et al., 2024). But this means looking far into the future, or rather its images painted in our minds, and almost guessing what could unfold after something that does not yet exist. In our academic works we want to sound sure, but we do not have any clear picture or mechanisms in mind as to how future will unfold. Using so-called scientific, pretentious language and jargon makes an appearance of prediction (after this comes this). But what I am feeling is that the discussions about social futures are more akin to crystal gazing (scrying).

As a social movement, degrowth is perhaps best seen as a combination of movements (Burkhart et al., 2020). There is also an overlap between degrowth and other movements such as voluntary simplicity, minimalism, zero-waste, deep ecology and many others. Realising this gives hope, as there are many humans contributing to the efforts of being in the world more sustainably, even if they do not explicitly identify themselves as part of the degrowth movement. Personally, I prefer to not see myself as part of the degrowth social movement, but I do see myself as part of voluntary simplicity, zero-waste and minimalism social movements. As I was reading this paragraph to my co-author and partner, he seemed very surprised. So, I want to clarify my statement. Even though I write about degrowth, I do not see myself as part of the degrowth social movement because degrowth does not have an agreed-upon definition, a set of agreed-upon principles or even a common vision of the future. Perhaps what makes degrowth diverse, interesting and fresh as a field at the same time makes it difficult for humans to commit themselves to degrowth. There are some aspects of degrowth that I appreciate and like, and others that I do not like. My fellow humans within the degrowth movements may like the aspects that I don't like.

At the same time, I have practised simple living, minimalism and zero-waste for a long time. In fact, I've engaged in these practices much longer than I have been doing research on degrowth. These movements always felt more defined, more concrete and action-orientated, though also philosophically and scientifically informed. To me, they have always felt hands-on and down-to-earth. Alongside advocating change in our systems, these movements have always proposed various concrete solutions. Though individual zero-waste practices are not the solution to ecological and social degradation, this orientation towards solutions and real changes in our mode of being in the world has always appealed to me personally. At times, such movements and individual actions are contrasted with the need to change our systems. What I notice in these movements is that humans are well aware of the need for change in systems. Over more than 10 years I have never met a fellow human within any of these movements who does not advocate, and desire, change in systems. There is acute awareness of the destruction capitalism causes. But there is also a felt desire to participate in transformations directly. Sometimes I think that I contribute more to change via my everyday activism as a practitioner of voluntary simplicity, zero-waste and minimalism than via my academic articles. It is not because my individual actions have a huge impact. They certainly do not. No practitioner of zero-waste or voluntary simplicity or minimalism would think that their personal actions have a huge impact. At least none of the ones I have met over more than 10 years said that this is what they believe. I think it is a big misconception about practitioners. But this practice started so many interesting conversations with fellow humans in all sorts of spaces – in trains, stores, hospitals, streets, cafes and universities, even online, as I made my practices public (https://beingofdeeptransformations.blogspot.com/). Thus, change in systems manifests via constantly trying to bring into being change in culture, trying to inspire others to relate with the world (the self, human and non-human others and nature) differently in their everyday life.

Within the broad and ever growing research field of degrowth, there are various strands and groups of humans working together in different places. When I was doing my PhD, I was not interacting closely with anyone. Here, I mean human rather than non-human beings. I was definitely interacting much with non-humans. In the business school where I was based, there was no one, apart from me, working on degrowth, and most of the time I was working from home. The university was an hour away from my home, and I did not want to walk there often. At home, I had freedom to structure my life in my own way. I could dedicate much time to practising, and writing notes about, zero-waste, voluntary simplicity and minimalism. I adopted kittens and was looking after them.

Importantly, I could open the window and have access to fresh air, unlike at the university with its air conditioning. I could work more in line with the rhythms of nature. In summers, I could wake up very early with the sun (I had no curtains) and start working immediately. In winters, I could read and rest more. This is a privilege that I appreciated immensely. I was observing my then-partner working standard office hours full-time and how this pattern of work negatively affected that fellow human who was a very creative person, longing for freedom, perhaps like any other human being.

My PhD was a monograph (Nesterova, 2020b) and most of my academic interactions were with books and papers, rather than with living fellow humans. After my PhD I began to work with my Danish co-author who then became my partner. At the same time, I was reading deep ecology literatures, much of which was by Arne Naess, and then moved to northern Sweden. My research was heavily influenced by the Nordics, Nordic scholars and Nordic nature that I love and where I feel safe. Jokingly, my co-author and I started to call what we were doing the Nordic school of degrowth. We connected via our appreciation of critical realism and a desire to develop a gentle and nuanced approach towards degrowth. We connected via the place. Being in the same region meant that we could think together in the same space. We could discuss in depth the social structures we were facing and observing in the Nordics. We could discuss politics in the Nordics and what we were seeing in the news in the Nordic countries. We wanted to outline our own definition of degrowth too, based on critical realism. We defined degrowth as

> deep transformations occurring on all four interrelated planes of social being [material transactions with nature, social structures, social relations, inner being], on different scales and in all sites, guided by gentleness and care, towards a society co-existing harmoniously within itself and with nature.
>
> (Buch-Hansen and Nesterova, 2023, p. 8)

This definition brings together critical realism, the need to acknowledge the role of all domains of society, the need to contemplate values and to have a shared goal. Critical realism is a philosophy of science that, in our view, can be useful for supporting degrowth research (Buch-Hansen and Nesterova, 2021). We also did not want to highlight only one system, e.g., the economy, or only one domain of social being, e.g., the psyche, education or the government. To us, it is always society as a whole that brings about change, including civil society (individual humans, groups, communities, movements, networks, academia and so on), the state and business. The scales of change are the psyche, the local, national and transnational. All of these scales need to be taken into account, as it is not so that a particular person, village or even a country can bring about degrowth on the global scale. Neither can each of these entities on their own become degrowth entities, as everyone and everything is interconnected and embedded within larger systems and structures.

Our definition of degrowth is underpinned by humanism and its belief in human goodness, human capacities for empathy, solidarity, care, awe, nurturing, compassion, self-transcendence and love. Gentleness and care in particular felt fundamental to us. Perhaps we could have used the word love instead of gentleness. We certainly thought and talked about it. At times, in our private conversations we say that love in central to degrowth. But the word love is so often used to either describe a feeling or a range of feelings towards a particular human individual. Or it is often used in a more casual manner to express appreciation towards an item, a place, a dish or an artwork. Perhaps our definition was influenced by our own story of being colleagues and then becoming partners, falling *in love*. Far from experiencing love as something purely beautiful, self-transcendent and magical, it was accompanied by and enmeshed with much doubt, pain, fear, anxiety and discomfort. As I am writing these words, I am feeling curious about how life's unfolding affects our scientific works.

So, in our definition of degrowth, we used the word gentleness instead of the word love. I do not know whether it was the right decision to use the word gentleness instead of love. Perhaps more humans would be able to relate with the world love. Perhaps this word would sound too unscientific to fellow humans. The general attitude of gentleness towards existence/nature/cosmos manifests itself in acts of care. We define degrowth society as a society co-existing harmoniously within itself and with nature. Our emphasis on harmony is to deviate from authoritarian, highly questionable or even unethical, prescriptive, top-down approaches exemplified in tradable birth permits and the like. In theory, a society where a group of experts in power assigns permits for the use of resources or reproduction may be sustainable, but certainly not harmonious, caring or loving. In my view, love and care need to come from within.

Challenges

Many challenges arise when theorising degrowth and imagining a degrowth society. To me, it feels that the necessary preconditions for degrowth to unfold are changes in humans' worldviews and how we relate with the world in our minds, hearts and in our actions. In short, felt and manifested in actions gentleness towards the world is essential – experiencing and manifesting in practice care, concern, empathy and solidarity; feeling oneness or interconnectedness with human and non-human others and nature in general. Perhaps these feelings seem abstract. Oftentimes I notice that when I discuss solutions to ecological degradation with fellow humans, they agree that changes in how we feel towards the world are necessary, but they still await for more solid and concrete solutions and suggestions. Perhaps for this reason humans turn to technological solutions that seem concrete and promise measurable outcomes. Or humans turn to policy proposals where change is brought about by someone else, and we would only need to vote better. Like many fellow degrowth researchers, I am curious about policies too, but it feels necessary to still experience gentleness towards the world to choose to vote for certain policy proposals. This is especially so considering that such proposals may require what humans can perceive as self-limitation. For example, maximum income comes to mind. To feel good about this proposal, or other restrictive proposals for that matter, a person needs to feel that nature, fellow humans they might not know or ever meet, non-human beings and future generations of humans and non-humans matter more than many of their wants.

On a personal note, I often wonder about degrowth in relation to individuals and their being in the world. Talking about individuals is not a popular subject within degrowth. Perhaps this is due to the rejection of individualism found in neoclassical economics, which degrowth opposes. This rejection of individualism is right, as no one is a fully separate self, detached and disconnected from the world around them. And yet humans are diverse and unique selves. Many solutions that degrowth proposes are community-based. These are beautiful ideas, and even personally I would like to take part in some of these practices. I feel inspired by community gardens, knowledge sharing, byttestationer (swap stations in Danish). But little has been said about how change can unfold on a very personal level, in diverse and unique individuals with diverse circumstances. It is important for all to develop deep and intimate relationships with nature and all her inhabitants. But how? As I was writing this book, what came to mind was that developing such a connection with nature requires at least at times spending quality time with the sea, mountains, forests, lakes and rivers. As I was contemplating this topic more, I realised that occasional trips to nature, even well-prepared, are not sufficient. Perhaps something much more than this is necessary, such as immersion in nature. Yet, proposing this as a sure path towards a better worldview may be futile. So many fellow humans live in cities. In a city, without immediate access to nature, without immersion in nature, love towards nature seems to be philosophical. I wonder if such love is enough.

There is also a question of how a genuinely sustainable society will arise from what exists currently. It felt to me that when degrowth started to take shape as an academic field, there was a sense of redoing everything. Everything had to be alternative. Our lifestyles, worldviews, how we consume, produce and exchange, how we think and feel. For this reason, it felt that we need to explore other types of organisations of production and service provision than businesses (Nesterova and Robra, 2022; Robra and Nesterova, 2023). Large corporations are destructive on many levels. They are impersonal, accumulate much power and are hierarchical. They are hierarchical in many ways, both within these organisations and in relation to others such as suppliers. This is not to say that humans within large corporations are bad, but it is to say that these organisational forms are not conducive to gentleness and care. Repair cafes, cooperatives, various libraries, swap shops, foraging and community gardens seem to be better and more beautiful alternatives. This interest in alternatives is understandable. If something is not working, such as the capitalist system and destructive production by large corporations, it makes sense to look elsewhere. It is easy to imagine an alternative world in one's dreams and on paper, to paint a beautiful vision of the world. And yet, new, hopefully genuinely sustainable, and more caring societies will arise from what exists currently. I wonder if fellow humans also feel sorrow when they realise that alternatives cannot simply be brought about from one's dreams and hopes. That is why my co-authors and I talk about transformation rather than transition (Buch-Hansen et al., 2024). There is no better world awaiting somewhere in the future. It must be created from what is. And what exists is not necessarily all bad. I find diverse economies scholarship (e.g., Gibson-Graham, 2006; Gibson-Graham and Dombroski, 2020) liberating for this reason. It brings our attention to the structures and other unfoldings in society that are not capitalist, that exist in parallel with, and even sustain, capitalism. These spaces need to grow.

In relation to business specifically, there are two questions that are still on my mind after many years of researching the role of business in degrowth transformations. These questions are worthy of contemplation, and they present a challenge to me. One is of scale, or what will happen in a genuinely sustainable society to large scale production and service provision. Another one is the question of profit. My contemplation of these questions is intimately linked with the nature of my own research and interest. I am interested in small businesses and in businesspersons, their motivations, values, modes of being in and relating with the world. When I say businesspersons, I mean fellow humans with diverse ways of relating with the world, dreams, hopes, circumstances rather than some stereotype or a model of a human being. These questions feel so important that I want to dedicate a section of this chapter to them.

Why not large businesses

Oftentimes, my fellow humans ask me why I don't research large businesses and what will happen to them in a degrowth society. Whenever potential PhD students come to me with a question concerning gaps in knowledge in degrowth business research, I always say that it would be interesting to contemplate large businesses and what will happen to them during transformations towards degrowth and in a degrowth society. From a philosophical and perhaps somewhat idealistic perspective, I find small or human scale society beautiful. (Nesterova, 2021b) I like Schumacher's (1993) contemplations on scale (small is beautiful). Something feels inherently uncomfortable and concerning about large-scale production. Long and obscure supply chains, treating humans as replaceable, severe hierarchies, low wages in supply chains, enormous remuneration for top managers, mechanistic approaches to management, intense and expensive advertising that tries to shape consumption patterns - there are so many reasons to dislike large corporations and large-scale production.

At the same time, there are many reasons that make me curious about small businesses and that lead me to believe that these businesses could be suitable for a degrowth society. I described these reasons in my PhD thesis (Nesterova, 2020b). Some of them include smallness or human scale of their operations, proximity between the business itself and its owner-managers. Generally, there is more transparency in small business. They are more in line with our human nature (Gowdy, 1998). Many of these businesses are inspired by local nature and local resources, they have local customers and employ locally, and localisation is such an important part of degrowth (Trainer, 2012). Small businesses offer more independence and flexibility to humans. Small businesses seem creative and good spaces for creativity and innovation in general. Here I do not mean innovation in a narrow technological sense. It can even be simplifying things, or it can be social innovation. Naturally, it can be innovation in design and processes, too. So, researching small businesses is both a personal preference and a result of professional contemplations. It connects to the idea of a society where I would like to live in, and the values that I would like to see flourish in this society.

Personally, I try to avoid consuming products of large corporations too. It is a form of consumer activism. In my own practice, I have noticed that living simply allows me to consume products made or grown by small, local, independent businesses. I use products made and services provided by large businesses too. For example, I use trains. At times, I use conventional medication. I use a phone and a laptop. When I want to buy food, I shop in supermarkets most of the time. Yet, in a supermarket I can still often buy items produced by small and local businesses. One issue with consuming products made by small businesses, especially ecological ones, is that those products are often expensive or niche. Practising minimalism and consuming less overall helps one with buying more expensive basic products, such as ones for personal care and household cleaning. But it would be unaffordable for me to consume more normally if I only consume products made by small, local, independent businesses. When I moved to Denmark, I began to live in Frederiksberg, a green and affluent municipality. This area is not something that I chose, but rather my partner and I had to live in this location for his family reasons. What I noticed in this municipality is an abundance of small, local stores. There are bakeries, cafes, clothing boutiques selling high-quality clothing, fishmongers, wine shops, cheese shops, small art studios and interior design shops. Could these be degrowth businesses? Some of them certainly had a sense of quality, durability, slow living about them. At the same time, it is unaffordable to most fellow humans to shop there routinely. I began to notice that most of the time, people would buy everything they need in supermarkets and then buy some treats and gifts in those small, local shops. In my household, we often did the same.

There are many other issues and nuance when contemplating small businesses, apart from their products often being unaffordable or affordable only under certain circumstances and decisions (e.g., a high wage or minimalism). Even when something is produced or assembled locally, often such products still require long supply chains. The ingredients may still be coming from all over the world. I am thinking about small businesses in the Nordics that make chocolate. Some of them are inspired by local, Nordic nature and flavours such as berries and herbs. And yet, the main ingredients still come from far away. The ingredients to make products locally are not necessarily ones made by small companies too. For instance, one can buy sugar from a large company that produces both conventional and organic sugar, to make sweets locally. The question is, are the sweets local and what makes them local? One business can combine ingredients from all over the world but be owned locally and assemble the product locally. One can make jam and wine from local fruits but growing and processing these fruits probably required chemicals, tools and equipment that are far from being local. This is not to say that nothing can be local. Rather, it is to bring our attention to nuance of local production.

While revisiting this chapter, I gave a lecture in Lund University. The lecture was about degrowth, food and mobility. I wanted to bring my fellow humans' attention to what I keep seeing in my research on small businesses, various nuances, contentious points, learnings, struggles of researching degrowth and business. A fellow human raised an interesting question that we then were discussing in his office. He noted that encouraging growth in the number of small businesses is a common growth strategy within capitalism. It is indeed so. In the beginning of my research career, I worked in a European project that was aimed at encouraging growth in small, low carbon businesses, both the number of such businesses and also the size of existing ones. The fellow human asked me what separates degrowth from non-degrowth. Small business is not necessarily degrowth, and this is so important to highlight. At the same time, growth in the number of small businesses and even the size of those businesses in some cases is not anti-degrowth, in my view. Consider local organic agriculture, for example, or local renewable energy production and storage. Perhaps it is the whole constellation of business, civil society and the state that matters (Buch-Hansen et al., 2024). What this constellation looks like, what it tries to achieve.

Over the years, I have thought about large businesses too. While many items can be made, and services provided, by small businesses, there are also large-scale services such as railways and large-scale production that needs to take place even in a degrowth society. I do not think that a degrowth society will be based on anarcho-primitivist principles, even though at times I contemplate this kind of society and imagine it as something idyllic, ultimately close to nature and to non-human beings, and less complicated. In my many conversations with fellow humans over the years, I have noticed that not many humans want this kind of society. Perhaps rightly so. And every time I face a health crisis due to my own autoimmune condition, I am grateful that we do not live in a technologically primitive society. When I say this to my fellow humans, some respond that perhaps I would not have this condition in the first place if I lived in a cleaner environment. Perhaps so, but I do not know with any certainty. The fellow humans who are sceptical about a degrowth society based on anarcho-primitivist principles mention, for instance, comfort, convenience and medicine as some of the reasons for their scepticism. I do not think that an anarcho-primitivist society is even possible, considering the path humanity has taken. For example, what will happen to the nuclear waste? This relates to my point above, that a genuinely sustainable society will not be wished into existence, it will unfold or be born from what exists right now.

Many degrowth business practices can be adopted by large businesses. Large businesses can produce durable and repairable goods, for instance. Oftentimes, large businesses have resources to develop better, more ecological products or schemes for, e.g., taking back the packaging. They can make more ecological products accessible to more humans, unlike the small, local businesses I mentioned above. Large businesses have financial resources for education. They can, at least in theory, become more humane and caring by, for instance, dismantling many of the hierarchies that exist within their own models. They can be owned differently. Perhaps large corporations need to be nationalised, and this is where the state can play an important role in degrowth transformations (Buch-Hansen et al., 2024). Much of what I say here though is either obvious or is my viewpoint resulting from contemplations of the role of business in degrowth transformations and degrowth society. I have not studied large businesses myself because I believe in the importance of diving deeper when trying to understand what unfolds in a business. For me personally it would not be enough to have an interview with a CEO or a sustainability manager. To me, looking at sustainability reports, vision and mission statements and plans (such as "we will be carbon neutral by some year") feels shallow. One way to get more acquainted with what unfolds in a large business would be to work there, preferably in different positions at different levels and for a long time. An autoethnographic project like this could bring to the surface the dynamics of the organisation, and what works and what does not work would become more obvious via autoethnography than just by asking one person various questions. Doing an autoethnographic research would be incredibly time- and energy consuming and psychologically difficult, not to mention the ethical aspects of it. I am doubtful whether large corporations would embrace this kind of research, and I have my doubts too about genuine openness that fellow humans would exhibit knowing that their fellow worker is a researcher.

The only experience of working in a large organisation I have is working in different universities. As I am writing these words, I have worked or been a visiting researcher, in England, Sweden, Finland and Denmark. For a while I was not connecting my own experiences of universities and my study of businesses. But over time I began to see much value in reflecting on my own workplaces as a researcher and not just an employee. This allowed me to understand much more clearly what would need to take place to genuinely understand the dynamics within an organisation. These days it is common that universities recycle, use energy from alternative sources, procure local products, encourage their staff to travel by train (in Sweden, for example), have sustainability-related degrees. At the same time, there are often strict hierarchies that prevent spiritual and professional growth. Business sustainability degrees often do not include what, in my view, needs to be part of business education, such as new materialism, deep ecology, nature and place-based teaching approaches. Short-term, precarious positions that are still commonplace in academia do not create spaces for genuine and lasting change. Oftentimes, proclaimed values do not seem to match reality.

Profit and growth

Profit can be a toxic institution and pursuit. Here I will discuss my reflections on profit and small businesses, as they are what I research and contemplate most often. In mainstream economics, it is assumed that firms try to maximise profit. When discussing profit with businesspersons, owners of small, ecological businesses that I research, it is not the case. Small business owners want to have some profit to be able to grow (if they want to grow) and to be able to get financing. In my view, growth in a small ecological business is not so problematic as long as it does not become the sole focus. We need more of such businesses and for them to be somewhat bigger so humans can consume their products rather than products made by large corporations. Perhaps I have an optimistic view of small business. But in my research, I find that such businesses often strive for transparency. They base their business on hobbies, craft, interest, curiosity or something that businesspersons feel passionate about. They develop close relationships with their customers and local communities. They are not performing sophisticated calculations to maximise their profits. If they want to grow, they often need external financing, which they cannot get if they are not profitable. This mechanism is part of the capitalist system, which is wrong and inhumane (more on capitalism below). But it is not so that businesspersons want to make a profit to serve the capitalist system, because they love it, believe in it strongly, want to destroy nature and exploit fellow humans and non-humans and wake up every morning with the sole goal to reproduce capitalism. They, like anyone else in society, often try to do their best within the framework the system provides while also trying to transform the system via their agency and practices. Oftentimes, the businesspersons I spoke to are in fact very critical of capitalism. Before I began collecting the data for my PhD, I naively thought that businesspersons would be explicitly supportive of capitalism, that they would criticise my anti-capitalist stance. I thought that those who are critical of capitalism would ask me not to include their stance in my research, as if it was a shameful thing to say. I was wrong.

Many small businesses do not want to grow at all. Their owners see growth as something detrimental to their lifestyle. They do not want to expand their production, hire more people and be responsible for their livelihoods. This is not anti-social or bad either. When I contemplate this, if I were to have my own business, I also would not want it to grow. Some businesspersons want their businesses to be "lagom" (just right in Swedish) in size, not too small but also not too big. Others see growth as something discontinuous and organic: there is time for growth and there is time for staying as they are. When a businessperson would say that they do not want to hire more fellow humans, I felt discomfort. Do they not want to help others? I would ask further questions, and what they said seemed to stem not from a lack of care, but rather from a conviction that more humans need to have their own enterprises. Many were willing to share with fellow humans their knowledge and experiences of establishing and running a business.

Because of my research of small, independent, local ecological businesses, I do not think that a for-profit business is necessarily bad. In itself, the form does not tell me much about the nature of a business. It is just a form, and on its own I cannot judge whether a business is destructive, and whether the owners are supportive of capitalism. I have researched other forms of enterprises, and oftentimes the attitudes and practices of humans who run different forms of enterprises are very similar. That is why, in my view, it is important to avoid simplifications such as for-profit equals bad, not-for-profit equals good. It can be a for-profit very small company that doesn't want to grow, is ecological, its products are useful for the practitioners of sufficiency and zero-waste, the owner is an activist or a practitioner of voluntary simplicity. They can be driven by a desire to take part in bringing about a better society, a desire not to have managers, to earn a living via engaging with their hobby or passion. Or it can be a cooperative with hierarchical structures and narcissistic personalities at its core. Perhaps anyone who has worked in academia knows how exploitative, competitive and hierarchical universities can be, and a university is not a for-profit business. None of it is to say that there can't be a small for-profit business with severe issues, or that there cannot be a cooperative with beautiful values. It is essential to avoid romanticising organisational forms. Everything depends on how exactly things unfold in every individual organisation, and it feels important to understand what practices take place in each of them, and why.

On foregoing the capitalism discussion

It was very tempting for me to start this book with yet another outline of the details of ecological degradation and capitalisms' role in it. As I am writing these words, my book co-authored with Hubert Buch-Hansen and Max Koch is in production. Much of that book is dedicated to exploring why and how capitalism is a destructive system. Degrowth is an explicitly anti- and post capitalist project, and I, like many fellow degrowth scholars, activists and students, find capitalism ugly. At the same time, my feeling is that there is enough literature that covers the topic of capitalism and why and how it causes and intensifies ecological and social degradation. I did not want to repeat the discussion here. To me, it felt wasteful to spend even more energy, time and paper on stating the same points that my co-authors and I have stated and that many others have outlined before and alongside us too (Buch-Hansen et al., 2024; Koch, 2012).

Works on degrowth oftentimes spend many words trying to convince the readers that capitalism is destructive. In my experience of interacting with those humans who are considered the target audience of these books (fellow scholars, students, activists and practitioners) are often very much aware of the issues of capitalism in both theory and their experiences. Oftentimes, in their everyday life, humans feel the detrimental effects of capitalism even stronger than many academics do. They are very intimately familiar with capitalism. Just like we, as individuals, are familiar with capitalism when we want to rent or buy an apartment, so are businesspersons very much familiar with capitalism when they want to finance their business externally. It is also so important to remember that those businesspersons are fellow humans who likewise contemplate growing their own food vs buying food in supermarkets, who rent apartments, take out student loans and mortgages in their personal lives. They see their children and friends participate in this system too. Before I started my research of small businesses, I did not know what to expect. I thought that everyone, apart from critical scholars and activists, would be defending capitalism, and I would need to explain to everyone I met on my path why capitalism is such a bad system. It was not so. Many humans from various walks of life were telling me why capitalism is bad and could explain in much detail the issues that I only knew in theory or had limited experiences with in my own life. They could also link capitalism with their own life experiences.

Something that I find helpful to contemplate in relation to capitalism is that capitalism is often painted as all-pervasive and larger than it is (Gibson-Graham, 2006; Gibson-Graham and Dombroski, 2020). Capitalism is often presented as a creature with a mind of its own that intentionally wants destruction and intentionally goes against those who disagree. Capitalism is pervasive, but it is a system of structures with certain tendencies, reproduced (but thankfully also transformed) by human beings. The writing duo J.K. Gibson-Graham noticed that there are multiple alternatives that exist in parallel with, and even sustain, capitalism. Such alternatives can be found in various domains of society. In production, it can be foraging, eco-social enterprises, household production and alternative organisations. In labour, it can be volunteering. In our mode of being, it can be care (see Gibson-Graham and Dombroski, 2020).

Apart from obvious alternatives (e.g., foraging), there are very normal social entities that are not necessarily capitalist through and through. To me it seems that small, ecological businesses very often combine elements of capitalism and elements of alternatives. For example, the same business can get external financing thus participate in the capitalist system. At the very same time, the business can be based on passion towards a certain product or a craft. It can make products that help fellow humans practise sufficiency rather than consumerism. Care towards nature, fellow humans and non-humans can be at the heart of this business. We can compare such business to an alternative, say, a swap shop. A swap shop (byttestation in Danish) is a place where humans can bring their unwanted or not needed objects that others can then take completely free of charge. One can take something from there too, if they need anything. I have taken some items to a place like this here in Copenhagen where I live. I like this idea a lot and am supportive of these places. A swap shop is an alternative, as when we go to a normal shop, we expect to pay. The swap shop gives one for a moment a sense of an alternative, money-free, sharing, caring and giving society. However, all those objects were initially produced in the capitalist system, many by large corporations. The swap shop I have in my mind while I am writing these words is very near a well-off area in Copenhagen. Perhaps to bring an item there was not a big loss or a sacrifice for the fellow humans who live in this area. Perhaps they could bring an old item to the swap shop and buy a new one in a conventional store. It is so important to avoid romanticising alternatives. I am afraid of sounding too pessimistic, especially about alternatives that are much needed but still marginal and fragile. At the same time, I believe that taking something to a swap shop can make a person feel good about the act and absolve them of a responsibility to keep and honour objects they live with. Knowing that some object is not going to a landfill may encourage more consumption and feeling comfortable about the consumption of new things.

Degrowth academics reject the notion of an economic [hu]man (homo economicus) from mainstream economics. It would be unfair to assume that while everyone is not a greedy, egocentric being, businesspersons are the ones who possess all of these qualities. Businesspersons are, like anyone else, just fellow humans. Those humans make mistakes, have doubts, face challenges, celebrate successes, take risks and try out new things, just like anyone else in society. They are not better or worse than anyone else. They are not necessarily agents of capitalism, or at least no more so than many others. Oftentimes I like to think that myself and fellow academics are agents of change who live almost outside capitalism. I used to think so especially in the early days of my PhD. Then, when I became more attentive towards my practices and my work, I saw with much more clarity that I very much dwell within capitalism. No less so than the businesspersons I was talking to.

I do not want to say that we should altogether stop criticising capitalism. To not critique capitalism is also wrong. Why and how capitalism is destructive is important knowledge that needs to be discussed often and in different domains of society. There are perspectives, including on how to do business better, that get much right. For example, they recognise bringing about a better society requires an effort from business, the state and civil society (see e.g., Porter and Kramer, 2011). They also recognise the importance of location and thinking beyond profit. However, they do not question capitalism as a system or material growth as a dynamic and a value. Such fields can benefit much from contemplating critique of capitalism.

The Nordics

In this book, I refer to the Nordic context. This is not because I find it to be overall the worthiest of attention, the most interesting, the most promising in terms of degrowth. Every context is interesting, every country and region is interesting and worthy of a deep and careful study. Every region needs to be contemplated in relation to degrowth, as every region has its own potentialities, social, cultural, political, economic, natural and other resources and faces its own challenges. I am interested in and study the Nordic context simply because I am based in the Nordics. It is where my life's path led me. I can study businesses here in much more depth than elsewhere, visit them and have in-person exchanges with businesspersons and fellow academics here without flying, which I have been avoiding for many years for ecological reasons. I also believe in place-sensitivity, in serious and long-term dwelling in a place to understand it, its constellations of structures and cultures and languages, and its inhabitants better. I feel more comfortable with some languages here in the Nordics too, which helps in studying businesses better. Apart from that, Nordic nature means much to me. I feel fondness towards nature that is familiar to me, that I have known since my childhood. Fir, pine, birch trees, juniper, moss, granite rocks, mushrooms, blueberries, lingonberries, sea buckthorn, lily of the valley, nettle – all of these are beings I have loved from a very young age and developed close connections with. I feel deep love towards the Baltic Sea. I will say more about being and writing in each of the three countries where I have lived (Sweden, Finland and Denmark) in the beginning of each of the chapters dedicated to the businesses in those countries, but here I will briefly sketch my relationships with these countries.

Being in Sweden

Sweden is the first Nordic country I lived in. I came to northern Sweden as a postdoctoral researcher and was based in Umeå University, at its department of geography. That move was intentional, as British academia felt hierarchical to me, and the society felt divided in terms of class, access to opportunities and wealth.

I wanted to be close to nature and have access to it (Allemansrätten or freedom to roam). I wanted to be in a less hierarchical academic system. I fell in love with magical northern Sweden and its nature. I will never forget my relocation to Sweden. I travelled by train all the way from the Midlands in England. I didn't book any tickets in advance and had never been so far up north before. It was the end of August 2021. As the train left Uppsala, I felt as if something shifted in my psyche. It felt like entering a different realm with vast expanses of forest. It was a fairytale setting if you could forget that many of these forests are planted and managed. It is a forestry industrial estate. In northern Sweden, it was easy to feel the power of nature and the conditions it imposes onto humans. It was also easy to see nature's abundance with so many gifts to forage, and to feel awe (Bonner and Friedman, 2011; Schneider, 2009) when watching northern lights. There were many small businesses that caught my attention quickly. There was so much creative thought, and many businesses were inspired by local nature and used its gifts and ingredients. I left Sweden willingly far before my contract expired. Partly it felt to be the right decision, but at the same time I was very sad to leave that country. Though I resigned from my job, I knew I would miss it and Sweden. I had a feeling that I would come back there. When I moved to Denmark, I received an invitation from a fellow human to visit his department at Lund University for three months and accepted that invitation. Sweden was just across the bridge.

Being in Finland

After being in northern Sweden for around a year and four months, I decided to relocate to a more southern area in the Nordics and return to a business school environment. Degrowth as an idea was very much welcomed by both teachers and students in the Finnish business school where I was based. While perhaps not everyone would agree with the degrowth discourse, many were ready to discuss it with curiosity, gentleness and understanding. While I was in Finland, I was not working closely with anyone at the university where I was based. I was not part of any project and was working on the ideas I developed during my PhD and while I was living in Sweden. As I was dwelling in Finland, I came to the realisation that for me and my research it was important to be in the space where I could have a closer relationship with the language. I find that my research is deeper and better quality when I understand the language of the speaker. My life is easier in the spaces where a Germanic language is spoken, where I understand, for instance, the documents from the authorities and websites of the businesses I am interested in for my research. I began to miss Sweden and less hierarchical Swedish academia. As my relationship with my line manager disintegrated and the university could not replace her, I realised that it was time to take my research elsewhere and relocate. I reached out to Aalborg University in Denmark to visit them and received an invitation from Roskilde University to visit them for a year and some months. I resigned from the Finnish university in October 2023. While I love Finnish nature and have met many wonderful fellow humans in Finland, leaving that university was the right decision. I travelled from Finland to Sweden by ferry. Stepping on that ferry felt liberating. I felt happy when I reached Sweden. At the very same time, leaving Finland was scary. I did not have a plan for my future and what others might call my career. But I knew I was doing the right thing and could not let fear stand in the way of my freedom. This quote from Rogers (1995, p. 10) resonated with me strongly: "I think I have always had a feeling that if I was given some opportunity to do the thing I was most interested in doing, everything else would somehow take care of itself". I realised that I could give myself that opportunity and that everything would somehow fall into place at some point.

Living in Denmark

I had visited Denmark many times before I had an opportunity to live here. I say *here* as when I am writing these words, I am living in Denmark. It's a country where I always felt comfortable as a visitor. My closest colleague Hubert Buch-Hansen, with whom we co-authored several works, was based in Denmark. We became a couple and as I relocated to Denmark, I developed a natural affinity for this country. I knew that I wanted to write the chapter on Danish businesses here.

In Denmark, I miss nature. Even though we live in a green area next to parks and a cemetery, this nature is severely transformed. In Copenhagen, I feel disconnected from nature, perhaps apart from the times when I am by the sea in Amager (the beach is artificial). As I stand there, I look at the bridge to Sweden that I have crossed so many times. As I was working some more on this chapter, I had a conversation with a fellow human. He brought my attention to some challenges he observed in my contemplations on degrowth. We talked about localisation and connectedness with nature. He mentioned that it is so common to think about spirituality in the context of nature, while it is also possible to be spiritual in a city. I experienced his words as humbling and thought-provoking. I have always associated nature with spirituality, and cities with artificiality and overstimulation. I began to think of many fellow humans I know who have spiritual and self-transcending experiences in cities. These are experiences with architecture, human-made music and art, places of worship, for example. While I can cognitively understand this, nothing in me resonates deeply with these thoughts. Like many others, I find some buildings beautiful, places of worship breathtaking, human-made music and art inspiring and evoking awe. But none of it felt as good as being with nature.

Oftentimes, when I try to share my journey with my fellow humans, I feel their curiosity and a positive attitude towards the path I took in my life. Living in all those countries contributed immensely to my spiritual growth. But it's so important to avoid romanticising it. Though I enjoyed living in each of those countries and learning from businesspersons in each one of them, I never felt completely safe and secure. My academic contracts were temporary and short-term. For this reason, I never felt I could settle in any country or commit to a place that I could call my home. I was afraid to develop deep friendships and close relationships with fellow humans, including businesspersons, as I knew I would leave at some point. I couldn't allow myself to have a family and children or even pets and plants. Something that helped me with living in many places, with relocation and financing these relocations was practising extreme minimalism. I practised extreme minimalism for ecological, spiritual and aesthetic reasons, and the financial benefits it brought were a welcome outcome too. Relocations are very expensive. Practising extreme minimalism meant that the objects I was inviting into my life had to be durable. They had to withstand everyday use and multiple relocations. Through this consumption practice, I learned about businesses that made sustainable and durable products. It is interesting how research on business and personal consumption interplay.

I do not hold on to my experiences of having lived in many countries. In the grand scheme of things, it does not matter. Something that has been a big part of my spiritual growth is feeling at home in the cosmos at large, in nature, and not in any particular country. As Salzberg (2008, p. 8) says:

> We can travel a long way and do many different things, but our deepest happiness is not born from accumulating new experiences. It is born from letting go of what is unnecessary, and knowing ourselves to be always at home. True happiness may not be at all far away, but it requires a radical change of view as to where to find it.

Intuitive and authentic writing

The process of writing this book, like the process of writing any other work I've written, including my papers and autoethnography, has been intuitive. I tried to avoid working according to a schedule or standard working hours. I simply worked on it whenever I felt that it was time to write, and whenever some thoughts and ideas crystallised in my mind. There were days of intense writing when I didn't even leave my home, and days I did not want to spend with this work at all. Sometimes I would write during weekends, sometimes during weekdays. Sometimes I would write during nights, at other times during early mornings. At times I wrote together with other beings (the sea, trees, rocks). At other times I wrote by myself in a somewhat austere space of the apartment where I live. Even though I had a deadline from my publisher that I proposed myself, I did not have that deadline in mind when I was writing. Writing intuitively is helpful because academic work, at least in my field and considering my philosophy of science perspective, is creative work.

At times, I wanted this book to be a summary of my thoughts, ideas and contemplations of degrowth business. But as I was writing intuitively, I realised that my mind was taking me in a somewhat different direction. While writing this book, I felt that it was becoming a combination of my research of businesses and autoethnography of this research. I could not ignore the intertwining of my research and consumption patterns. I was a consumer of the products those businesses produced. Those businesspersons were parts of the same social movements as I was. When I started my PhD in 2016, I would not dare to write this way, to explicate this intertwining. Like many others, I was encouraged to separate my research from myself and my own journey. A paper or a book was supposed to be a final and perfect product, unaffected by feelings, moods, emotions and one's own story. For this reason, when difficulties unfolded on my path, my first reaction was to write to the publisher and ask them to change the date when I had to submit my draft. But I did not do that. I decided to write while the challenges were unfolding. The time of challenges is so valuable and important. In my experience, it increased creativity and sensitivity to others' struggles and hopes. Challenges remind me of ephemerality and discontinuity. It would be a waste to wait until a challenging time in my life was over. I wanted to write authentically.

Though various ideas for this book were present in my mind ever since I started to contemplate the link between degrowth and business in 2016, I started writing this book only in the beginning of 2023. The months before May 2023 were challenging because I just moved to Finland and my now-partner and I were contemplating being a couple. We were colleagues and friends for a while but then our feelings towards each other changed. We were based in different countries. I was in Sweden and then in Finland. He was in Denmark. Being in a long-distance relationship was psychologically challenging. Afterwards, my presence at the Finnish university became challenging. Resigning from the Finnish university felt liberating, but moving to Denmark was still stressful. Gathering all the necessary documents, applying for a residence permit, waiting and then getting accustomed to a new country is never easy. And yet I experienced much spiritual growth. Realising my own vulnerability made me even more empathetic and sensitive to others' vulnerabilities, including the persons I was interviewing for this book.

Somehow, I feel that if I wrote this book in an environment that was calm, the book would be less rich and nuanced. Books are very often large works. They also need to be consistent and coherent at least in some ways. At times, when I read a book, it comes across as if it was written within a short period of time. This is because there is no sense of continuity of the author's own journey and how it affected the writing process and thoughts that crystallised into words in that book. It is not how it is in reality. Books take a long time to contemplate and write, and the way this writing unfolds is often inconsistent and discontinuous, messy and turbulent. It unfolds in parallel with other aspects of life. Apart from undergoing the struggles I mentioned above, while writing this book I was working at the same time on my autoethnography. Autoethnography is akin to keeping one's finger on the pulse of one's life. It makes a person very aware of their own thoughts that go through one's mind, one's state of being, one's emotions and generally the world within and around them. I wish every researcher of business would do an autoethnography at the same time as doing works that are more central to their field of specialism. Autoethnography is an incredibly humbling activity which results in much empathy towards the self and, perhaps most importantly, others and their journeys. Thanks to my autoethnography, I became aware of various influences that my life exerted on this book.

This book itself at times provided a refuge. Writing it was therapeutic and healing. As I am writing these words, I am also hoping that many of the challenges are in the past. I am contemplating life as a space where challenges are interwoven with joy. I am weaving my life and lessons from it together with my research.

It is liberating to read works that embrace more authentic, reflective and raw writing styles (e.g., Helin et al., 2023). For a long time, I have felt fear to write authentically. I have been fearful of using words in my academic writing that I felt comfortable using in my everyday life – spirituality, gentleness, ephemerality, simplicity, love, discontinuity and vulnerability. Somehow it never felt like these words belonged in mainstream economics and business studies. At least these were not the words used often by my lecturers when I was studying, or in the papers and books I was reading. Only some years after my PhD, I felt I could use whichever words I wanted, whichever words were most authentic and communicated most clearly what was in my mind. It is not my intention to downplay messiness and nuance, or to sound more scientific or supposedly objective and detached. Mainstream economics papers may look scientific, but too often they have very little to do with complex, messy and emerging reality. Vulnerability is one of these words that felt uncomfortable to use for a long time. I began to think much about it when I was writing my autoethnography and when I was talking to businesspersons. We are taught that our research needs to be robust somehow. Why not vulnerable and emotional? I wanted to write intentionally in a way that is vulnerable – raw, personal, emotional and imperfect. Anything other than that feels inauthentic, as if not written by humans who sweat, eat, cry, fall in love, become ill, lose and gain hope.

Main themes of this book

This book constellates the three themes of degrowth, depth and hope and focuses on sustainable businesses and their journeys. I chose the word "reflections" deliberately. So first I want to comment on why I chose this rather gentle and casual word rather than a more scientific sounding phrasing such as findings or results.

Reflections

It has been essential for me to frame this investigation as reflections – reflections rather than a literature review, an analysis and synthesis of existing discourses, reporting someone else's thoughts and findings. While there are places for such things too, there is also place for reflections. Reflections, in my view, are always humble and in becoming. Reflections are not final thoughts or perfect findings. Reflections are a space where one's research, one's self, one's own journey, places, observations, intuition and many other things intertwine in a beautiful and meaningful way. Oftentimes, researchers share their own reflections in private conversations and to a much lesser degree in academic papers. For this reason, papers often come across to me as somewhat artificial pieces of writing and lacking in something extremely important. Combined with a lack of explicit statement of one's philosophy of science and engagement with philosophy more generally, papers are not as humane as they could have been. Because of this, in my research journey I derived much more inspiration not from academic papers, but rather from classic works of philosophers, humans outside my area and from conversations with fellow humans such as businesspersons, students and many others. In terms of a format (but also content), my favourite book is "*Power of Gentleness: Meditations on the Risk of Living*" written by the French philosopher Anne Dufourmantelle. I wish more books were written this way. In my book, reflections refer to both reflections of businesspersons' own paths and my own reflections. My collection of data for this book was accompanied by reflections. While I was engaging in conversations with businesspersons, I was not trying to find something out, to make anyone ashamed of not doing enough, to question their existing practices. Rather, I was trying to understand their path better, to create space where both, them and myself, could be willingly and safely vulnerable. I was sharing openly my own experiences as a practitioner with those businesspersons, just like they were sharing their experiences with me.

Degrowth

Above, I outlined what I mean by degrowth. A degrowth society in this book is synonymous with a genuinely sustainable society. By sustainability I mean harmonious and long-lasting co-existence between humans and nature, and within humanity itself. This includes beings beyond humans. It also includes human selves. That is to say, a sustainable society is not simply one that exists within nature's limits. In theory, this could be done in a totalitarian, top-down manner. To me, degrowth is not simply a question of numbers. If so, it would not have been so difficult to bring it about. It would be possible to calculate exactly what is sustainable and assign allowances to countries, businesses and individuals. This approach is certainly not something I embrace. While I do believe that some policies could be useful (such as maximum income and universal basic income), I also believe that the best option is when a genuinely sustainable society stems from deep transformations within humans, facilitated by policies. Degrowth society to me is a society that experiences gentleness towards nature and others (humans and non-humans), a society where humans are offered, have access to, and use, countless opportunities for a more harmonious living.

Even though I advocate degrowth, research it and write about it, my feelings about degrowth are conflicted. I am hopeful that degrowth will be an even more inclusive field, embracing genuinely interdisciplinary dialogues. At the same time, it is important to understand what cannot be part of degrowth to avoid degrowth becoming a meaningless concept.

I am worried about unrealistic proposals and exclusion of large groups of humans from contemplating degrowth. It is easy to dream about a radically different society, and perhaps partly it is a function of the social sciences and education. But apart from this, we need to think about bringing about a genuinely sustainable society from what exists currently. We need to understand better how businesses can become part of degrowth and what they will look like. Perhaps in the future businesses will not exist as an organisational form, but they do right now, and I am curious about their journeys towards degrowth.

Sustainable business

These days, sustainability is a mis- and over-used word, but while disagreements exist in terms of what a sustainable society entails, how it is governed and how to get there, there still appears to be a general understanding, irrespective of a person's position, of what sustainability might mean. Sustainability is luckily something that many humans contemplate these days. Humans outside academia often have nuanced understandings of sustainability too. At some point on my research journey, I felt sceptical about this word. Perhaps many degrowth academics feel this way too. Then I came to the realisation that it is always more helpful to not be immediately dismissive when someone mentions sustainability. It is always better to ask what they mean by it and say what you mean by it too and then try to find some common ground. When I started using this approach instead, many beautiful, empathetic, thought-provoking and humbling conversations unfolded with so many different people.

I am often asked, what do you mean by "sustainable business"? Often it feels vulnerable to use this phrase. There is so much greenwashing. As a practitioner of voluntary simplicity and zero-waste, I am a consumer of sustainable products. And there is no shortage of situations where something is presented as sustainable when it is not, or not as sustainable in the end of the day. So, the term "sustainable business" can feel unsafe from a theoretical and consumption perspective. I do not think that anyone knows what a perfectly sustainable business is. Overall, I believe that there is no perfectly sustainable business. Every business is on its own sustainability journey. Some of those journeys are rather beautiful, such as those of some small and local businesses. Such businesses often approach as closely as possible the somewhat idealistic degrowth business framework. They use local, natural materials, only employ a few people, they are based on passion towards some product and love towards local nature. And yet, even these businesses require long supply chains for their equipment, they rely on services in other countries, use high technology. Often, they produce niche products which are rather expensive, such as jams and wine. In contrast, there are obviously "unsustainable businesses", often large firms operating in destructive industries such as fast fashion. Many businesses are not in one of these contrasting groups, they are somewhere in between. The situation is complicated by the fact that oftentimes businesses are trying to improve, and if we imagine sustainability as a scale, they move along this scale.

Depth

Depth in my contemplations refers to several things. It refers to the depth ontology of critical realism. Critical realism encourages us to contemplate things more holistically and beyond the surface. There is more than what can be perceived by our senses. There is more than our own research interest. For example, critical realism assumes that everything that exists unfolds on the four planes of social being: (1) material transactions with nature, (2) social relations, (3) social structures and (4) inner being (Bhaskar, 2008). As someone interested mostly in the inner being of humans, I cannot ignore the fact that we, humans, are embedded within social structures and relationships that constrain and empower and we transact with nature. This is humbling, and I believe research is better when we take various things into account that transcend our own interest. I try to pay attention to the other planes of social being, and how the plane I am most interested in is affected by what unfolds on all the other planes. Having deep conversations with researchers who specialise in the other planes has been incredibly useful for me. Having deep conversations with businesspersons is as useful and humbling. Having deep conversations with those who do not embrace degrowth has been one of the most important experiences on my research journey.

Depth also refers to deep ecology (Sessions, 1995), the need to think more broadly about being, which encompasses other beings beyond human. As I was writing these words, I came across a book called *The Handbook of Solitude: Psychological Perspectives on Social Isolation, Social Withdrawal, and Being Alone* (Coplan and Bowker, 2014). On the cover, there were the stars, the moon, water and trees. It was so interesting to me that the book was about solitude. As an individual, I spend much time alone. That is to say, without my fellow humans in proximity. But I never feel lonely or solitary. There are always other beings present – trees, animals, stars, mountains, rivers. I feel that deep ecology captures this attitude well. It expands fellow feeling, the feeling of kinship to many others, far beyond our human kin.

Depth refers to the need to contemplate and consider everything more slowly and with much more care. Science is not slow these days. There is pressure to publish, to produce more. It is incredibly difficult to write deep contemplations under such pressure. Because of this pressure to publish, many works appear every year, so it is difficult to keep up with everything that comes out, to engage in deep contemplation of those pieces, even when they are relevant and interesting. It is difficult to find opportunities to spend quality time with books and articles, to discuss the topics with the authors. Having genuinely deep, long conversations feels like a luxury and a treat rather than the norm. And even though I try to engage with depth in my works, I still feel hope that there will be space for more depth in academic spaces.

Hope

Hope comes from different sources. Partly, in my case, it comes from the worldview I have developed throughout my life. Philosophically, hope comes from humanism. I've always felt hopeful about humans, human nature and what we are capable of as human beings. This includes not only businesspersons but also humans in the state apparatus and hope in consumers. Hope in human communities, networks, groups and alternative organisations. Even hope in academia that I, perhaps surprisingly, still feel. In my teaching, autoethnography and increasingly more so in my writing in general, I prefer to talk about human beings rather than different roles they play in society. For example, to separate consumers from businesspersons is just a thought exercise. In reality, all businesspersons are also consumers. In addition to that, they are also family members, partners, friends, sometimes even academics and activists. In the end of the day, everyone is a human being. While it remains important to study social entities (such as businesses and other organisations) on their paths of degrowth (or how they could step onto such paths), more attention should be paid to *humans* in general. Paying attention to humans, their development and inner transformation is especially important for a degrowth society. In a degrowth society, humans will be playing different roles. If we imagine that in degrowth humans will have more free time, e.g., due to universal basic income or shorter work week (Buch-Hansen et al., 2024), then the same persons might be small business owners, take part in repair cafes, community gardens, volunteering and caring. Thus, it is not unreasonable to assume that humans would be trying out different roles in such a society. In some chapters of their life, a human being might want to be a businessperson, in another a gardener, in yet another they might want to focus on care work. Even in my contemplations about my own path, at times I think about the roles I would play. Without the current pressure to sell my labour in academic spaces, perhaps I would dedicate much more time to care and community work. For this reason, it makes less sense to me to talk about what kind of people businesspersons should be. Or what kind of people academics should be. It makes much more sense to think about underlying principles and us as humans.

What are the sources of hope in the degrowth discourse currently? In my experience and engagement with the field, not as many as could be. Ecological degradation, overconsumption, inequalities, injustice, persistence of capitalism and its structures are routinely highlighted. It is heartbreaking to hear from my fellow degrowth academics that they feel little hope that a better society will actually come into being. Instead of dwelling in the space of hopelessness (and indeed there are so many reasons to feel hopeless too!), I believe we need to seek sources of hope and spend more time and energy researching these sources.

2 Degrowth business

As I was working on this chapter after having published several works on degrowth business and having done many lectures on this topic too, I was contemplating if I had anything new to say. I was afraid that there would be nothing new, that I would be repeating what I already said in my other works. And simply repeating what I have said elsewhere is one of the biggest fears of mine as an academic. After publishing my degrowth business framework in 2020, I naively thought that for a long time, if ever, I would not have any new reflections on this subject. Perhaps it was even worse when I only started my PhD. Back then, I thought that in some years I would have concrete answers to my research question, that I would know what exactly degrowth business is or should be.

I was so wrong. My contemplations never stopped, and new ideas came to my mind as I moved from England where I wrote my initial paper on degrowth business to Sweden. Even more new thoughts came to mind as I moved from Sweden to Finland, and especially when I engaged in deep conversations with businesspersons and began to connect my study of business and my autoethnographic work. I began to see much more clearly how social and natural structures affected businesses, how personal journeys of businesspersons intertwined with businesses' paths, how businesses and consumers were connected. I began to recognise my own struggles in the capitalist system in the struggles of businesspersons. Diving deeper into new literatures such as humanistic geography (Tuan, 1976), humanistic psychology (e.g., Schneider et al., 2014), deep ecology (e.g., Sessions, 1995) and interacting with new cultural, socio-economic and natural spaces inspired so many new thoughts. New spaces included new countries and places, conversations with academics coming from different fields, conversations with businesspersons in different countries and conversations with fellow humans who often are, like myself, practitioners of sustainable living, voluntary simplicity, minimalism and zero-waste.

Various approaches

It is difficult to talk about the connection between degrowth and business. There can be different approaches. We can say that a degrowth society must differ so substantially from what we currently have that there should be no business at all. And

DOI: 10.4324/ 9781003452300-2

within the broad field of degrowth, it has indeed been suggested that businesses should not be part of degrowth, that a business is an inherently capitalist entity and that our scholarly interest should be directed more towards alternative forms of organisations (Robra and Nesterova, 2023). In some ways, this line of thinking is understandable if one thinks about large corporations that exploit humans, non-humans and nature. Many of their sustainability efforts are tokenistic if not laughable at the face of severe ecological degradation. In me, it provokes sorrow to witness claims of sustainability in, for instance, fast-fashion companies. I observe that it provokes sorrow in many, if not all, persons who are part of the same social movements that I am part of, such as minimalism and voluntary simplicity. Large, fast-fashion companies relentlessly offer new products that are often poor quality, while at the same time having recycling schemes or producing some of their goods from, say, recycled and organic materials. Arguably, they do not make sustainable products more accessible but rather use humans' concern about the future to increase profit. Imagining that such businesses can be part of degrowth feels futile. And while it is easy, at least in theory, to say that such businesses are certainly not degrowth, there are so many other businesses where it is not entirely clear what their relationship with degrowth could be. For example, they could produce good-quality, necessary products and make them accessible to more humans.

It can be beautiful to imagine radical alternatives, such as living in idyllic, primordial settings as hunter-gatherers (Gowdy, 2020). Everyone would be healthy and not in need of modern medical technologies, not burdened by possessions, not interested in conspicuous consumption and not bombarded by advertising. No planetary boundaries would be crossed. The water and air would be clean. Hunter-gatherer communities are imagined to be close-knit, caring and less hierarchical (Gowdy, 1998). It is easy to romanticise living in such communities and while engaging in dreaming about a seemingly perfect world to forget the benefits that modern life provides. As someone living with an autoimmune condition, at various times in my life I have relied on conventional medication, something that I usually take for granted in our technologically advanced society. And there are many other fellow humans in need of modern medicine and other modern technologies.

Alternatively, our mind can take us to a more modern society, but one where technology is appropriate, where only alternative forms of organisations exist. All production and service provision would take shape of cooperatives, repair shops, and tool libraries. Food would be grown by communities, households and foraged (Trainer, 2012). Humans would engage much more in sharing, community work, borrowing and giving. Perhaps it would be a highly localised society. There would be some large-scale production and service provision, perhaps owned by the state. But overall, when we think about these alternatives, it is hard to know what could happen to large corporations and service providers. The main issue with this society, where the vast majority of production and service provision is done by alternative or nationalised organisations, is that it is unclear how it could arise from the current society soon enough. One important issue with alternatives is that engaging with alternatives can be discontinuous, while it has to be deep and consistent, if not exclusive, to make a real difference. I've walked a path of a more ecological living for over 10 years, and what I notice at times within ecological movements is engaging with something discontinuously. That is to say, using a repair shop, using a swap shop or buying vegetable boxes from a local farm can be a one-off activity or something a human being engages with for a limited period of time. I have met so many fellow humans who would subscribe to a vegetable box from a local business, just to return to shopping in a supermarket afterwards for convenience reasons. My fellow humans would use alternatives when it is the most convenient option. I am certainly guilty of this myself. For example, I know well that getting clothing from a swap shop or a second-hand shop is a more sustainable, better option than buying new. And while I have taken clothing to a swap shop and donated clothing to charity shops, I still bought new items. No matter how sustainable these new items are, using the items that already exist is always the most sustainable option.

I often think about alternatives and what a genuinely sustainable society could look like. A thought that started my path of theorising degrowth business was that businesses exist currently. In my research of sustainable businesses, I notice that more often than not, such businesses are good at what they do. They have expertise and knowledge. They have ideas, plans, experiences of failures and successes and dreams. The unfolding of ecological degradation is intensifying, and everyone must participate in bringing about a genuinely sustainable society. This includes businesses and businesspersons too (Buch-Hansen et al., 2024). A different form of society cannot be manifested into existence just by theorising beautiful alternatives or placing responsibility and hope into one domain of society, such as spirituality of individuals, spirituality of politicians or policies. We need to work with the messy, complex and sometimes ugly reality. I think it is important to involve businesspersons into conversations about change. It is important to listen to their existing struggles and to offer suggestions for improvement.

When I started contemplating the possible role of business in a degrowth society, I asked myself what business should be like for a degrowth society to be possible. It's been many years since my degrowth business framework paper came out, and I still contemplate this question, on my own and with my fellow humans who agree and disagree, who like and dislike my original framework. It feels essential to avoid claiming finality of knowledge, and instead dive even deeper into this question.

Degrowth business framework

In 2016, when I asked myself the question of what business should be like for a degrowth society to be possible, the first thing that came to mind, both intuitively and through reading a lot of different literatures, was that such business needs to be small. Whenever I say this to my students, I can feel their sorrow about this proposal. It is not realistic. Yet, small businesses are more human-scale, closer to their customers and communities, the distance between the owners and the employees is not as dramatic as in large corporations. Oftentimes, small businesses are craft, lifestyle and family businesses, or businesses run by friends. In comparison, large corporations feel impersonal, they are powerful, often destructive. Their supply chains are incredibly complex and rarely transparent. Their remuneration for the top management is often obscene. For these and many other reasons, in my PhD I focused on small business.

I still struggle to see how large capitalist corporations can become harmonious parts of a degrowth society. Here, some things that come to mind are a different kind of ownership, educating the public about the impact of corporations on societies, heavy regulation and phasing out many of such corporations through first nationalising them (Buch-Hansen et al., 2024). On a personal note, perhaps as someone who comes from an anarchist perspective, I felt uncomfortable contemplating many questions concerning large corporations and degrowth. This is because actions by the state (nationalisation and regulation) seem necessary to make production and service provision by large corporations sustainable. Yet, the question "how about large corporations?" is one that my fellow humans ask me most often.

After realising that (most) businesses in a degrowth society should be small, I began to think about the principles of an ideal degrowth business (Nesterova, 2020a). Though it took me some years, looking back I realise that it was not an enormous challenge to identify those principles. After overviewing post-growth and other compatible and sympathetic literatures, I arrived at three groups of elements: the environment, society and non-humans, and deviation from profit maximisation. Looking back, I wish I found better names for all those three groups. When I revisited these groups years later, I certainly felt unhappy with how I named them. The word "environment" sounded too detached, as if it is something that surrounds us. Perhaps *nature* would be a better word. Society and non-humans would be named, for example, "beings" instead. Deviation from profit maximisation is about relating with the world.

The elements within those groups were rather self-evident. While I derived them from various literatures, and during my PhD years I read a lot, I am sure that a very similar set could be derived from simply sitting down with fellow humans to contemplate those three groups. It would have perhaps been an even better, deeper and more beautifully mapped set of principles if I thought about this question collectively, with fellow humans coming from different walks of life and backgrounds, different disciplines, those fellow humans who agree and disagree with my views. In some ways, those three groups of elements correspond to the domains everyone is the field of sustainability contemplates: nature, society (including the self) and the economy. To me, it was imperative to include non-human others and to question how we approach "the economic". As for the economic part of my contemplation, deviation from profit maximisation seemed obvious. Once a fellow human asked me a provocative question about these groups of elements. He asked me what the difference was between degrowth business specifically and other discourses within sustainability that addressed business. In fact, there was not so much of radical *difference*. But at the same time there is definitely more, such as sufficiency and aiming at the satisfaction of genuine human needs. There is honouring non-human beings and honouring the diversity of motives behind doing business. More importantly, perhaps is it not emphasising business itself but rather emphasising the constellation of business, civil society and the state, how this constellation works together towards genuine sustainability, what roles businesses play in humanity's journey towards genuine sustainability. But this manifested more prominently in my later works.

I embedded my framework within something broader based on the philosophy of science of critical realism that underpins my work. That something broader are empowering and constraining social structures (Collier, 1994). Later on, I came to the realisation that structures are not only social but also natural. This is when I decided to dwell in a geography department and in an area where it is impossible to not notice the effects of nature on humans. In northern Sweden nature imposes limits, for instance, on agricultural activities and mobility. That region is characterised by cold and long winters and short and mild summers. In fact, the food industry is one where it is so easy to see how business and nature relate. As I was writing these words, somewhere in the middle of writing this chapter, I went to a supermarket here in Denmark to pick up some food. It was already cold, days were short and it was snowy. In the supermarket, one could find cucumbers and tomatoes grown in Denmark. Even though the tomatoes were packaged in cardboard, I was contemplating the energy that was required to grow them. Even though they are technically local, they are absolutely not seasonal. They were also not delicious at all. They were so much less tasty than the tomatoes I bought in southern Europe in summer months. I was looking around the Danish supermarket and saw seasonal vegetables such as the celery root, Jerusalem artichokes, leeks, potatoes, parsnips, beetroots and apples. These were delicious and kept better at home than those tomatoes. Situations such as this make me think about nature's limits and messiness of degrowth business. It can be local and unsustainable at once.

Despite conflicting feeling about my own degrowth business framework that I mentioned above, constructing the "ideal" framework of a business for a degrowth society was very interesting and thought-provoking. At that time, I thought that if only all businesses were what I called degrowth businesses, then, providing other domains of society would also do their part, we would have a degrowth society. I was thinking, if only all consumers began to practise voluntary simplicity, if only all politicians dropped their personal power and status ambition and would begin to feel love towards human and non-human others and nature. Of course, such thinking is naïve. The naivety of my thinking came to mind when I was writing my first autoethnographic paper. As I was living an extremely minimalist lifestyle and consumed very little, I could not help but think that the world would be ecologically speaking in a much better place if everyone lived the same way. But all humans are different, and there is such a great diversity of ecological modes of being, though the underlying principles are perhaps the same.

So alongside contemplating and writing about degrowth business I was myself practising a lifestyle that combined elements of extreme minimalism, zero-waste and voluntary simplicity. This practice has been humbling not only in terms of feeling empathy towards others' journeys (including businesspersons' journeys), but also in terms of realising that there is no one perfect way or a benchmark. While practising extreme minimalism, which included living on my own in a very small dwelling, without furniture, pets and without common home appliances, I was witnessing that others' sustainability lifestyles looked very different but were no less legitimate and no less sustainable (in many cases even more sustainable) than mine. Thus, it is rather naïve to paint a picture of something supposedly perfect and say that everyone needs to comply. Apart from, I believe, getting the broad dimensions of degrowth business right, I still assume that these practices are common sense when certain values are adopted. These values broadly include, as my co-author and I later captured in our common works (Buch-Hansen and Nesterova, 2023), gentleness and care towards the world. Something that helped me, apart from my own autoethnography (Nesterova, 2023a), was studying businesses and having conversations with businesspersons, both those whose businesses I formally studied and more generally. Talking to practitioners is humbling. I learned a lot from them. Talking to practitioners, and listening to them, is the fastest way to bring nuance and imperfection to the surface. I also think that it largely depends on a business what elements of the degrowth business framework they can use, what elements apply to them. For example, the elements that a consultancy business can use are different to what a manufacturing business could consider. Perhaps this is something that did not come across as prominently in my earlier theorising.

Process

After constructing the degrowth business framework, I began to think so much more about businesses being on paths of sustainability rather than adopting or not adopting some framework. I came to the realisation that it was not as simple as assigning a business into a degrowth group or not-degrowth group. Rather, it was more useful and realistic to think about businesses in non-binary terms. I came to see businesses' journeys as processual. Implementing degrowth business practices is a process of navigating existing social landscapes, natural structures and inner landscapes. It is also a process of navigating capitalism. As I said in the Introduction, it is not my aim to one more time offer a critique of capitalism. But it is important to acknowledge capitalist structures and how they specifically affect businesses and businesspersons. The process of navigating these landscapes is imperfect and nuanced, animated by very human capacities for creativity, concern, care towards fellow humans and nature. The process is not linear. It is a journey of learning. Making mistakes, having doubts is natural and part of the process. This process does not unfold in a vacuum. It always unfolds within frameworks of society, nature and place-worlds, within their structures which pre-exist businesses. While businesses can participate in the shaping of those structures, the structures are powerful and can be constraining.

Talking about degrowth business can be useful in abstract, even wishful and idealistic, terms. Degrowth business is what a business should, ideally and in theory, look like in a degrowth society. But there are limits to this theorising. To transform in reality, it is more helpful to talk not about degrowth but *degrowing*. Yet, because the word degrowing is associated with decline, becoming less or smaller (which does not have to be the case in a degrowth society), it is even better to talk about the journey of a business towards degrowth. This journey entails multiple processes such as sufficiencing and transcending (Jungell-Michelsson and Nesterova, 2024). In relation to non-linearity and a processual nature of degrowth business, when I came across this quote by Bhaskar (2008, p. 159), I related deeply to it: to "be developmentally consistent is to know when to be inconsistent, when to grow, when to mature".

Human needs

Businesses and other organisations in a degrowth society need to focus on genuine human needs. If our economic activity needs to reduce, what should be sacred are the needs rather than wants. Many scholars said this, including my co-authors and myself (Buch-Hansen et al., 2024), and the deep ecology scholarship (Sessions, 1995). It also feels intuitively true. But the question of needs is difficult to navigate. Once, when I mentioned to a fellow scholar that human needs is a challenging topic to navigate, their response was that we know what the needs are. While this is true, when we start diving much deeper into the topic, we can discover much nuance. For example, food is a human need. But food satisfies not only our nutritional needs as biological bodies, but also many other needs, such as social and cultural. When we think about food, we think about ritual, tradition, celebration and holidays. Coffee and wine are not needs in a strict sense. And yet, consider the Swedish institution of fika (Jungell-Michelsson and Nesterova, 2024). It contributes to bonding between humans. It can be a degrowth practice (Nesterova, 2023c). When I moved to Sweden and joined a Swedish university, I did not take part in fika rituals very often, but the times when I joined were special and wonderful. During those times, I had an opportunity to discuss local news, understand the local culture much better, learn about my fellow academics' life stories and journeys, their hopes, dreams, struggles and successes. I learned so much during fika breaks. It feels unnecessary to propose that coffee and wine should not be produced in a degrowth society. And while it is true that at the heart of fika is perhaps social bonding rather than necessarily coffee (indeed, some drink tea and water during fika breaks), my feeling is that in the Nordics coffee consumption is still an institution.

I appreciate Maslow's outline of human needs. When it comes to a degrowth society, the satisfaction of physiological human needs for air, water, food, shelter, warmth and sleep is non-negotiable. I believe that in the case of basic human needs, adopting a normative position unapologetically should be normal. What causes sorrow and at times even hopelessness is that basic needs are still not universally satisfied.

My feeling is that generally needs are not discussed enough within business schools. Surely, they are discussed superficially, but considering the importance of the question of focusing on needs, such discussions must expand. Personally, at times I feel lost when contemplating needs, even my own needs. While I have a sufficiency list, supposedly capturing my needs apart from the very basic physiological ones, I still contemplate the question of needs often and cannot claim that

I have a perfect answer or a perfect list. I will discuss this in more depth in the Chapter 9 of this book.

In what follows, I want to revisit my original degrowth business framework together with my readers.

Environment

The first group of elements in the degrowth business framework is Environment. The elements are the following:

- reorientation towards environmental considerations
- material and energy throughput and waste reduction
- waste avoidance/reduction, pollution minimisation
- frugal, efficient use of energy and resources, eco-sufficiency, recycling, sharing of resources
- renewable energy and resource use
- durability and repairability
- appropriate or simplified technology
- localisation of sourcing, production and exchange
- pro-environmental behaviour in the workplace, including travel by employees

When I revisited my degrowth business framework after some years, the first thing I noticed was the vocabulary that felt imprecise or too detached from my own practices and emotions. Reorientation towards environmental considerations is perhaps better phrased as manifesting through one's business genuine gentleness and care towards the self, human and non-human others and nature. It is a deep and acute realisation of being in the world with others and with nature. In a degrowth society, every businessperson would care. The "environment" as a word is too abstract. In this case, we should think about the place where business is and the places it affects. We should also think about nature as a whole, and perhaps even about the cosmos at large. Where does nature end?

Material and energy throughput is a phrase commonly used in the degrowth literature. I took this phrase for granted as it was used so commonly, but later I began to contemplate what we mean by materials. Oftentimes, materials are fellow beings such as trees and rocks.

Waste reduction hints at the circular economy. When I was writing my PhD thesis, like many fellow humans interested in degrowth, I did not like the concept of the circular economy as it did not question capitalism seriously or at all. Later I came to the realisation that interesting and thought-provoking conversations can unfold with circular economy scholars, and circularity can be thought of differently.

I liked the term frugality used in earlier literatures. The term efficiency somehow feels mechanistic and technological. Perhaps frugality has a sense of foregoing something or sacrificing. When it comes to efficiency, it is often contrasted with sufficiency. It seems that opposing these practices by saying that efficiency signifies a weaker form of sustainability while sufficiency signifies a stronger form is unnecessary. Both are essential.

Sharing of resources is perhaps easier said than done. I have met many businesspersons who like the idea of this practice but find it challenging to implement it in reality. When it comes to sharing, it is much less challenging to do it as a consumption practice.

Renewable energy still requires the use of resources, say, for the production of wind turbines and solar panels. It is important that using renewable energy is seen as part of a constellation of practices rather than sufficient on its own.

Producing durable and repairable goods is also a practice that makes sense when genuine human needs are contemplated. It is not in line with degrowth to produce durable goods that are not needed in the first place.

The question of technology is challenging. In my research, I notice how technology use should not be seen in binary terms. For instance, a business is rarely high-tech or low-tech. Even the businesses I studied that were low-tech used the internet and social media which are high-tech.

The question of localisation is likewise difficult. There are many reasons why localisation is appealing to degrowth theorists. Localising production, consumption and exchange allows us to contemplate local resources, live with the rhythms of nature and build close connections with local communities. It allows us to avoid participating in long and complex supply chains, questionable practices in far-away places with weak environmental and labour legislation. There are many issues with localisation too. It is not specified within the degrowth literature as to what "the local" constitutes, whether it is one's local town, region or country. It could depend on the nature of the product too. Somehow, Danish carrots and beetroots seem local. But so does clothing that was produced in the Baltic states. Moreover, even locally produced products often rely on long supply chains. I often give an example of soap bars that became almost a symbol of zero-waste life. There are many such soap bars that can be bought here in Sweden and in Denmark, made locally by small, local and independent businesses. However, looking into the list of ingredients makes one realise that many of those ingredients travelled very far. It is possible to get local lettuce and herbs in northern Sweden in winter, grown via vertical hydroponic agriculture, but it is very energy intensive. A more sustainable way to do "local" in winter in Sweden is to consume root vegetables rather than local salad vegetables.

Pro-environmental behaviour in the workplace is not enough. What needs to change are the worldviews of humans and how they relate with the world. If their worldviews are based on gentleness and care towards the self, human and non-human others and nature, then pro-environmental behaviour would be organic and also coupled with caring behaviours towards fellow humans. If a human being remembers to switch off the light when they leave a room or recycle properly at work, it is good but not enough.

Travelling by employees should be minimised. Being in academia, I observe so many fellow humans who study sustainability and fly, for example, from the Nordics to the US. At the same time, it is a controversial topic in academia and perhaps other fields. Having international experiences and attending conferences hosted in far-away countries could be good for someone's career. Some fellow humans might be worried about compromising their career. Around 2013, I decided to stop flying for ecological reasons. Since then, I flew only once to Finland from England, the trip I had done by trains and ferries too. Afterwards, I decided to focus on my local region, the Nordics, and attending conferences as rarely as possible and only those I could reach by train. Even if it might in theory disadvantage my career, living harmoniously with nature feels more important.

People and non-humans

The second group of elements in the degrowth business framework is people and non-humans.

Workers:

- production orientated towards happiness and wellbeing, e.g., via de-specialisation, meaningful jobs, reduction in working hours, orientation towards fulfilment and the development of human potential
- decreased productivity
- democratisation of decision-making

Community:

- orientation towards societal wellbeing
- embeddedness within communities
- serving the needs/desirable sectors
- no public coercion via advertising
- democratisation of technology

Non-humans:

- consideration of non-human life

When we contemplate businesses as spaces for spiritual growth, it is essential to remember that this is not simply down to employees to create these spaces. There is a systemic issue of highly specialised production, jobs that are not sources of meaning, working hours that leave very little space for spiritual growth outside the workplace.

Reduction of working hours is not something that employees can institute themselves. Rather, there needs to be a policy that makes it mandatory to reduce working hours in a working day and to reduce a work week. In some industries, this would work differently. For instance, speaking with a German farmer who grows organic fruits about this policy idea made me realise that in organic agriculture one works with nature's rhythms rather than rhythms of society.

The question of productivity is also systemic. It is impossible in many spaces for one employee to reduce their productivity without compromising their employment. Productivity can be decreased in very small businesses, and especially craft-based ones where it takes much time to produce objects. But such businesses are exceptions rather than the norm.

Democratisation of decision-making is something that many more businesses can implement. It relates to the idea of flat hierarchies rather than top-down management.

As for communities, businesses are parts of them, and it is important that they behave as such. Production for human needs is essential, and it can be easily overlooked in the degrowth business framework, while in fact it can hardly be a degrowth business that produces objects that humans do not need. It feels controversial to suggest that whole sectors should be gone. Yet, suggesting that sectors should be gone does not mean failing to recognise that fellow humans have positive experiences even in undesirable sectors, or that these humans should not be cared for if an organisation closes down. For me personally, contemplations of undesirable sectors are difficult because for many years I have practised extreme minimalism. Such pattern of consumption excludes a great number of products. I challenge myself to navigate the space between assuming that the world would be a better place without these sectors and understanding that there exists a diversity of needs. Some categories of products that I exclude from my consumption are, for instance, clothing for special occasions, makeup, home decorations, jewellery, fast anything (food, clothing, furniture) and cars.

Advertising and degrowth do not go hand in hand. Advertising is too often a tool to stimulate demand, to encourage humans to consume more.

More democratic technologies have been part of degrowth discussions since the roots of the degrowth discourse emerged. The question of technology is challenging. Some ideas include open access, low technology and appropriate technology. Low technology is appealing because it is not as energy intensive. However, perhaps the most popular situation that is offered when discussing low vs high technology is medicine. Conventional medicine is high-tech and necessitates high-tech equipment for its production.

Apart from caring about humans, businesses need to care about, and seriously take into account, non-human beings. This should not be a tokenistic thought but something that requires so much more contemplation within the degrowth discourse. Non-human beings within the degrowth discourse are included in categories such as nature, ecosystems and the environment. But these categories are abstract. There is an urgent need to recognise that flourishing must be "more-than-human" (Phillips, 2016, p. 468). And yet when I contemplate degrowth business literature, there is not much in defence of non-human beings, including animals and other life forms such as rivers, lakes, trees and mountains.

Deviation from profit maximisation imperative

This is the third group of elements.

- focusing on qualitative change: rethinking of production, deviation from productivism, drivers other than profit, success other than material success

- shift in values: cooperation and collaboration, simplicity, responsibility, wider belonging, solidarity, non-violence
- changing attitudes to growth: smallness/human scale, non-growth, sufficiency in productive capacity
- alternative business models and ownership patterns: cooperatives, social enterprises, grassroot economic practice

I find it interesting to think about degrowth business practices as organic and intuitive. If one genuinely cares about the self, others and nature, it would make sense for them to implement degrowth business practices. For this reason, I think that knowing what these practices are is not sufficient. What is equally important are the principles from which these practices arise. These principles would make the practices more sustainable. For instance, if one genuinely cares about nature, one would take only as much from it as needed, while considering other beings. One would be inclined to use natural materials. If one genuinely cares about fellow humans, one would treat them with kindness, love, care, respect and compassion.

I believe there is a causal relationship between the mode of relatedness with the world and the practices: the mode of relatedness causes certain practices to be manifested. Some may say that it doesn't matter how one relates with the world, what matters are the actual practices where humans use materials and energy. In other words, nature does not care what is going on in humans' minds, what matters is the material aspect since this results in ecological degradation. For this reason, stricter frameworks (taxation, caps, etc.) would need to be instituted. And yet, I do not find such arguments convincing. Practices should be manifested "out of love" (Steiner, 2011, p. 138) rather than out of a sense duty or fear of authorities or punishment.

Planes of being

The planes of being framework originating in critical realism and Roy Bhaskar's writings is incredibly useful for thinking about degrowth and business. My co-author and I used it multiple times in our work (e.g., Buch-Hansen and Nesterova, 2023; Buch-Hansen et al., 2024). We also combined it with our "less and more" approach to degrowth to create space for thinking about degrowth in terms of both growth and reduction, as a dialectic of both (Table 2.1).

While theorising degrowth business, my co-author and I (Buch-Hansen et al., 2024) used the classic version of the four planes framework. To me, it seems that material transactions with nature could benefit from being expanded to transactions with nature, since not all of them are material. For instance, experiencing awe and a sense of wonder in a natural environment, such as a forest, the sea or the mountains. It relates to business too. Whenever possible, businesses and other organisations should allow employees to work in natural environments. While this may not be possible for every profession, from my experience it is possible at least in universities. In my experience, the best ideas came to mind not while sitting in a shared office with an air conditioner and a view on a car park and buildings outside. Rather, they came to mind while I was with the sea, the stars, the northern lights or in a forest, with trees and other beings.

Table 2.1 Planes of being and degrowth business

Planes of being	*Less*	*More*
Material transactions with nature	Production for wants Creating demand Long supply chains Energy consumption Globalisation	Production to satisfy needs Localised production Reduced food miles Local, renewable materials Efficiency Sufficiency Place-sensitivity
Immaterial transactions with nature	Utilitarianism	Awe Wonder Gratitude Sacredness
Social relations	Hierarchies Exploitation Utilitarianism Useful relationships	Flat hierarchies Teamwork Mentorship Care for others Kindness Empathy Compassion Relationships based on interests
Relations with non-humans	Utilitarianism	Care Consideration
Social structures	Large-scale production Fast (fashion, furniture, food) Advertising Social media as an advertising tool High technology	Alternative forms of organisations Small business Social media to receive feedback and engage in dialogues Appropriate and diverse technology
Inner being	Business growth as success Monetary success Pursuing social status Disconnection between self and work	Spiritual growth Lagom Comfort with less Curiosity Playfulness Being adventurous

Relations should likewise not be constrained to human, inter-personal relations. Humans need to develop relations with other beings, including animals, trees, mountains and rivers.

As for social structures, these are rather self-explanatory, and the value of thinking in terms of less and more is in avoiding saying that something must not exist at all, though we can say this about some things such as fast fashion. For example, while there needs to be less large-scale production, avoiding thinking of it in terms of "none" or "zero-tolerance" can help us avoid unrealistic scenarios and proposals.

When it comes to inner being, my favourite plane of being, I believe it is easy to identify what there needs to be more of. It is by no means a secret or a new proposal. The issue here is implementation.

Why do such businesses exist?

During one of the discussions of my work on degrowth business, a fellow human asked me about the existence of the businesses that I am curious about, whether they exist to fulfil some existing demand on the market. In my experience of interacting with small businesses, it is not as simple as businesspersons doing market research and then attempting to sell their goods or provide services to a certain audience. It is much more complicated than that. Oftentimes, what is fulfilled are things like passion for something, desire for independence, flexibility, curiosity and hope for a better future. Most often, it is many of these things at once. Of course, in the current system, there is a desire or hope for some profit. But it is only one consideration amongst many. Business plans and strategies are intuitive or experimental and always in becoming. This is especially so with the businesses that start very small.

In general, those humans we call businesspersons in fact play a large constellation of roles. They are at once civil society members, friends, family members, activists, consumers and participants in various groups and communities, who fulfil plural desires, duties and hopes. When seen this way, it becomes difficult to reduce these humans to a one-dimensional character who wants to maximise profit. It likewise becomes difficult to reduce their businesses to a tool for maximising profit, and to reduce their role in society and in nature to someone who instrumentalises everything to achieve the end goal.

At times, I think the reasons for such businesses' existence and paths are as diverse as reasons for personal sustainability practices. I found it easy to comprehend the diversity of motives behind a business's sustainability paths when I thought about my own practices and my own work. For example, while in my personal sustainability practice and autoethnography I often emphasised the ecological reason, I then realised that there are many more reasons than that. There is a financial reason. I notice that extreme minimalism and voluntary simplicity allowed me to have some savings. Down the line, saving helped me move countries freely and resign from an academic position in an act of activism. There is an aesthetic reason. I enjoy living with less objects and with more light and space in my home. I enjoy natural fabrics and materials. There is a health reason. Due to my autoimmune condition, I use natural textiles which are also more sustainable. There is a spiritual reason. Living with less allows me to focus on things such as my relationship with the universe. As for my work, there is a financial benefit. It is also a space where I can contemplate and create new knowledge. It is a space where I can share my knowledge and learn from others, where I can participate in bringing about a better society. The fact that I need to "earn a living" within this capitalist system does not mean that other motivations are less strong or non-existent.

Degrowth consumption

It feels odd to talk about degrowth business and degrowth compatible production without talking about consumption. In my academic journey, I focused primarily on degrowth and business. At the same time, I have been trying to live a more degrowth compatible life as a practitioner and a consumer. In many conversations with businesspersons, I noticed that they emphasise how more ecological production and consumption interlink. Most, if not all the businesspersons I spoke to, themselves practiced ecological consumption or a different mode of being in the world in many ways. But it took me a while to write about consumption more explicitly and concretely. I wrote about my own consumption in my autoethnographic work, as contemplating my own consumption revealed much nuance and struggle of trying, and oftentimes failing, to live a more sustainable life. Doing autoethnography revealed multiple reasons behind living more sustainably. I realised that apart from the ecological reason, there is also a spiritual reason, the aesthetic reason, the financial reason and the health reason. And perhaps there are more reasons that I will understand in the future as I contemplate consumption more.

Degrowth business and degrowth-compatible consumption are interrelated so deeply. It is hard to imagine businesses stepping on degrowth paths while consumers desire fast fashion, fast furniture, fast food and do not care about nature and human and non-human others. It is also odd to imagine a world where consumers buy much less, seek local, durable and repairable products, while the only types of businesses that exist are large corporations providing low-quality, not durable, mass-produced goods using components or ingredients from dozens of places. When I think about a degrowth society, a harmonious picture comes to mind, where the desires and paths of producers and consumers are compatible. The way it is currently in the capitalist system is of course not as simple and binary as I have just described. There are both small and independent businesses providing high-quality goods. There are also consumers who seek to consume goods offered by such businesses. There are also large corporations and consumers who do not deeply contemplate and question their own consumption patterns. I believe that oftentimes consumers do not step on paths of transforming their own consumption not because they love large corporations, do not love nature, fellow humans and non-humans and do not want to support small local businesses. Rather, it is because a more sustainable lifestyle can be more expensive and thus exclude many humans from participating. In my own life, I notice that practising this lifestyle requires one to be in a privileged position. For example, it helps to live in an area where everything is reachable on foot or by good public transport. Many alternatives do cost more. And even if they last longer, the initial investment can exclude many people. It feels vulnerable to say this, but it must be said. I found it easiest to practise a more sustainable lifestyle when I lived on my own but close enough to my friends with whom we could share various objects. It was when my wage allowed me to consume zero-waste and organic products. This is not to say that there are no ways to live a more sustainable lifestyle while also spending less. But some things are expensive still, such as trains here in Denmark where I live, or organic food, or home textiles made from organic cotton, or handmade soap bars. Things such as affordability and accessibility need to be discussed explicitly.

I think that a simple way to contemplate consumption is via yet again employing the four planes of being framework, combined with the less and more framework. When I was writing my autoethnography, I was wondering what could be a good way to outline my own practices. I used the four planes as this framework makes it possible to focus on a variety of practices and not forget or ignore some. For example, it reminded me that so many practices are possible because there are fellow humans around me. I also realised that so many practices that facilitate sustainable consumption are not strictly material but rather spiritual. But contemplating practices across the four planes did not feel sufficient, so I added the less and more framework too. The less and more framework in this case, just as is the case when we contemplate degrowth business, reminds us that degrowth is about a dialectic of less and more. It is not simply about reduction. In fact, very often it is about growth.

When I was sketching ideas of practices of degrowth compatible consumption as I was contemplating it, yet again I had the feeling that these practices are rather common sense. As I have practised voluntary simplicity and zero-waste for a long time, I noticed that many fellow humans within these social movements adopt these practices. It is not so that it is possible to adopt all these practices at once. Even in my own life, I started doing ethical banking only much later. But I was contemplating inner growth far before I went to a university. When I had something to give, I would. At other times, I was not giving as much. Or I was giving in non-material and non-monetary ways. The process is really messy, non-linear and discontinuous. Somehow, I believe that no one, even within the degrowth movement, is perfect in practising a more sustainable consumption pattern. At the same time, I have hope in human nature, though such hope needs to be moderated (Maslow, 1970), and to be hopeful about human nature is not to claim perfection. I think that more humans can alter their consumption, and for that there needs to be assistance from the state.

As I was writing this section, I intended it to be small, and only when I started writing it, I realised that so much more needed to be said about degrowth and consumption. I dedicated Chapter 9 to this, so those of my readers who want to dive much deeper into this subject, and engage with an example from my autoethnography, are welcome to spend some time with that chapter.

Policies

As I am working on this book, I get a feeling that policy for degrowth is becoming and even more popular topic (see e.g., Fritz and Lee, 2023; Khan et al., 2023). For good reasons. As we have seen above, it is easy to theorise what businesses and consumers need to do. But they do it within certain social structures that constrain and empower. It is naïve to assume that change would arise solely from one's will or one's mind. Policies need to empower transformation, create space for thriving of small, independent, local businesses and alternative modes of being. It makes sense to talk about policies, as better business and better consumption are so interrelated.

At times, my fellow humans ask me what policies need to be there. I think this knowledge is not secret. Policies for a degrowth society have been outlined and include, for instance, income caps, wealth tax, UBI (universal basic income), UBS (universal basic services), shorter workdays and shorter work weeks (Buch-Hansen et al., 2024). This is not to say that policies are not contentious and that these are exclusively degrowth policies. For example, some within the degrowth discourse note that UBI can be used to encourage consumerism. There is also a question of quality. For example, free education for all could be a UBS. But education is not always good or compatible with degrowth. For example, educating humans in mainstream business studies and neoclassical economics is not going to help.

I am not a policy scholar, and this is not necessarily the topic that has interested me the most. I am much more interested in inner being of fellow humans, in our spiritual transformations and how they can manifest in concrete practices, and how they do it already. So, I do not want to speak about policies with a voice of authority. However, it seems obvious from my own research that a UBI and UBS would be helpful. A UBI would allow humans to, for instance, take time off work to contemplate their modes of being in the world. It would allow them to resign from the jobs and spaces from which they feel disconnected or where they are exploited or harassed. It would allow them to make better choices (e.g., organic food and durable goods). Perhaps it would allow them to try and make a small business out of their hobby or craft. Naturally, policies should work together. For instance, even if one had time to start a small business, they would also need access to financing that is fair, non-exploitative, does not alienate the person from their business and that is easy enough to navigate.

I think we should contemplate UBS in depth. Services such as healthcare, education, transportation and housing should ideally be free. However, a more degrowth compatible policy could be, for instance, making local travelling free while also taxing long-distance flights to holiday destinations. Housing that provides lagom space should be free, but large spaces should be taxed. Education that is genuinely useful and helpful for a better society should be free, while education (e.g., in economics) should be heavily transformed. Perhaps outlining such directions of thought raises more questions than it answers. For example, it restricts people's freedoms, requires heavy government intervention. It requires, essentially, groups of humans to make decisions for others. There could also be controversial situations and exceptions such as having family members living in those holiday destinations or humans living with non-human beings they adopted and who require space.

3 Depths of relatedness, sufficiency and circularity

I hope that sometime in the future, thinking in terms of disciplines will become obsolete. In a better world, it seems, better answers could be reached when one starts with a research question, genuine curiosity, willingness to read far beyond one's own discipline, willingness to listen and to work with fellow humans coming from various backgrounds. Staying within the limits of a particular discipline may feel safe. There are certain theories, recognised names, journals and methods. What is outside of them may feel scary and unknown. At times when I walked out of the limits of some discipline or a field of knowledge, it was a humbling experience. What I thought to be new and unexplored was discussed intensely and extensively somewhere else. For example, when I started to investigate consumption in relation to degrowth, there was not much out there linking these two fields. At the same time, many questions degrowth might have about more sustainable consumption were discussed and answered beautifully by various scholars of sustainable consumption, deep ecology, voluntary simplicity and other fields. It takes time to dive deeper into another discipline and long conversations with others, but it is so important. Pressure to publish does not help. I feel that it leads to a utilitarian approach to science and knowledge. It does not allow humans to take time to contemplate something at length. In this chapter, my main message is that business is not isolated and cannot be understood as an entity in itself. Neither can it be understood by studying economics, organisation and management literatures only. Perhaps such literatures are not even essential to understand business. Some of my students studying business came from various scientific backgrounds, not necessarily economics and business studies. It never was a disadvantage. Perhaps, it was even an advantage in the world where new thinking is so necessary. Business can be understood as a social entity that is deeply related with the world. And the world includes consumers, families, activists, animals, trees, rivers, mountains and many other entities and beings. Business can be understood even better in conversations with businesspersons rather than as an abstract entity. Such conversations inevitably lead to realising the depths of relatedness of business with the world.

Relatedness

A business as a social entity exists in the world in deep connections with others and with various social and natural structures. This includes other social entities such as

DOI: 10.4324/ 9781003452300-3

organisations, individual human beings, non-human beings, various social systems (finance, education, transportation, policies, norms, rules) and nature. Even though disciplinary thinking (e.g., business studies) encourages us to focus on connections that a particular discipline is interested in, this approach is not holistic and not useful for bringing about a genuinely sustainable society. Disciplinary thinking in business studies, for instance, focuses on the relationship of a business with other businesses in various networks, with suppliers, distributors and customers. Focusing, for example, on non-utilitarian relationships between a business and non-human beings is not yet within the premises of mainstream business studies. In mainstream business studies, non-human beings are seen as service providers, resources, materials or even ingredients, but not as fellow beings or kin with whom we share this planet, our common home.

Looking at the state of affairs from an existentialist perspective reveals the depth and multiplicity of relationships of a business with the world. This does not mean that more traditional focal points associated with business studies, such as business networks or supply chains, should be ignored. Rather, it means that a much broader range of topics deserves our curiosity, and a much broader range of research questions can be considered. Within business school contexts, oftentimes students wonder if researching a particular topic for their thesis is sufficiently business-related or business-orientated. Such students are exhausted by mainstream economics and mainstream business studies contents. Often, they recognise that conventional approaches cannot solve the issues of, for example, ecological degradation. Embracing a more holistic, existentialist approach expands our view of business. It results in more interesting and diverse research journeys and illuminates our understanding of plural and diverse ties between a business and the world, or even the cosmos. This diversity may be concealed and overlooked if only investigation of more traditional business topics is allowed and encouraged.

There are three or even four interconnected dimensions of our being in the world that existentialism, and the fields inspired by existentialism, captures (Nesterova, 2021c; van Deurzen and Adams, 2016). These dimensions can be also called "worlds", the Eigenwelt (the self-world), the Mitwelt (the with-world), the Umwelt (the surrounding world). In other words, they include the self, others and the environment. The fourth dimension can be referred to as the spiritual dimension (the Überwelt). It concerns, for instance, the universe or even God, if one is religious. I do not consider myself religious but certainly I consider myself spiritual, so personally I feel comfortable using terms such as the universe or the cosmos in my inner dialogues and in my academic writing. Some fellow humans, including businesspersons, fellow academics, and students, that I have spoken to on my research journey are religious and prefer to use the term God. I felt that we had a common understanding of the Überwelt despite these different approaches and worldviews.

While the first three dimensions may feel justified, intuitively or experientially true and scientifically acceptable and comfortable, considering the state of social science, still largely and unfortunately influenced by positivism, there is a chance and a risk that the fourth dimension will be overlooked or mentioned in passing. One may fear to come across as unscientific if they become interested in this dimension or feel ashamed of bringing the spiritual into their scientific pursuits. However, the notion of spirituality in this, or any other context for that matter, should not make anyone feel uncomfortable. Oftentimes businesspersons mention their own relationships with something bigger than us, be it the universe or God, something that allows them to transcend themselves, see beyond the mundane, or to see magic, meaning and value in the mundane. I always felt that it is unreasonable to exclude this beautiful, complex and meaningful relationship out of fear of being judged by some humans in the scientific community. I also wonder if it is reasonable to exclude this dimension if it motivates fellow humans to behave in ways that are kind, caring, loving, gentle and considerate. Hence, I will start this discussion on relatedness with the spiritual dimension first.

To me, this dimension seems foundational. It has a deep and significant implication on how we as humans relate with the entities in the other three dimensions: the self, human and non-human others and the environment. Businesspersons are, like any other persons, beings with certain philosophical, spiritual and religious convictions that influence and sometimes even guide the way they relate with the world and how they choose to exercise business practices and personal practices, which practices they wish to include in the way they do business, and which practices they wish to avoid. There is a wide variety in the constellation of principles, as every businessperson is a unique human being. I've met some businesspersons who explicitly based their businesses on certain religious principles and guidelines, and those who simply experienced self-transcendence and tried to live according to this realisation of oneness and connectedness between themselves and the cosmos. They did not connect it with any particular religion and simply wanted to run their businesses in a way that honours something "larger than us". And one does not exclude the other. That is to say, some combine religious and other (spiritual, philosophical) beliefs successfully to form beautiful worldviews, modes of being and constellations of personal and business practices.

The spiritual dimension in relation to degrowth seems very important, as stepping on a degrowth path necessitates self-transcendence of some kind, i.e., experiencing care and concern for something beyond and larger than one's own life. It includes experiencing these attitudes towards fellow humans and other beings that one will never meet, towards places one will never visit. It is interesting and puzzling that this dimension has been largely overlooked or mentioned in passing within the degrowth discourse, including in relation to business and degrowth. Within the field of sustainability, oftentimes fellow academics highlight, in personal conversations and during *fika*, their own spiritual journeys, the importance thereof, and their personal desire to bring together spiritual convictions and research. Yet, their research remains more aligned with traditional and safer topics and subjects.

On many occasions, especially earlier on in my research journey, I also felt hesitant to talk openly about my relationship with existence, the universe or the cosmos, and about my spiritual beliefs in general. I did not want to come across as unscientific or acquire undesirable labels. I was afraid of not being taken seriously. Later, I felt more comfortable about it and do not feel ashamed of my beliefs, expressing them in academia and beyond academic spaces. I feel more comfortable using a much broader vocabulary in academic settings than I felt was possible in the beginning of my PhD and before that time. Trying to conceal my beliefs and the importance of my relationship with the universe could result in a failure to acknowledge an extremely important, if not central, generative mechanism behind my own practice of ecological living. As years went by and as I contemplated my own practice via an autoethnographic study, I realised that practising the mode of living I describe in my autoethnography is not caused by more knowledge about ecological and social degradation and various facts about it. Rather, it is caused by a certain way of relating with the cosmos and seeing my role in existence. This is not to say that knowing more or being exposed to facts about, say, biodiversity loss, does not encourage, motivate or empower me to act further. It certainly does. But knowing more is, in my experience, not the reason. It would be purposefully misleading to say that learning more made me step on a path of a different mode of being. Perhaps for other humans, it is different. In multiple conversations with fellow humans, I realised that some changed their modes of being purposefully as they learned various facts about ecological degradation.

I notice that the language humans use to describe relating with the world differently is very much shared between many spiritually inclined sustainability academics that I talked to and sustainability-orientated businesspersons. In my own experience, some of the most vibrant and intimate conversations unfolded between myself and businesspersons not on the topics of concrete business practices such as using renewable energy, natural materials or implementing circularity. Rather, they unfolded on the topics broadly falling within the premise of spirituality, self-transcendence and our (human) connection with the world at large. It is most interesting to understand how spirituality, self-transcendence and attitudes to connectedness of everything with everything else manifest in practices.

Studying spiritual aspects would, at least to some extent, explain why businesspersons, for instance, try out alternative business models, are genuinely curious about such models, take risks to try something new and different. It would also help us understand what systems need to be in place, apart from the more obvious ones (e.g., green finance, UBI (universal basic income)) that we have discussed elsewhere (Buch-Hansen et al., 2024) to support degrowth transformations in relation to business. For instance, perhaps it is the case that philosophy needs to be taught more seriously at schools, economics departments and business schools.

Oftentimes, how a human being relates with the world is left outside the premise of education. It is assumed that it is one's personal matter, not a matter of formal education. On so many occasions, I've seen students wanting but feeling hesitant to connect their spiritual beliefs with their scientific journeys and projects. Like myself some years ago, they feel uncomfortable about it, expect judgement, expect not being taken seriously. It takes time to create a safe space where topics such as self-transcendence, spirituality and being in the world can be discussed, especially in the realms of business schools. Philosophy beyond philosophy of science is not a common subject in business schools either. In my view, this approach is deeply mistaken. This is not to say that a certain spiritual or philosophical doctrine needs to be instituted. Rather, a range of philosophical tools needs to be offered to humans so they can more seriously and intentionally reflect on and construct a healthier (gentler, more caring and loving) way of relating with the world at large.

As I am writing these words, I am thinking about some encounters in academia that I've had over the years. At times, I would meet a fellow human in an academic space who also considered themselves spiritual, who practised spirituality and was seeking ways to weave together their research and spiritual beliefs. After some moments of hesitation, we would always feel that it is safe to discuss topics such as self-transcendence, oneness and intuition with each other. We would feel safe to use the words we wanted and that felt right rather than the words that sound scientific or feel appropriate in a business school context. Such experiences were magical and liberating.

The self, others, nature

All the four dimensions of the self, others, nature and the spiritual are interrelated. The way humans relate with each of these dimensions has implications for how we relate with the remaining dimensions. For instance, since the self is part of existence at large, it is difficult to imagine an unhealthy relationship with the self co-existing with healthy relationships with others. It is likewise difficult to imagine someone experiencing deep and genuine care and concern towards fellow humans and disregard towards non-human beings.

A business as a social entity relates with the selves of humans in many ways. This connection is perhaps most obvious in small businesses, and even more so in micro businesses. In very small businesses, it is difficult (and even unnecessary) to separate the business from the human being who operates it. Oftentimes, such businesses grow from their founders' own passions, crafts, skills and interests (Nesterova, 2021a), as well as a desire to derive income from engaging with one's passions, crafts, skills and interests rather than from selling one's labour to someone else and navigating working for someone else. This is understandable and should not be seen as commercialisation of one's passion. Such passions and interests can include local ingredients, food, wine, natural body care, even sustainability consulting that considers local culture, place and local social and natural structures. Perhaps those fellow scholars, to whom writing is their passion as much as their job, can identify themselves with these words. At least, I see much similarity between craft-based, small-scale production and the approach to research and writing some fellow academics have.

Moving further up the scale of business, away from micro businesses and towards larger ones, this oneness between a businessperson and a business may start to dissolve. For instance, some businesses are passed down generations, bought and sold. Involvement of external finance may have implications on how a business is operated. In all these cases, a business is not a manifestation of one's worldview as is the case with almost idyllic, personal and humane micro businesses but a more obviously economic and legal entity. Yet even in these situations, the self and business relate. The self of each human transforms or reproduces social dynamics within business and participates in decision-making on various scales.

However, it is interesting to note how different the modes of relatedness with the self are in micro businesses and large ones. In a micro business, there is often a sense of amalgamation or identity, while in a large one a person might feel replaceable and powerless. This is something that still needs to be untangled within the degrowth discourse.

Micro and small businesses appear to be perfect forms for degrowth, and much has already been said on this. I have discussed this topic above too. Large-scale production has been acknowledged as necessary and various degrowth ideas and ideals have been applied to this kind of production. Perhaps, nationalisation could be an option. Yet, nationalisation does not solve the issue of scale in relation to the self. Social dynamics of power manifested in authoritarian supervision can be reproduced in a nationalised business. The self might not thrive in this situation and be encouraged to manifest its best in such spaces. Considering this, contemplating reductionist policies and solutions seems lacking in nuance. Policies often overlook the quality of a space.

Humans are in the world with others (Heidegger, 2001). In itself, a business is a social entity, a community of humans (Lawson, 2015), if it is not a sole proprietorship. A business interacts with other humans as well. They include customers, humans in other businesses, communities, activists, academics, artists, as well as businesspersons' and employees' families and social circles and random persons who crossed their paths but were in some ways influential. Needless to say, a business that is on a degrowth path would take all of these humans into account. It would take future humans into account too, even if it sounds philosophical and abstract. This is easier to accomplish for a small business. Some of the most beautiful modes of interactions with others I have observed in very small businesses operated by family members (or couples, or close friends) in the UK and in Sweden where I did my research. The relationships seemed genuinely harmonious, values were aligned and skills were complementary. Those businesspersons interacted well with each other, had a somewhat playful and adventurous approach to business, overcame challenges together. Their mode of relating with each other expanded to their customers, activists, academics and many others. The feeling of a family extended to their employees if they had any. When friends and other like-minded individuals were involved, relationships within those businesses likewise seemed harmonious and non-hierarchical, though perhaps more formal. As I was studying businesses run by either families or friends, despite occasional challenges that every human faces on their journey, I could not help but think that if I was to establish my own business, I would do it with my partner or a close friend.

As I mentioned in the beginning of this book, I have never studied large businesses as part of my research, though as anyone else in academia I experience structures of universities as large organisations. The contrast between large organisations I have worked for and small ones I studied is dramatic. It is more difficult and less intuitive to apply the term "organisation" to a small business. The way humans relate to one another changes as the size of organisation increases. A large organisation seems more grounded in roles and hierarchies than in humanness and genuine and authentic relationships, though naturally there are pockets of very human ways of interacting such as when co-workers become friends or partners. But overall, I always feel sorrow when I contemplate small and large businesses. As I contemplate this topic, it always becomes clear that a degrowth society cannot house only small businesses. Yet at the same time, I don't see much beauty in large businesses. This is not to say that their products or services are not necessary – indeed some of them are – but I always doubt that large businesses can be genuinely humane, that they can, thoroughly and universally be based on kindness, affinity, care, concern, love, empathy, solidarity and other human qualities and capacities.

Degrowth scholars hope that a degrowth society will be based on very different values that guide how humans relate with one another, including in business contexts. For example, competition is often cited as one of the principles of interaction that will not be part of degrowth. While at this point in the degrowth discourse it is almost self-evident that cooperation is desirable, it is yet unclear how this will be achieved in social interactions within businesses. Many, if not all, humans in larger organisations perhaps have experienced how deeply ingrained competition is. Perhaps differences in wages between those lower and higher up in hierarchies should be abolished, alongside strict hierarchies themselves. Not to mention differences in the stability of employment. Perhaps anyone in academia is familiar with enormous differences between poor and short-term contracts that early career researchers often have and comfortable and safe conditions offered to professors. Businesses should be spaces of exploring, thinking, learning and working together, and this becomes difficult when differences in conditions are very large.

Apart from other humans, there are also non-human others with whom businesses relate, whether they recognise it or not, whether they see it as a relationship or not. In the degrowth discourse, relationships of business with non-human beings have not received enough attention. As I am writing these words, I am hopeful that at some point these words will become untrue or dated. Here, as elsewhere in my works, I use the term "non-human being" in a very broad sense, to include not only other animals but also trees, rocks and what is usually seen as features of nature or even ecosystems (rivers, lakes, mountains). To view, say, lakes as beings to some may come across as unscientific or poetic at best. Yet, to others it makes perfect sense, such as to the advocates of deep ecology such as Arne Naess who adopted a mountain as his father. Interestingly, to some seeing a lake or a mountain as a being seems mystical and obscure, while seeing the same entities in a utilitarian way, as a collection of resources, is somehow justifiable. It is difficult for me to see why the utilitarian view should be maintained and embraced, seen as normal, clever and scientific, while viewing a non-human being as kin should be discounted as abstract, poetic, unscientific or childish.

There is certainly some evidence of taking non-humans into account in different kinds of businesses. Businesses that avoid, for instance, animal ingredients and ingredients that harm non-humans are certainly on a path of relating with non-humans differently. Yet, there is still a long way to go. It remains rare to hear businesspersons' contemplations about other beings and forms of life that are not animals. More often, such contemplations fall within the premise of talking about "nature" where nature is a system that includes beings and various relationships between them. But those beings are not usually singled out. It could be that contemplating beings individually is a more mindful and intentional approach, but it is not common and prevalent in the contexts where I have done my research (England and the Nordics).

Businesses are also related with the environment or nature. Businesses' impact on nature has traditionally been a concern of the degrowth discourse. The general idea is that this impact needs to reduce. Many ideas of practices exist within this discourse (Hankammer et al., 2021; Nesterova, 2020a). These various ideas outline how a better mode of relating with nature can come about. Producing sufficiently to satisfy human needs, producing locally, using natural materials, implementing circularity as a principle to keep resources in use as long as possible – all of these are examples of practices. In reality, every business has its own, unique constellation of practices it implements and practices that businesspersons would like to implement on their ecological paths. Every aspect of a business's existence entails interacting with nature.

It is interesting to contemplate where more ecological practices stem from. They may, in a degrowth society, stem from legislation and duty. However, even in this diverse social system that combines many elements of capitalism and many elements of humanness, there are humans and businesses that do much more than what is generally expected from them. From my conversations with these fellow humans, seeking and implementing such practices stems from a certain worldview those humans hold. That worldview can be captured and expressed using various words such as concern, care and gentleness. In very simple terms, they do it out of love. Roy Bhaskar (2000, p. ix) seems to be right in saying that "the most appropriate (correct, best possible) ethical and political stance is one of unconditional love for our essential selves, and that of each and every other being and the environment we inhabit". And while it might be easy to relate to this statement, the challenge is to nurture this worldview.

The same domains of relatedness that existentialism captured were captured by critical realism and its four planes of being that I and others (Buch-Hansen et al., 2024) have found very helpful in our works to think about being and becoming in a more nuanced and holistic way. I mention the four planes often in my works and in this book, just in case a fellow human reads this book in their own way, starting where they wish to start or engages with it creatively and discontinuously. The planes include material transactions with nature, social relations, social structures and inner being. While material transactions with nature and inner being correspond to the domains of the environment and the self, respectively, being in the world with others highlights both inter-personal relations and social structures, both of which are constituents of society alongside agents (human beings) themselves.

Recognising and contemplating our own relatedness with the world and social entities' relatedness with the world is not enough. It is essential to manifest this understanding in practice. This has been on my mind since I started my PhD and went into academia. It felt important to me to go far beyond saying that I understand our relatedness with nature and our dependence on it. It was imperative to manifest it in my practice and to understand how others do it. In this chapter, I decided to focus on sufficiency and circularity specifically, as these are complementary practices that are central to transforming both business and consumption.

Sufficiency

Currently, there is much discussion of the principles that are central to a genuinely sustainable society. Sufficiency is one such principle. In simple terms, sufficiency is an alternative to "ever more". In fact, sufficiency is both a principle and a value (Jungell-Michelsson and Nesterova, 2024). It is a principle as it can guide the way we produce and consume, and it is a value as we can come to see it as beautiful and meaningful in itself. Sufficiency feels better than less, as less may make us think about deprivation, going without, poverty and sacrifice. Sufficiency also feels better than more, as it makes us more respectful towards nature and its limits, others and the self. Here I want to expand on the link between sufficiency and the self. As opposed to self-limitations, I view sufficiency as finding joy in the feeling that one is enough, and that one has enough. Looking for "ever more", striving to buy and accumulate comes across as seeing oneself and one's life as always deficient in something.

Sufficiency requires more contemplation of what enough may be. And such contemplations can be playful and thought-provoking, as well as good in themselves, as they may evoke feelings of solidarity and empathy. In my practice, I notice that sufficiency orientation is calming and makes living more manageable, joyful and mindful. There are several words associated with sufficiency, such as "enough" and "limits". But also a Swedish word lagom (meaning "just right") captures sufficiency well, in my view. A good and simple example from everyday life to illustrate the meaning of the word lagom is a situation where you may serve something to a fellow human. As they recognise that they have received enough, they may say that it is lagom for them. Lagom is not something a group of experts decides and tells humans what lagom is for them. Rather, lagom is subjective. What is lagom for me may be different to what is lagom for a fellow human. In itself, what is lagom is not necessarily a perfectly sustainable quantity or amount of something, but contemplating it allows us to avoid extremes and look for what is right for oneself. It is important because certainly the capitalist system does not seem to have many proposals based of the notion of "enough". It always pursues more. I use the word lagom often in my everyday life as I find it very useful in relation to having the right amount of food, the just right number of objects, walks and so on. It feels so useful that I brought it with me to my Danish household.

Sufficiency overall has a positive connotation and is a welcoming concept. The principle and value of sufficiency is shared across multiple strands of ecological thought, including degrowth, deep ecology and American environmentalism. While degrowth may be associated with reduction, perhaps due to earlier definitions and calls for reduction and downscaling, sufficiency is more about contemplating what suffices and what is unnecessary, how to live well while having enough for a good life. It appears that the sufficiency discourse, which generally also falls within the post-growth direction of thought, attracted those who found degrowth to be too confrontational and alienating. Some of the most wonderful and thought-provoking conversations that I have had in my academic journey were with scholars of sufficiency. There appears to be so much gentleness within that field of thought.

Sufficiency is not something that businesses can bring about on their own (Nesterova and Buch-Hansen, 2024). It requires effort from multiple domains of society. With my co-authors, we considered three domains in our works: civil society, state and business (Buch-Hansen et al., 2024). Naturally, there is overlap between the domains of civil society, state and business. Humans who are members of civil society can also be businesspersons and work for the state. However, the roles and functions of these domains are still somewhat distinct. Perhaps in every domain, relationship with sufficiency will look different. The state can nationalise and phase out industries that oppose sufficiency, such as fast fashion and fast furniture businesses. The state can also ensure that education that humans receive is of high quality and suitable to both address ecological degradation and live well as individuals playing various roles in society and in nature. It can impose better regulations on advertising that encourages humans to consume more. And the state can provide guidance in terms of what limits are, based on expertise and evidence. One role of businesses is, for example, to design products in deep conversations with customers, that will allow humans to practise sufficiency in everyday life. It is also a role of business to produce enough to satisfy needs of all. One role of humans in civil society is to develop modes of being that embrace sufficiency. Civil society can develop modes of being to which sufficiency is central and practise lifestyles that are sufficiency-orientated, such as voluntary simplicity, simple living, zero-waste, slow living, minimalism or some constellation of those. Together these pursuits will result in a society and economy based on the principle of enough.

In the civil society, the concept of "lagom" seems most appropriate. Lagom is subjective, thus it provides freedom for every human being to figure what is "just right" for them, hopefully without resorting to entitlement and disinterest in the wellbeing of fellow others, including humans and non-humans. Stating that everyone, including the state, civil society and business, needs to be involved in seeking sufficiency shows the breadth of effort. Apart from recognising how broad the effort should be, it is interesting and necessary to consider the depth of effort. The depth goes all the way from inner being to transactions with nature. Here I will use the critical realist four planes of being.

Transactions with nature

Degrowth discourse stems from the recognition of nature's limits, of ecological degradation resulting from disregarding those limits and a felt need to do something about it. Overall, this entails reducing production to what is enough or sufficient for all. Generally, only production to satisfy genuine needs must take place, but the question of needs is difficult and messy, as I mentioned earlier. Alongside this, individual humans' material transactions with nature need to be reduced where individuals consume at an unsustainable rate. It always feels vulnerable to me to discuss the topic of individual consumption. In my own life, I chose a constellation of minimalism, voluntary simplicity and zero-waste as a mode of being. I understand that not every human being wants to live this way. At the same time, I do not think that a genuinely sustainable society can be possible if humans pursue living with ever more objects and using ever more services that require materials and energy to be provided. Naturally, there are more ecological ways to live with more than I and fellow practitioners of minimalism do. It can be done via, e.g., second-hand shopping, keeping items for a long time, keeping inherited objects, storing useful items such as tools and food. But "more" achieved via consuming new items is unsustainable. As a practitioner, I avoid keeping inherited objects and even useful items because I prefer to borrow objects from friends and family when I need them, and I always think that someone else would use some items much more than I do. At times, I am somewhat sceptical about living with ever more even when the objects were obtained in ecological ways. For instance, I avoid second-hand shopping. Though it is a more ecological way to consume, say, clothing, I want to take part in normalising wearing the same outfit every day if one so wishes. For my fellow humans, it would be hard to tell without asking if I bought the item of clothing I wear new or second-hand.

On this plane of transactions with nature, usually it is the material aspect of production that is highlighted. However, our transactions with nature go far beyond the material, or us taking resources from nature and returning wastes to nature. We transact with nature in many different ways, including immaterially. For example, self-transcendent feelings such as awe and wonder result from us interacting with nature. Nurturing such feelings and dwelling in such experiences may be conducive to adopting sufficiency as a value. On my own journey, I notice that immaterial transactions with nature are linked very closely with practising sufficiency. When I spend quality time with the sea, the sun, forests, rivers and lakes, everything is put into perspective. Somehow wearing the same outfit every day feels normal, advertisements look repellent, tasteless and forceful, and I want to take from nature only what I genuinely need.

Social relations

Sufficiency can be brought about via interactions between human beings. For example, contemplating together what sufficiency is, our experiences with sufficiency, how to share existing objects and make them last longer together has benefitted me greatly as a practitioner. As a practitioner, I have countless sufficiency-related conversations with others regularly, and they give me hope and provide new ideas. I do not only talk to my fellow academics about this. There is so much that I learned from humans from different walks of life and of different ages, in different spaces. Practising sufficiency is joyful, and it can be a safe space when long conversations about ecological degradation become intensely anxiety-provoking. Businesses can participate in such conversations too. Small businesses have a privilege of intimate connections with their customers and can learn much from them. They can develop inter-personal relationships with customers and step on sufficiency paths together with them. As some businesses that I research are also businesses that make some of the products that I consume in my everyday life, I often share my contemplations on sufficiency with these businesspersons. A very important aspect of practising sufficiency in one's everyday life is living with objects that are durable and repairable. I also want to say beautiful. By providing feedback to businesses, I believe it is possible to direct production towards these types of objects.

Beyond social relations, there are relationships between humans and non-human others and even with objects. Businesspersons producing wild berry wine in Sweden that I spoke to were contemplating the amount of berries available and noted that there are enough berries for both wine production and for the animals living in that region. Apart from non-human others, I am wondering about *things*. Too often we do not honour the things we live with. Everything is seen as replaceable. But practising sufficiency requires a very different, more caring, approach to objects.

Early on in my minimalist journey, I sketched a playful "sufficiency list". It was a small, personal experiment that eventually led me to autoethnography. At that time, I asked myself what items I could not live without. That is of course an exaggeration, as I could probably live without most of those objects, but they certainly made my life easier and more comfortable. When I practised extreme minimalism, I lived with those objects and not many other ones. As of August 2022, the sufficiency list included my laptop, phone, headphones, passport and other documents, notebook, pen, shoes, backpack, bank card, personal care items, towels, sweatshirts/T-shirts, trousers/shorts, bowl, fork, spoon, knife, stockpot, dish brush, tote bag, jacket, handkerchief, scissors, blanket, lunch box, mug, scarf and mittens (Nesterova, 2023a). The list changed somewhat over time, but it didn't change much. As of December 2023, it includes my laptop, phone, passport and other documents, shoes, backpack, bank card, personal care items, towels, shirts, trousers, cotton tote bag, reusable water bottle, jacket, scissors and scarf. When I moved from Finland to Denmark, that was everything I brought with me. In Finland, I lived without furniture and all the kitchen items were borrowed from friends. The climate in Denmark is somewhat milder, so I don't have mittens. All the kitchen items belong to the fellow human I share this space with. At times I think it is odd that at 34 I do not even own a mug. At the same time, I have never had difficulties borrowing a mug from friends. More recently, I started using a simple glass jar that was home to pasta sauce as a mug, and it works well. When I was revising this chapter, which was just after Christmas, I wanted to note that my partner gave a reusable coffee cup to me as a gift. It was not an absolutely necessity, but it would allow me to eliminate single-use coffee cups when I'm out. I began to use the reusable cup at home too, alongside the glass jar. Because there are so few objects that I live with, I developed a close connection with them. This is not to say that I would feel bad if they were taken away from me by a fellow human. Indeed, it is not the worst unfolding that could happen. But I am grateful that the scarf that I acquired in Sweden lived with me in three Nordic countries and kept me warm in all of them. This scarf is sufficient even if it develops imperfections. It has a story and shared a life and experiences with me for some years. I don't keep many sentimental items, but in this situation, it appears that an everyday, useful item acquired sentimental meaning.

Social structures

Humans and social entities such as businesses exist within social structures and constantly interact with them. Social structures can both empower and constrain. For sufficiency to thrive as a principle, as a practice and a value, those social structures need to be in place that empower sufficiency pursuits and exploration. Social structures need to make sufficient production possible, create spaces for sufficiency-orientated social interactions, and spaces for personal growth towards a worldview that incorporates and celebrates sufficiency. Currently, social structures are more geared towards materialistic growth and encourage accumulation and attachment to things, money and status (Fromm, 2013). One critique that I hear very often from fellow humans in general, but especially from my students, is that degrowth is still very abstract. They want to discuss possible solutions. Something that comes to mind in terms of social structures and sufficiency is the following. More humans need to be given opportunities to start small businesses, turn their craft and skill into a business. For this, they need time and financing. They need time to reflect on a business idea, on their skills and their development and their journey. For this, policies such as reduced working hours, shorter work week, paid leave, or UBI could be helpful. When I contemplate my own consumption, I realise that so many objects could be or are produced by very small, local businesses. While their products may be more expensive than the ones produced by large corporations, oftentimes they are much better quality and made from better materials. These objects are beautiful, and they last longer. The question of financing has not been addressed sufficiently in degrowth. Borrowing to start a new business, especially with an intention to not grow, may be challenging.

Alternative organisations such as swap shops and repair shops can facilitate sufficiency, keeping the same objects in circulation in society. It is interesting to contemplate why humans would engage in such organisations. In my view, there needs to be a strong constellation of values that would encourage humans to do it. Sufficiency is just one of these values. Oftentimes, going to a swap shop requires commitment and dedication, as it is a much less convenient option than buying. It might require time to visit several swap shops to find exactly what one is looking for.

Education needs to become much better at encouraging humans to contemplate sufficiency and weave it into the fabric of their worldview. Importantly, such education needs to begin much earlier than at the level of higher education. As I was revisiting this part of the chapter, I was thinking about my partner's four-year–old child whom I met recently and other young humans of her age. Sufficiency often gets overlooked as the parents and other adults use material objects as one of the ways to manifest love. When young fellow humans are exposed to such patterns of consumption, I believe it will be more challenging for them to adopt sufficiency as a value later in their lives.

Sufficiency of locations (Nesterova and Jungell-Michelsson, forthcoming) could be discussed much more in society. Ideas could be, for instance, local and seasonal food and local travelling and holidays. When I contemplate sufficiency of locations, what comes to mind is that developing this value also takes time. Perhaps, it takes time to fall in love with some place, to appreciate non-humans who live there, to see staying in that place not as a sacrifice but genuinely as the best choice, to see local and seasonal food not as a sacrifice for the climate and nature but as desirable and delicious.

Inner being

The plane of inner being goes all the way into the depth of human psyche, what matters to us and how we as individuals relate with the world. In my view, this plane of being is the most fascinating one. There seems to be a causal relationship between how humans, including businesspersons, relate with the world and what practices they choose to exercise. At least this is what I notice in my own autoethnographic study. While knowledge about ecological degradation empowers my practice, what motivates me to live differently (e.g., practise voluntary simplicity, zero-waste, minimalism) are not negative emotions such as anxiety and fear about ecological degradation (though they are constantly present too), but rather feelings such as oneness, empathy, love and care towards nature and fellow beings, both humans and non-humans. Naturally, relating with the world happens within social structures that impose constraints, so oftentimes it is possible to see a mismatch between one's worldview and one's practices. For instance, businesspersons often share with me the obstacles they face. During my PhD journey I researched a very small business, run by a woman and her husband. They produced natural dyes. It was a tiny, craft-based business, something one could imagine as part of degrowth society. In degrowth business terms, almost everything was in place. In addition to their ecological business practices, they did not want to grow their business. Many aspects of the business were intertwined with art and passion for colours and nature. The only aspect that these businesspersons were struggling with in the process of production was using plastic to store and ship the natural dyes. They mentioned seeking an alternative, but they could not find anything that performed as well. It was not due to indifference, or a lack of care, or a desire to support the fossil fuel industry or a desire to reproduce capitalism, but rather because at that time there were no better alternatives. I felt empathy towards their story as I observe much imperfection in my own everyday life and practice. For instance, leading a perfectly zero-waste lifestyle can be a full-time job depending on one's circumstances. I find it challenging to buy zero-waste food. There are no zero-waste shops in the area where I live, farmers' markets are seasonal and food markets are far. As I walk back home from the train station, I go to a supermarket to pick up food. This is also not due to a lack of care, or a lack of knowledge or a desire to reproduce capitalism. Rather, a better option is not readily available. It is not even available when I consider a slightly longer walk.

Oftentimes, in situations when businesspersons say that they try but cannot currently do better, researchers become sceptical about businesspersons' worldviews.

I tend to trust my respondents and become more curious about what prevents them from aligning closely or almost perfectly their worldviews and practices. Often it is social systems, beliefs and norms, fear, doubt and lack of something such as finance, knowledge or access to expertise. Discussing various constraints can lead to contemplating helpful policies and changes in the social system.

And while manifestation of sufficiency in practice may not be perfect, for it to manifest in practice at all, it needs to feature as a value. Ideally, and perhaps more sustainably, sufficiency is a value that is part of a constellation of values or a system of relating with the world. Deep ecology (e.g., Naess, 1995), in my view, provides a good starting point and a system of values that embraces sufficiency. Sufficiency becomes an obvious and organic principle if the premises of deep ecology are embraced. It may be so that a human being is not inspired by deep ecology specifically. Then, developing a worldview that emphasises the interconnection of everything with everything else, or oneness, could be helpful.

In the words of Steiner (2011, pp. 207–208, original emphasis):

> The single human individual is not actually cut off from the universe. He is a part of it, and between this part and the totality of the cosmos there exists a real connection which is broken only for our perception. At first we take this part of the universe as something existing on its own, because we do not see the belts and ropes by which the fundamental forces of the cosmos keep the wheel of our life revolving. [...] we can believe in this independence only so long as the things we perceive are not woven by our thinking into the network of the conceptual world. As soon as this happens, all separate existence turns out to be mere *illusion due to perceiving.*

Another important value, apart from oneness, that is also related to oneness, is gentleness. My co-author and I strongly emphasise gentleness in our works on degrowth (Buch-Hansen, 2021; Buch-Hansen and Nesterova, 2023). Gentleness concerns our being in the world, our general attitude and acting towards the world. *Our* includes not only the members of civil society or academia but also businesspersons and humans occupying various positions in state apparatuses. While gentleness may be perceived as abstract, ephemeral and hard to define (Dufourmantelle, 2018), it is best captured in existential terms of lived and felt experience (Schweizer, 2022). Gentleness (as opposed to, for instance, care) is not a widespread concept in the study of business and other organisations (Mumford et al., 2022). However, it is not an unusual term in other fields such as philosophy (Dufourmantelle, 2018) and political thought (Mendham, 2010). Being gentle "means not wanting to add to suffering, to exclusion, to cruelty and inventing space for a sensitive humanity" (Dufourmantelle, 2018, p. 15).

Circularity

In theory, a sufficient for everyone amount of goods can be produced, thus satisfying the criterion of sufficiency, while the design of such goods might be wasteful. For example, the product or the packaging might be difficult to recycle, the materials used might not be biodegradable, the processes used in the production of the product might be linear. I am reminded of my sufficiency list, a playful list of objects that I sketched many years ago to identify the items that were necessary for me to live a comfortable life. When I sketched that list initially, I was in the process of living with less and stepping on a minimalist path. I did not want to buy new objects until I used up the ones I lived with, so I kept the ones I had in my household and gave away and donated the rest. I noticed that some of those products that I kept were rather conventional. Many came with plastic packaging, some were not made by local small companies, others contained ingredients that were not biodegradable. Over time, as I ran out of some products or had to replace some objects, more and more of them were in line with my ecological and aesthetic values and principles. But comparing the composition of objects at the beginning and currently made me see the distinction between sufficiency and circularity more clearly as well as experience it myself.

Overall, circularity complements sufficiency: it is important to produce enough and also produce it well, i.e., not wastefully. Personally, I do not advocate the circular economy as a model of economy. Focusing solely on circularity can lead to ignoring very important aspects of transformation, such as a different mode of relating with the world and self-transformation. The economy is so complex and inherently social that circular processes (such as reducing, reusing, recycling) come across as just a part of the economy. At the same time, it makes much sense to me to talk about circularity as a principle and try to make economic processes and product designs in ways that are circular rather than linear.

Elsewhere (Nesterova and Buch-Hansen, 2023) my co-author and I discussed the depth of circularity in detail, but here I want to reflect more on it. There has been much discussion on whether degrowth and the circular economy are compatible. I believe that degrowth and circularity as a principle are compatible. The principle of circularity is more aligned with degrowth than the notion of the circular economy. Degrowth is both anti- and post capitalist. It encourages us to think about a better future for humans, non-humans and nature, to be adventurous and creative in our theorising and modes of being. The circular economy is generally not explicitly political or radically adventurous. This is not to say that fellow humans who advocate the circular economy are capitalist or not adventurous. Just as it is with degrowth, there is a diversity of views within the circular economy community.

The circular economy is often contrasted with the current linear economy. However, it appears reductionist to see the whole economy as linear. Principles of circularity have existed for much longer than the concept of circularity has been around. In fact, when I talk to fellow humans from older generations about circular economy, zero-waste and other related concepts, they find it entertaining since what we see as new and highly innovative thinking was something those fellow humans knew and considered normal when they were young. Oftentimes, they use other words to describe circularity, such as frugality or not being wasteful.

Circularity is an ideal, but in my own research I notice that no business is fully circular. In fact, such binaries (circular vs not circular, sufficient vs not sufficient) applied to production are not helpful. Even those businesses that implement circularity are also engaging in less than circular activities. For example, a business engaged in vertical hydroponic agriculture that I studied in Sweden implemented circularity in terms of its water use. Yet, to catch insects, they had to use less than circular methods. The businessperson I spoke to felt bad about it and knew that it was not an ideal solution, but at that time they had no better solution than to use sticky insect tape. It might seem a trivial issue, but for a small business that grows greens and herbs indoors, in a very small space, insects could become a big challenge. Not to mention the contemplations that inevitably arise in one's mind in relation to growing salad vegetables in winter in northern Sweden.

Rather than avoiding talking about circularity in relation to degrowth due to differences in approaches, the principle of circularity is interesting and worthy of contemplating in depth. Circularity should concern far more than design that aims to make a product and its components more easily reusable and recyclable. When circularity is contemplated in depth, it is easier to find links between circularity and other important sustainability principles, and to see how it fits within degrowth.

Transactions with nature

Material transactions with nature is the home domain of circularity, as circularity is primarily an ecological principle. Circularity presupposes seeing waste as a resource, rather than something to be returned to nature as a byproduct of our economic activities. The principle encourages us to design products in such a way that the products are easy to reuse and recycle. It is important to not limit circularity to one process, such as producing fibres from plastic rescued from oceans. Such fibres, as they wear and are washed, release microplastics. So, while the initial idea is good, it does not seem to go far enough. Circularity as a principle of dealing with materials appears to go together with the practice and lifestyle of zero-waste in civil society.

Social relations

Circularity, just like sufficiency, as a principle cannot be brought about by individual actions. This principle should be nurtured in relationships between humans. One example can be learning together and developing connections between businesspersons and academics specialising in circular designs and circular business models. Another example is developing relationships between businesses and their customers. For instance, developing closer relationships may encourage customers to return the packaging or refill it.

Social structures

Circularity cannot be brought about via individual actions of a business as a social entity. It requires structures in place that will help businesses implement circularity as much as possible. Supporting structures can include regulations, infrastructures, networks of businesses, financing for new businesses that have circularity at the heart of their business models. Education system can be a supporting structure for businesses too. While I am writing this book, I observe many courses that incorporate circularity. Within business schools, I have met many fellow academics who specialise in the circular economy. Unfortunately, it has not always been so. I remember the times when the circular economy was not taught widely in business schools. But teaching circular economy is not enough. It needs to be taught together with alternatives such as degrowth and philosophy that allows the students to develop worldviews to which gentleness and care towards the self, human and non-human others, and nature are central.

Inner being

The realm of inner being is something that the circular economy scholarship tends to overlook. Bringing about the circular economy, and implementing the principle of circularity, often feels mechanistic, a matter of better processes and designs. In my view, implementing circularity is to a large extent a matter of inner being of humans, naturally with the support from social structures. Circularity requires a completely different attitude to nature and fellow others, including both humans and non-humans. This is because circularity requires effort. At the very least, stepping on more circular paths and normalising them rather than conventional ways necessitates contemplation, questioning the mainstream, seeking alternatives and establishing conversations with others. It also requires financial investment. What is required from businesspersons can be mobilising creativity and adventurousness, willingness to work with others, seeking creative solutions far beyond tokenistic pro-environmental actions, taking risks. Consumers need to feel comfortable with reused and recycled materials, feel passionate about engagement and cooperation with other humans to improve production together (e.g., writing to businesses, giving feedback). Consumers need to take time to participate in circularity practices, such as returning or refilling packaging.

As a practitioner of voluntary simplicity and zero-waste, I have always observed that participating in circularity practices takes much time. Even after more than a decade of practising voluntary simplicity and zero-waste, not all my practices are automatic. At times, it feels much easier to replace an item, and it requires an inner dialogue and reminding oneself of one's values. Repairing takes time, as does careful recycling. Returning packaging takes time, as does sharing items with friends and family. As I was writing these words, I went to a swap station (byttestation in Danish) with my partner here in Denmark. We went there with an intention to share some objects with fellow humans. I was contemplating how much time it takes to go to a farmers' market or a food market to buy seasonal, unpackaged vegetables, to go to a small, local bakery to buy unpackaged organic bread and to go to an eco-store for some local unpackaged soap. It is incredibly time-consuming. I was thinking about my privilege, that I could at times, though not always, go to such places to avoid waste because I had very few care responsibilities. I had no children, pets or elders to look after. Perhaps it could be that convenience plays an important role: circular economy systems and organisations must be readily available and considered normal, or humans need to be able to work less and thus have time for practices such as repairing, sharing and recycling mindfully. At the same time, I was contemplating what I observed when I took my waste to the recycling place near the house where I live. In the mixed waste bins, one could see obviously recyclable objects such as cardboard boxes and glass jars. Just a few centimetres from these bins, there were the bins for cardboard and jars. Convenience was not the only factor. It could be knowledge and worldview too.

Developing a worldview to which gentleness and care are central is essential. Having this worldview would encourage humans to take time, to express support for policies that free up time. I do not think that having a beautiful worldview will necessarily result in perfect practices, but it will certainly improve our practices. And the goal is perhaps not to have perfect practices, but for more humans and organisations to step on genuine sustainability paths, to start somewhere.

It also seems important that such worldviews are developed genuinely so actions can be free and organic rather than done out of duty while feeling sorrow about the need to perform this action. In his exploration of the philosophy of freedom, Steiner (2011, p. 138, original emphasis) notes that:

> An action is felt to be free in so far as the reasons for it spring from the ideal part of my individual being; every other part of an action, irrespective of whether it is carried out under the compulsion of nature or under the obligation of a moral standard, is felt to be *unfree*. A person is free in so far as he is able to obey himself in every moment of his life. A moral deed is *my* deed only if it can be called a free one in this sense.

Table 3.1 Sufficiency and circularity

Planes	*What it entails*
(Material) Transactions with nature	Producing for needs Producing sufficiently (not less or more) Localisation Reducing wastes Natural and recovered materials Designs for durability/extending the product and materials' lifetime
(Social) Relations	Sharing Deepening connection with customers Deepening connections with fellow businesspersons Deepening connections with activists, researchers and local governments Collective learning about sustainability
Social structures	Shaping political-economic conditions Engaging in formal and informal networks spanning private and public sectors Creating infrastructures to handle waste Policies addressing overconsumption
Inner being	Self-transcendence Transformation in the self and one's worldview Care towards others and nature

Bringing together sufficiency and circularity

Sufficiency and circularity can exist separately in a business. Generally, it is difficult to talk about sufficiency and circularity in business as a whole. These terms can describe certain processes and practices in a business. For example, a business can pursue sufficiency in size and remain non-growing. The same business can produce a wide range of products and constantly explore new options. This can be the case with craft and artisanal production. The business can explore new colours, textures and flavours. In this case, sufficiency applies to the size of business but not to the product itself.

Sufficiency and circularity need to go hand in hand. Currently, just as it is possible to imagine producing enough goods and designing those goods poorly, it is also possible to imagine overproducing goods based on the circularity principle.

4 Humanism and hope

Why humanism and hope

In the sustainability discourse, much has been said about destruction that humanity, and in particular certain parts of humanity, such as the materially wealthy, caused and continue to cause to nature. Messages such as "we are transgressing planetary boundaries" are there to encourage us to act and have a sense of urgency and concern. It is important to feel concern and to act now. And yet, such messages need to be supplemented and balanced with positive messages of hope. Overemphasising destruction leads to feelings of disempowerment, futility of our actions, resignation, shame, guilt, anxiety and eco-anxiety and fear. During many years, since I began to do my research on degrowth, I had many conversations with my fellow humans in academia. So many of these fellow humans said that they have very little hope. They feel pessimistic about change and about degrowth society ever coming into being. At times I felt this way. Even these days, sometimes I still feel this way too. I feel it strongly in the spaces with many shops. I feel it when I walk around central Copenhagen around Christmas time. Around that time, I receive many messages from my fellow humans who also advocate change, and I notice that the feeling of joy connected to holidays and seeing friends and family co-exist with deep sadness and sorrow about overconsumption and ecological degradation. I feel pessimism even stronger when I read the news about violence and destruction that takes place in the world.

When I speak to my fellow humans within movements such as voluntary simplicity and zero-waste, and when I speak to businesspersons, I notice that there is much more hope than in academia. When I teach, I never want to misrepresent the severity of ecological degradation, but neither do I want to rob my students of hope. I believe that hope inspires and motivates humans to act.

It is my hope that more fellow humans will join our conversations and efforts within the broad degrowth movement. Some of the most beautiful messages I receive are the ones from my fellow humans who consider writing their PhD about degrowth and business. They are genuinely curious and want to join the effort. Oftentimes, they are hopeful and believe that something can still be done about ecological degradation. Some of those fellow humans have experiences in industries outside academia or with running a business. I cannot say to these fellow

DOI: 10.4324/ 9781003452300-4

humans who reach out to me that we cannot think together or that it does not matter anyway. My feeling is that for more humans to join our conversations, we need to offer so much more. Recent years have seen more diversity, more sensitivity towards places and cultures, more dialogues with various philosophies, sciences and concepts, more practical solutions and policy proposals within degrowth. This is just the beginning.

We need to offer something beautiful. I am not ashamed of using the word "beautiful" here. Some may say, there is no need to sugarcoat degrowth. And indeed, we need to remain honest about degradation and accept the full range of emotions we are feeling about it, including anxiety, anger, fear and even hopelessness. At the same time, there is so much beauty in humanity. There are alternative organisational forms that exist in parallel with capitalist forms (Gibson-Graham, 2006). Within capitalist institutions, there are humans with beautiful worldviews. There are friendships and other deep connections between humans. There are empowering networks of likeminded humans. There are beautiful human capacities that manifest every moment. They are, for example, care, love, empathy, creativity, compassion, solidarity, altruism and self-transcendence. There are beautiful emotions such as joy, awe and contentment. There are so many beautiful ideas. There are so many beautiful spaces that can and should be nurtured. So many reasons to feel hope.

Humanism

Humanism as a stance, rather than a doctrine or a school of thought, has much to offer in terms of hope. In the minds of many, humanism is associated with the somewhat controversial human potential movement (Stone, 1978a; 1978b). To be inspired by humanist ideas and use humanism, it is not necessary to advocate for the human potential movement. When it comes to human potential, I do not think that it is helpful to judge it as "unlimited", as this feels narcissistic. But we do have great capacities for love, creativity, freedom, care, concern and empathy (Bhaskar, 2012). At the same time, we have capacity for humility, reflection and recognising our own imperfections. And we have capacity for growth and self-transformation.

At times when I contemplate the degrowth movement, I think that most humans within this movement would judge themselves to be good people, doing their best in academia and outside academia, and often in their personal lives, to contribute to bringing about a degrowth society. I certainly see those fellow humans as that too. Then I wonder, why there is so little hope in other fellow humans? To me, it has always been hard to see my fellow academics as inherently good and fighting against capitalism, and businesspersons as inherently motivated by money, profit and by some inner desire to reproduce capitalism. So many businesspersons I spoke to recognise issues with capitalism and are part of various movements such as voluntary simplicity, zero-waste and regeneration. So many businesspersons practise spirituality with an aim to nurture love and care towards the world.

At the heart of humanism is seeing humans as *generally good* (Maslow, 1970). I want to spend some time with this phrase, generally good. What does it mean? First of all, this phrase may feel uncomfortable. Perhaps the beauty of the "economic man" model was in its simple, though wrong and misleading, approach to humans. There is nothing concrete about saying that we are generally good. It is more philosophical than useful for quantifications. And considering that the social sciences have been dominated by positivism, to some it may seem useless to talk about our goodness. Yet it is essential. Saying that we are generally good may be polarising. When I discuss this topic with my fellow humans, it seems that some believe that we are generally good, while others believe that we are evil. I find that it is rather difficult to change humans' minds about this. This of course applies to me as a human being too. I have always seen humans as generally good. It was not a result of me attending some lecture on humanism or reading a particular book that inspired me or changed my mind. This is a belief that I hold dearly despite having seen and experienced the evil parts of humanity too. It is interesting how personal beliefs lead one to read certain literature and feel affinity with it. In the social sciences and philosophy, there is no consensus on human nature. It is very easy to find literature and schools of thought that can reinforce one perspective or the other.

At times, perhaps like any other human being, I have seen, heard about or experienced myself something so evil, violent or abusive that I began to think that my beliefs about human nature were wrong. But those moments of deep and overwhelming frustration, disappointment, sadness or even anger about evil within humanity never lasted too long. Whenever I looked at the world around me, goodness eventually feels overwhelming. Oftentimes, I thought that this is because I have not experienced severe trauma, such as surviving a war. In every traumatic experience I lived through, there was always a dialectic of goodness and evil. As I am writing these words, I am thinking about my Jewish grandmother who survived the Second World War. Many of her relatives and community members were killed during the war, but she, like me, believed in human goodness. If she became a degrowth theorist, I think she would feel drawn to humanism too. She certainly felt drawn to it in her life's philosophy and worldview. And while she is just one human being amongst billions, thinking about her and her life experiences makes me reflect on humanity in general.

Humanist scholars (e.g., Maslow, 1970; Tuan, 2008) highlight human goodness rather openly in their writings. For instance, Maslow (1970, p. 118, italics original) notes that "our knowledge is sufficient to reject any claim that human nature is, in its essence, *primarily, biologically, fundamentally* evil, sinful, malicious, ferocious, cruel, or murderous". When I read these words, I wonder what would happen if these words were spoken during economics classes, if students were taught this in business schools, if they were encouraged to contemplate this.

While this approach to humans may be labelled as pollyannaish, none of the humanists are naïve about human nature. None would assume and claim human perfection or sainthood or deny the existence of evil, violence and wrongdoings. As Maslow states, "Nor dare we forget that human nature itself generates much evil, if not from inborn malice, then from ignorance, stupidity, fear, miscommunications, clumsiness, etc." (Maslow, 1970, p. 257).

I believe that mainstream business and economics education can generate much evil too. This is not to say that those fellow humans who attend mainstream economics, business and marketing classes are evil or do not care about fellow humans, non-humans and nature. I do not want to say that they do not have agency and merely absorb what they are told by their teachers. But many students come to classrooms with hopes, a desire to learn. They come with much trust towards their teachers and their knowledge. Perhaps they trust the person who tells them that humans are egoistic and greedy, or that humans can be and even should be manipulated to buy unnecessary goods and services. Too often we hear in business schools that we (students) should be on the side of banks and corporations rather than consumers. This is absolutely wrong, and I am not ashamed of saying this. We, humans in business schools, economics departments and elsewhere, should be on the side of care, oneness and love. And I do not think it sounds naïve and unscientific and do not care if someone thinks that it does. We need to take these capacities seriously, study them deeply, understand them, feel them within ourselves, recognise and celebrate them in others and look for ways to nurture them.

Hope

Hope, in my view, lies within human goodness and human capacities for love, empathy, compassion, solidarity, self-transcendence, creativity, care and concern and human ability to differentiate between good and bad. All these, if deeply felt and manifested in practice, work to bring about a better society. I believe that hope is implicit in degrowth. It is necessary to assume that we, humans, can bring about a better society. Otherwise, why are we theorising degrowth? Why are we seeking alternatives?

While seeing beauty in humanity it is important to, at the same time, recognise that we operate within social and natural structures. It goes without saying that there are limits to human agency. Even those who believe that humans are essentially free (Bhaskar, 2000) acknowledge that structures can not only empower but also constrain (Bhaskar, 1989, 1998). While I admire human agency and have much hope in human capacities and potential, every day I contemplate social structures. It is hard to ignore them when you try to live an ecological life or when you move countries. Even when structures are not actively preventing one from practising an ecological life or manifesting one's worldview in business practices, they may dictate the pace and conditions of these unfoldings.

I always find it interesting when my fellow humans in academia gravitate strongly towards agency-based or structure-based explanations. Perhaps it is due to their personal interests or beliefs. Something that attracted me to critical realism, amongst other things, was that it transcends agency-structure dualism by offering a model of interaction between agency and structures. In this view, agents reproduce and transform social structures (Buch-Hansen and Nielsen, 2020; Collier, 1994). Social structures constrain and empower agents. Importantly, social structures pre-exist agents. So, for example, we do not choose to be born into capitalist structures. They simply exist. They were there before we were born. But the fact that they exist doesn't mean that they are immune to change, that they are here to stay. We either reproduce or transform them. While I recognise both, agency and structures, individuals, individuals' motives, actions and potentials have been of particular interest to me. Doing autoethnography made me more inclined to transcend this interest and to recognise the structures and their power so much more.

Humanism and different strands of thought: sketches

Humanism and small businesses

I share with humanists a positive attitude towards human nature, including the nature of businesspersons. Over the years, I have spoken to many businesspersons, especially those running small businesses. The conversations I share in this book are just the tip of the iceberg. I want to oppose the view that businesspersons are bad, exploitative and utilitarian people, driven by a desire to accumulate and by self-enrichment. That they are people who do not care or particularly want to reproduce capitalism and destroy nature. It simply is not what I am finding in my research, which I will share more in the chapters on Danish, Finnish and Swedish businesses. Businesspersons are human beings, not different to the rest of humanity and capable of so many beautiful things. Having said that, I also do not want to say that businesspersons are better than anyone else or that violent practices do not exist at all in small businesses. It is important to avoid romanticising both small businesses and businesspersons. Like anyone else, businesspersons make mistakes, make bad decisions.

Humanism and ecological thought

Once Bookchin (1982, p. 38) said that "we are the very 'knowingness' of nature, the embodiment of nature's evolution into intellect, mind and self-reflexivity". It reminded me of Emerson's writings that celebrate both human goodness and nature. In particular, this quote that I came across, I found thought-provoking: "What is a [hu]man but nature's finer success in self-explication?" (Emerson, 2009, p. 297). Human goodness is a property of nature itself. My co-author and I developed similar thinking and theorised human beings as nature itself becoming self-conscious (Schmid and Nesterova, 2023). We contemplated our human capacity for intentionality, for unlearning and learning, healing ourselves and our societies and letting the rest of nature heal itself. I hope that it does not sound narcissistic, as claiming superiority of humans amongst other species and beings. This was not our intention. Consciousness and intentionality do not make us, humans, *better* than other beings. There are diverse ways to *be*. This kind of contemplation that Ben Schmid and I wrote about requires a humanistic stance, recognising our abilities to see both our spiritual and material side, to both self-transcend and to see ourselves as beings of the Earth, as nature itself. I feel drawn towards the strands of humanistic thought that honour both human goodness and nature, and such thinking is what could potentially help us develop ecological worldviews for degrowth. I want to offer to my reader another quote by Emerson that weaves together human goodness (here manifested as demand of harmony) and admiration of nature:

> The Gothic cathedral is a blossoming in stone subdued by the insatiable demand of harmony in man. The mountain of granite blooms into an eternal flower, with the lightness and delicate finish as well as the aerial proportions and perspective of vegetable beauty.
>
> (Emerson, 2009, p. 20)

In my reading, harmony refers to so much more than aesthetics. It refers to harmonious being.

Humanism and existentialism

Existentialism influenced my thinking a lot throughout my journey (Nesterova, 2021c). There are many overlaps between humanism and existentialist philosophy, and they interest me more than possible differences, especially when oftentimes differences reveal themselves in concrete authors' positions rather than being at the core of some direction of thought. Existentialism, amongst other things, emphasises choices that we, humans, make within the given world. The universe is seen by existentialists as inherently without a meaning (Camus, 2005). Thus, it is every human's responsibility to infuse their existence with meaning. Allowing, philosophically, for so much freedom in our choices and decisions, existentialism aligns with humanism which is likewise hopeful about humans' thinking and capacities.

This speaks to critical realism's role of agency in reproduction and transformation of social strictures. To remind, in critical realism humans reproduce or transform social structures (Collier, 1994). They do it within the framework of these structures but still they do it freely and perhaps very often intentionally. The intention though is not necessarily to, say, destroy nature. For instance, though a flight contributes to nature's degradation, a human being likely chooses to fly for other reasons. Yet taking that flight is a free choice. Here I am not referring to, for instance, young children who by definition have less agency than adult humans. Because humans are to a large extent free (existentialism), have potential (humanism), can affect the unfolding of reality (critical realism) and have a responsibility to identify for themselves (rather than necessarily find somewhere) meaning (existentialism), there is a choice between reproduction and transformation of social structures. Hope lies within humans making consciously a choice to reproduce good structures and transform bad ones. By good structures, I simply mean those that nurture genuine sustainability and bad ones are the ones that do not.

Human nature

To me, humanism is inseparable from contemplating human nature. The question of human nature is difficult. Ecological economics, the original scientific grounding for degrowth, did not give clear answers as to who we are apart from assuming that a human being is not "economic man" of neoclassical economics. A long time ago, Becker (2006) in the journal *Ecological Economic* noticed just that. I don't think much has changed from the time Becker was writing. The same words could have been said this year.

The question of our nature has occupied our, human, minds for a long time. Naturally, in this book I do not claim to have answered the question of what human nature is. But at the same time, I always felt the need to contemplate this question, not least to be able to theorise degrowth transformations. I always wondered why we assume that such transformations are even possible. To assume this possibility, there needs to be a belief that we, humans, are capable of changing ourselves and our systems. There needs to be a belief that we are willing to take part in changing our system while knowing that it might be difficult, that it might disadvantage someone's life, financial wellbeing and their career.

In the social sciences, of course depending on the knowledges and teachers we are exposed to in various places, we get acquainted with different perspectives on human nature. We also come to conclusions about human nature in our lives, simply via living and experiencing society and the self.

I was educated in economics and business studies. The first model of human nature that was discussed explicitly and coherently during economics classes was that of an "economic man" of neoclassical economics. Some would say that it is not fair to assume that "economic man" is a model of human nature. It is just an abstraction. But it is still a model that tries to approximate humans, to distil who we are to certain attributes. And these attributes, such as selfishness and greediness, are certainly not what other traditions would say lies at the heart of humanity. Surely this is also not what I see around me in society. What I see, despite also seeing violence, that humans are generally good and caring being. I often think about the effect teaching neoclassical economics has on humans. If we tell fellow humans, especially young persons, that at the heart of us is selfishness, what will that do to their minds? I studied economics at school, before I went to the university. At that time, I thought it was good to be able to study economics at the university. Only later I realised how detrimental it can be.

Behavioural economics made a step further by saying that we have emotions and various biases. That is to say, we do not make perfect decisions, based on sophisticated calculations and rationality, but our decisions are affected by conditioning, limitations, feeling and even the weather. While thinking this way initially felt liberating to me, behavioural economics was a step towards further contemplations rather than an end point. It never became a school of economics where I felt at home.

Humanism was where I felt most at home when it came to thinking about us, humans. Each one of us has an affinity for some theories and attitudes about ourselves that exist within philosophy and sciences. Here I refer to humanism in a broad sense. There are many fields such as humanistic psychology and humanistic geography that adopt humanistic assumptions. Other spaces of knowledge also seem to adopt deeply humanistic assumptions. For example, deep ecology (Sessions, 1995) seems to have a very hopeful view of human beings. Another one is metareality, the third moment of Roy Bhaskar's philosophy of critical realism (Bhaskar, 2012). My reading of Bhaskar's metareality is such that metareality shares much with humanism. Both of these traditions, deep ecology and philosophy of metareality, assume general human goodness and human potentials for care and self-transcendence. As I was reading these literatures (humanism, humanistic geography, metareality, deep ecology), I was yet again thinking that so often essentially the same thing is expressed using different vocabularies.

Still, accounts of human nature differ much, and below I will share some contemplations that to this day have crystallised in my mind. We, humans, are biological beings, social beings and individual selves, at once. It is both intuitively true, and something that various philosophical and scientific traditions highlight. Some traditions focus more on some aspects than on others. And while an individual scholar's interest may lie within any of these aspects, it feels important to think about all these aspects, at least to acknowledge them. It allows us to avoid reductions, such as reducing ourselves to biological processes, or reducing societies to individuals or individuals to sponges of some kind who simply absorb society's dominant ways of thinking and being.

My interest has been mostly within the realm of the individual selves. Perhaps this is because for a long time I lived in a remote area with not many fellow humans around. Society was something very abstract for me for many years of my life. At the same time, I was contemplating individuals' connection with nature often. It is only much later in my life that I acquired a more sophisticated vocabulary to describe human connection with nature, such as biophilia (Wilson, 1984), topophilia (Tuan, 1974), self-transcendence and oneness. When I came across these concepts, automatically this vocabulary made sense to me and caught my interest. As for us being social beings, or selves in society, this is something that I began to contemplate more deeply when I started working with my fellow humans in academia who study political economy and sociology. Even then, my first inclination was to include non-human beings too and contemplate interplays between agency and structures.

I want to expand on each of the dimensions of our being.

First and foremost, we are **biological beings**. We are animals, made of flesh and blood, and we are mortal. We are of nature and in nature. We have biological needs such as needs to sleep and eat. We feel pain. This materiality of us, I feel, has not been receiving sufficient attention within the degrowth discourse. It is true that in degrowth, the limits nature imposes onto our economic activities have been acknowledged, as the need to satisfy humans' basic needs, many of which are biological. But still the traditions that address our materiality and embodiment are only now beginning to find their ways into the degrowth space.

Some suggest that we feel a natural affinity towards life, i.e., experience biophilia (Wilson, 1984), and towards places, i.e., experience topophilia (Tuan, 1974). I do not know whether it is a universal experience. I surely notice these feelings, including on the somatic level, within myself. To me, it is a feeling of deep comfort, safety and trust in nature, a feeling of gratitude for the abundance nature provides, a feeling of awe that the conditions on this planet are so welcoming towards life. This feeling manifests most strongly in the places I am familiar with, where I know how to orientate myself, what mushrooms, roots, nuts, seeds, vegetables, berries and herbs to forage. These are the places to which I want to return upon my death as a biological body.

We are **social beings**. This is a condition of our existence (Heidegger, 2001). Even if we decide to live in the woods, to withdraw from society and live self-sufficiently, such a withdrawal only partly separates one from society. Perhaps it does not separate us from society at all but only reduces the number and intensity of interactions with fellow humans and with social systems. We adopt the language, patterns of thinking and social norms. We *become* as individuals in society. It is likely that if we decided to live in the woods, into the woods we would carry all the memories of living with others and our education. We would still be subject to society's operation and laws. Perhaps we would still use the internet or basic tools, which are of society.

There are deeply intertwined layers of social being. There are one's family, social circle, communities one is part of. There are social structures and systems within which we are embedded. Society is something that constrains and empowers at the same time. It can be disappointing to be part of society that is organised on capitalist principles. Yet, society houses various alternative spaces too, and they can be empowering.

It feels vulnerable to write about this aspect of being. For a long time, I feel that I gave this aspect of being insufficient attention. While growing up in a remote area is good for facilitating connection with nature, non-human beings, nature's rhythms, possibilities and limits, unless there is a community of humans too, it is not good for facilitating connection with, and observation of, society and its diverse functions and spaces. When I was growing up, for 10 or so years of my life, until I was in my mid-teens, seeing society and how it functions was akin to snapshots rather than immersion. I thought to myself that I would fail sociology at the university.

Because of this, I chose methods that allow me to focus on small-scale entities and individuals, and also on my personal practice via doing autoethnography. Yet, it is via my autoethnography where many social structures came to prominence. Many sustainability practices (sharing, borrowing, learning together, consuming, recycling, repair) are enabled by society. I have to interact with various social systems, such as the educational system, the finance system, the system of public transportation, migration laws and regulations on a daily basis. Recognising this deep embeddedness within society, how it affects each one of us makes me think that personal growth is not so personal after all. Being with nature feels like a powerful source of self-transformation and personal growth. But oftentimes, access to nature depends on society, as does acquisition of philosophical tools that makes interactions with nature growth-promoting.

We are also individuals or **selves**. Here I assume human uniqueness and general human goodness of human individuals. Talking about the self does not mean assuming a self that is separated from society. It is rather self in society and in nature. As I was writing this chapter, I received a call from my stepfather who learned that I moved from Finland to Denmark. He asked me "what do Danish people do every day?" It seemed to be such a benign question, but it stayed in my mind for many hours, and even after that I had a feeling that I would be thinking about it for many weeks. I was contemplating it in relation to what I was writing. Is there one thing that all Danish humans were doing every day? The first thing that came to mind was that, like anyone else, they were sleeping and eating. But when exactly they were sleeping and what they were eating depends on a particular individual. Many would be working but working in different jobs. Many would be commuting but use different modes of transportation. I realised that the fellow humans I was thinking about were the ones in my area, in Frederiksberg. Perhaps the lives of farmers would look very different. There is such a diversity of modes of being, ways of thinking, constellations of feelings and emotions humans experience, constellations of circumstances. Those humans all have different stories, talents, hopes, dreams and desires. I struggle to think about a model of a Danish person. I thought about myself too and how Denmark is only a part of my journey.

It feels to me that the selves of individuals have not been spoken about enough within the degrowth scholarship. Perhaps this is understandable as somehow thinking about selves is associated with individualism. Perhaps there is fear that thinking too much about individuals may distract us from thinking about changes in systems. Of course, it does not have to be the case (Buch-Hansen et al., 2024). But not thinking about the self may lead to unhelpful generalisations. It can lead us to assume that every human being in this society is overconsuming and has internalised capitalism. This is an unfair assumption. Human beings are different. Some may overconsume, others do not consume enough due to financial pressures, yet others consume less for ideological reasons. Some support capitalism, while others are indifferent, and yet others oppose it. Some would like to participate in alternatives but do not know how or do not have access to resources (e.g., social capital or money). Recognising that humans are different and generally good is an enormous source of hope.

Growth

Growth seems to be an important aspect of being human – not only growth in the biological sense but also growth as development, spiritual growth. It feels vulnerable to me as a social scientist to talk about spiritual growth. When I mentioned it in my teaching to my students, I often felt the need to explain what I mean and almost apologise for the use of this concept. It is strange that it feels natural to talk about it in everyday life but less so in academic contexts such as writing a book and teaching. Yet this concept is precise, and I do not think that there is a need to reinvent it, to try and use another term just to seem more scientific. Perhaps the discomfort in secular spaces arises from a religious connotation of the words spirit and the soul. Some may feel that there is no place for such things in science. While I am not affiliated with any organised religion, the words spirit and soul make sense to me, as synonyms to the mind or the psyche.

In the beginning of my theorising of degrowth and business, I realised that change in our worldviews is absolutely essential for a degrowth society to come into being.

But changes in worldviews are likely not something that happens abruptly, once, or as a shift. Even though many fellow humans shared with me about some events or particular times that made them step on ecological paths, this "stepping" was only the beginning of the journey. Likely these journeys began much earlier and the act of "stepping" itself was a culmination of some processes that had been unfolding in the minds of these fellow humans for a long time, perhaps both consciously and subconsciously.

Even when I think about my own path, at times I refer to particular moments in my life, for simplicity, to say when my worldview changed. At times I think it was when I moved out of my family home and could practise a different mode of living. At other times I refer to the beginning of my PhD when I finally acquired the necessary vocabulary to describe my worldview. In reality, it did not change abruptly from one thing to another. It was more so that the circumstances changed, I felt more freedom, many learnings constellated in my mind, many practices became possible, I had more time for internal dialogues. I began to read more literatures (voluntary simplicity, deep ecology, critical realism) that aligned with the way I saw the world. The stepping on the path was gradual, and then the growth itself was intentional. I believe that growth is a process. It is grow*ing*.

With my co-author Hubert Buch-Hansen, in many deep discussions about degrowth transformations, we came to a conclusion that spiritual growth is essential for a degrowth society to come into being. This is not to say that other changes in society do not matter. They matter just as much, so spiritual growth is not sufficient on its own. But it is necessary. Growth, in a sense, is central to degrowth. For this reason, we began to think about "deep growth" or self-transformation enabled both internally and externally. Internal enablement refers to, for example, inner dialogues, contemplations and meditation. External enablement refers to eco-social policies that can create conditions for personal growth in humans of all ages and walks of life. External enablement also refers to free and lifelong education opportunities, supportive communities and networks, supportive relationships. There are some notes about personal, spiritual growth that I have been taking for many years and that I want to share below.

Spiritual growth is **not liner**. It is definitely a journey. At times, we experience periods of active growth. At other times, we simply live. It is not so that we can expect that the next month or the next year we will be more "enlightened" than before. It is not to say that experiences do not matter, but rather it is to avoid putting pressure on oneself and others to derive as quickly as possible some quick learnings from one's path or to become immediately better at one's practices. At times, this "better" is very marginal, at other times significant. Perhaps growth will look different for different humans. In my own life, I made many changes in my early 20s when I fully left my family home and could choose to live my life the way I wanted to. At that time, I became vegan, started my extreme minimalist journey, decided not to drive or fly and to step on the path of service via going into academia. I started to actively explore movements and modes of being, such as voluntary simplicity, zero-waste, simple living and slow living. Those changes were still gradual but because they unfolded in a relatively short space of time, perhaps to an outsider they looked like a change or a shift. At times, living that way felt like a routine. At other times, I felt I was learning a lot. I felt growth almost on a somatic level. That is to say, I embodied the feelings of joy and peacefulness. Growth was processual because there was no end goal. There was not a certain number of possessions I wanted to live with, or a certain number of citations that I wanted to get to feel that my degrowth theorising finally reached a certain number of fellow humans. During some periods of my life, I thought I was not growing any more. But then something else unfolded that contributed to growth. It could be something big and significant such as moving countries, or it could be something small such as gathering delicious spruce tips and feeling intense gratitude towards nature for the abundance she provides. At times, growth resulted from something positive such as seeing the northern lights in northern Sweden or sunlight here in Copenhagen after many days of rainy weather in winter. At other times, it resulted from difficult times such as quitting my job as an act of non-compliance with violence in academia. In many conversations I've had with businesspersons, I noticed that my experiences of being on a growth path and their experiences resonated. These paths were never straightforward. Our paths involved rest, reflection, stagnation, going back, making mistakes, failing, trying again.

Spiritual growth is, despite the emphasis I put on human individuals, is a **collective undertaking**. This is because humans are social beings. The society constrains and enables spiritual growth and does it at the same time as there are different tendencies operating within the same society. For example, movements that advocate alternatives may enable spiritual growth. Likeminded humans enable it too. Work that does not feel meaningful may constrain spiritual growth. Some systems do both. For example, education, in my experience, constrains and enables growth. Over many years in academia, I observed various dynamics in this field. It is inspiring to see teachers who see it as part of their work, to facilitate the students' spiritual growth and development. They see their work as something involving far more than giving some information to the students and examining the extent to which they absorbed this information and listened to the instructions.

Something meaningful unfolds when different groups of humans who try to grow intentionally come together. For example, many businesspersons I spoke to note that for a genuine transformation in society to happen, what they are doing via their businesses is not enough. They need consumers to be on board with transformations. They enable each other. Oftentimes, small businesses develop close connections with their customers and engage in transformative conversations. They discuss sustainability and bringing about a more sustainable society. They learn from each other. My personal growth is also enabled by businesspersons and engaging in deep conversations with them. As an academic, I find it humbling to learn about their journeys, to learn about something I do not experience in my everyday life, such as running a business and navigating capitalism as a businessperson. This humbling and realising clearly that someone knows more than I do about some aspects of life is a part of spiritual growth. Above I mentioned enabling rather a lot. Eco-social policies create spaces that can enable humans to grow spiritually. There needs to be spiritual growth in the humans in the state apparatuses too (Buch-Hansen et al., 2024), so that eco-social policies could be implemented sooner.

Spiritual growth is not only an **abstract concept**. At times, I have heard from my fellow humans that this concept is frivolous, obscure, even mystical and occult, that we need to focus on the change in our systems rather than on something so abstract as spiritual growth, growth in our soul that some do not believe even exists. I empathise with the need to change our systems. But there is a mechanism behind change in systems. In critical realist terms, change in our systems happens as a result of transformation of systems by humans (individually and collectively) and reproduction of those parts of the system that are good, sustainable and nurturing. Systems do not change from nowhere or from without. Rather than discounting spiritual growth and labelling it as something frivolous and obscure, the task becomes to de-mystify it while still seeing magic and beauty in it and being open to new experiences and learnings. Spiritual growth is very concrete in many ways. It can be experienced on the somatic/bodily level via felt self-transcendent emotions such as intense gratitude, awe, oneness, love and wonder. It can manifest in concrete practices such as living more simply, withdrawing one's support from oppressive structures, quitting destructive pursuits such as having much money and making time for meaningful activities. Spiritual growth manifests in a realisation that growth is not strictly personal. It is about growing and helping others grow as well. To de-mystify my own spiritual journey, I decided to use autoethnography as a method. It was helpful to bring to the surface various mechanisms behind my personal growth, how interactions with nature and non-human beings facilitate growth and how various social structures constrain and empower me. Many fellow humans, including businesspersons, engage in similar activities via taking notes and journaling. They do not call it autoethnography, but at its heart what they are doing is very similar to it.

Spiritual growth is **lifelong and deep**. One of the most important learnings in my academic journey so far has been realising that so many things are on a spectrum. That is to say, businesses are not "degrowth" or "not-degrowth", "low-tech" or "high-tech", "sufficient" or "not-sufficient". Becoming comfortable with this messiness is important. Likewise, humans are not unenlightened or enlightened. Perhaps like any other fellow human being, I can think of someone who in my view is violent and abusive. In my life I have noticed that fortunately such humans are rare to come by, and it is my hope that they can also step on paths of self-transformation and growth. On the other end of the spectrum, there are fellow humans who have engaged in spiritual practice for a long time and authentically manifest their spiritual learnings in their everyday life. But perhaps most humans are somewhere on a spectrum, though much closer to the second group than to the first one. They are always learning and growing, in diverse, imperfect and discontinuous ways. And because this process is so complex and multidimensional, it would be naïve to assume that doing a lecture on ethics in a business school would be sufficient. Naturally, a lecture can be inspiring, thought-provoking and interesting. It may affect a human being deeply. But for genuinely deep and lifelong growth to manifest, education needs to start much earlier than university education. Growth should be seen as a lifelong undertaking, from birth to death.

5 Imperfection of the journeys

It is not difficult to imagine what a perfect degrowth business should look like. It would probably be a business producing only for human needs (e.g., basic but healthy and nutritious foods, simple and durable houses), using natural, affordable, renewable, reclaimed and local materials. The business would rely as little as possible on long, global supply chains, since it is challenging to know at any given moment what exactly is going on in those supply chains, in far-away locations. The business would be a pleasant, kind, caring and stimulating place to work, conducive to humans' professional and spiritual growth. Competition between humans and strict hierarchies would no longer exist. Instead, humans would feel a genuine desire to help one another and work together. It would have close, long-term and kind ties with its customers and local community in general, with its suppliers and distributors. It would carry an environmental message and help customers step, and remain, on, transformative paths. This, for example, would be done via encouraging sufficient rather than excessive consumption and sharing knowledge about making the products last longer. It would be sensitive to the place where it is, including non-human beings. Ideally, this business would be run by persons who are on spiritual paths, and these personal paths of self-transformation would support their creativity and constant quest to make the business even better. The closest business to this vision that I can think of is a small, family-owned farm growing local, organic vegetables.

Yet even such idyllic and, in theory, almost perfect businesses are not without aspects that point at unsustainability of some kind. Such businesses' products would very likely be expensive or more expensive than conventional products. Likely, they would be available only to a very small number of people, and perhaps only people from certain groups, such as those with large enough disposable incomes. Perhaps such business would not grow or grow only slowly and organically. What I often notice in my field work is that growth, such as in number of employees, or varieties of products or the amount of land the business owns, comes with challenges that some owners prefer to avoid. Moreover, these products (say, local and organic vegetables) would supplement the consumption or diets of people rather than satisfy all their nutritional, social and cultural needs. It is difficult to imagine that in the current society, all humans would want to or be able to survive consuming only local, seasonal food or that such diets would be able to satisfy nutritional

DOI: 10.4324/ 9781003452300-5

needs of all. Such patterns of consumption are niche and require time and dedication if not sacrifice. As a practitioner of sustainable living and voluntary simplicity, I empathise with the consumers who cannot limit themselves to local, seasonal and organic foods bought strictly from small, independent, family-owned businesses. Sustaining such a pattern of consumption as perfectly as possible, in addition to sustaining other sustainable practices as perfectly as possible, is a full-time commitment and is expensive. Perhaps it is possible to become an influencer and make a career out of living this lifestyle, but for most fellow humans living a perfectly sustainable life is impossible within existing structures.

Just like almost perfect sustainable lifestyles are very rare and very challenging or even impossible to achieve for most humans, especially those living in a city without access to land as is currently the case with me and many other fellow humans, business journeys are also imperfect. Recognising this should not be a source of frustration or an invitation to give up. Rather, it is a source of empathy and being humble about what we, researchers, propose as solutions. Towards the end of the book (Chapter 9), I will dive deeper into my own journey to show why I experience empathy towards the businesses I research, and to highlight systemic constraints. In what follows, I want to bring our attention to loose ends, nuance and overall imperfection of business journeys towards a genuine sustainable society.

Needs

Above, in the chapter about degrowth business, I touched upon human needs. Here I want to say more in relation to contemplating imperfection. Degrowth literatures highlight that production should focus on satisfying human needs. It is common sense: if we as humanity overproduce, it is the production of less necessary or even harmful goods and services that needs to stop. The concept of human needs, basic human needs and genuine human needs is somewhat unclear. There are various ways to capture these needs. Max-Neef's framework (Max-Neef, 1991) is referred to in degrowth literatures and degrowth-related conversations (Buch-Hansen et al., 2024). While I appreciate the writings of Max-Neef, I find that framework somewhat convoluted to use in my works. Maslow's hierarchy of needs (Maslow, 1943) is very simple and intuitive. This is not to say that one is better than the other, but since I appreciate simplicity, for my own contemplations Maslow's framework is more suitable. Yet, as long as the focus of sustainability researchers and businesses is on production for needs and not wants, perhaps any framework would be useful that allows us to start somewhere and reflect on needs rather than wants.

First and foremost, production should focus on basic needs such as food, shelter and warmth. Such production should be sufficient or enough for everyone to satisfy these needs. It should also be place sensitive, i.e., suitable for the constellation of natural and social structures in a location. Moreover, it is easy to see how other needs such as a need for creativity and esteem could be accomplished in the process of production of such commodities. It is possible to come across a view within sustainability academia that even though local food production is desirable, it somehow does not seem appealing, at least less appealing than working from academics' offices. Food production is hard work, but talking to businesspersons engaged in local food production revealed an interesting picture to me. It is a creative activity that requires much knowledge, practice, learning and growth. Researching local varieties of fruits and vegetables, how these plants provide habitats and to whom, how climate change affects crops, all of this is no less demanding than academic work and often perhaps even more so, since it always combines research and practice.

While degrowth highlights humans' vital needs, people have other needs too. For instance, Maslow (1970) noticed aesthetic needs. Is a business producing various home decorations from local, natural materials a degrowth business? Such items might not be necessary (i.e., they are not basic, vital needs), and they may be rather expensive as many hours of human labour and creativity go into such artistic pursuits, but in many other domains this business may be in line with degrowth principles. There are also various ways to approach, for example, daily necessities such as home textiles and plates. They can be made as simple as possible with a focus on durability and natural materials. They can also be made aesthetically pleasing, which perhaps requires more materials, more time and these products would be more expensive.

Overall, aesthetics in relation to degrowth has not been addressed enough. Within a broad sustainability movement, there seems to be a less than gentle attitude towards aesthetics. Aesthetic of, say, a more sustainable lifestyle is seen as a way to encourage consumers to simply buy more green goods (whether they are actually green or not). To me as a practitioner, the aesthetic component is incredibly important alongside the ecological and spiritual components of a more sustainable mode of dwelling in the world. Hence, I find it challenging to advocate for production that satisfies only the most basic needs in the most simple way while disregarding the aesthetic component. Though naturally, simplicity can also be beautiful. None of it is to say that locally grown vegetables or simple houses made from local, natural material are not beautiful. They are. Yet, there needs to be space for arts and making products in a more than the simplest way.

Many non-material needs can be satisfied within business if the way the business is operated is intentionally conducive to their satisfaction. For example, a business can be a space for thinking together, learning together, belonging, support, personal growth. It can be a safe space.

Technology

Within the degrowth discourse, at least in some spaces of it, there is felt discomfort with high technology. Some strands of thought within degrowth question technology openly and discuss high technology's role in ecological degradation (Heikkurinen and Ruuska, 2021). Such views within a post-growth discourse are not recent. Schumacher advocated appropriate technology in his book called *Small is Beautiful* (Schumacher, 1993). Moreover, there are also philosophical directions of thought that question technology, such as anarcho-primitivism (Perlman, 1983). Such discussions are thought-provoking and important to nurture. They contribute to diversity of views within society and bring to the surface valuable points of critique. I see much value in discussing low and appropriate technology not necessarily as something that is the most suitable option for all domains of society and all circumstances, as something to strive towards. Rather, I see appropriate and low technology as something that can co-exist with high technology such as that needed for medicine production and railways. Appropriate and lower technology can also be emancipating when high technology is too expensive or can be avoided. In different periods of my life, I lived without running water and without devices (vacuum cleaner, washing machine) that are so normalised in our society. I used extremely primitive technology for my daily needs when I lived in Finland, such as a cloth to clean the floor and a bucket to wash my textiles. I used rainwater too earlier in my life as an experiment. And at those times, my quality of life was not worse than now when I live in Copenhagen with access to high technology.

It is not my intention here to dive deep into discussions on technology. On a very personal level, I like to contemplate an idyllic society living in perfect harmony with nature, without 9 till 5 jobs, advertising, monoculture, nuclear waste, instruments of war and so on. Anarcho-primitivism, in my view, is a beautiful school of thought. However, it often comes across as a fairytale rather than an actual pathway that can stem from where we currently are. And there is no other way to bring about a more ecological society than from where we are: a different society cannot be simply wished into existence. Even if it was possible, whose vision would be manifested? Technology and high technology are parts of society. It goes without saying, and I believe that most in the sustainability discourse would agree, technology is not neutral, and every technology needs to be evaluated from an ethical perspective.

In terms of business, it is important to transcend the binary of low technology vs high technology. While some businesses rely on or even produce high technology, many businesses combine both low and high technologies. This concerns also seemingly nearly perfect sustainable businesses such as small farms producing local, seasonal and organic goods. Oftentimes, they have websites or use social media to sell their products and communicate with their customers. And both social media and websites rely on very high technology. Using high technology at least somewhere seems unavoidable. Even if a business such as an organic farm doesn't have a website and avoids social media and sells their products only to their local community, in their farming they use tools that they did not produce themselves. Those tools require high technology to be produced. Consider, for instance, steel required for production of garden and harvesting tools.

Ephemerality

Ephemerality is a characteristic of sustainability journeys, in both businesses and individuals, that I have been noticing and been curious about since the start of my academic career. Practices are impermanent. Getting many things right doesn't mean it will be like this the following month or year. Change in ownership, employees, business networks and even changes in nature, all that affects how sustainability practice unfolds. Everything is always in becoming, and though it is nice to think that this becoming unfolds towards something better, and often with good intentions it does, it is not always so.

Oftentimes, I contemplate what happens to the businesses that I research or come across on my path when they change ownership. I believe that many of my readers can think of some businesses that started very small, were sustainable in many ways, but that then were bought by some large corporation. There are also businesses that were sustainable but then ceased to exist. I will contemplate this more in relation to one Danish and one Finnish case later in this book.

Lack of knowledge

Even in those businesses that I studied, whose owners had their heart in the right place, there was a lack of knowledge. It concerns multiple domains. For example, it is difficult for small business owners to know what is unfolding in the supply chains. They tend to trust what their suppliers say and trust the certifications those products and ingredients carry. Much is based on trust or even hope that others share the same convictions. It is often impossible for those persons to go and check how things actually unfold in those suppliers' factories. And even if they could, a one-off visit would only give a snapshot of practices rather than any deep understanding of the unfolding of ecological and social sustainability in those spaces.

There is also lack in knowledge in terms of processes, technologies and techniques. This is a space where businesses can collaborate with universities, but it does not always work in the way conducive to genuine sustainability. For instance, when mainstream academia advises small businesses on what they should be doing, the results can be disastrous. Genuinely beautiful views, experience and knowledge of businesspersons are questioned by those promoting mainstream views on economics and business. Businesspersons are encouraged to borrow to grow without realising the pressure such path brings. A much better and more useful path would be listening to what these businesspersons want, where they face issues and why and offering an alternative of a more organic growth (or even non-growth).

Growth

At times, a business grows, at other times it may not. I do not think that a degrowth business is necessarily a non-growing one, though non-growth is also a valid choice for a degrowth business. The businesses I research are often very small, and what they do is compatible with a degrowth society that I imagine. If these businesses grow, it is not bad in itself, and perhaps it is even good. Some of the businesses I researched or came across on my path were so caring towards human and non-human others and nature that I was thinking that it would be great if they wanted to grow even a little bit, by involving more fellow humans in what they do. But often they did not want that. Instead, the businesspersons envisioned that more fellow humans should start similar businesses or make products at home. Some of the businesses I researched grew very slowly. For them, to introduce a new product, a flavour or employ a new person is a big and important decision that comes with new contemplations and responsibilities. Sometimes such contemplations take years.

Limits

There are limits to what businesses can do on their own. Customers need to exercise their efforts. Governments need to create spaces where new businesses can be established and where existing ones can thrive on their sustainability journeys. For this reason, my colleagues and I theorise degrowth transformations as transformations unfolding at the same time in business, civil society and the state (Buch-Hansen et al., 2024).

Stories and emotions

Humans in businesses are on their own journeys. These humans are imperfect, their paths are also imperfect. They make mistakes and experience anxiety and worries. Businesses are operated by real humans. One businessperson I spoke to some years ago was going through a challenging personal situation with their partner. They established the business together but then decided to go their separate paths. It was a difficult, emotional situation, deeply intertwined with the business itself, its financing, its operations and its story. The business, understandably, contracted at that time.

My journey

It is only when I started writing my autoethnography in a consistent way, almost every day, I began to have a much deeper understanding of individual journeys of human beings, irrespective of who they were. They could be businesspersons, students, fellow academics and other humans. I began to feel deep, genuine empathy and compassion towards the complex journeys of others. When I began to theorise degrowth business, the outcome of that was a framework. I was thinking that if only all businesses complied with this framework, the world would be a better place. It is likewise not difficult to imagine perfect consumption to match degrowth business. Would it not be good, would the society not be sustainable, if every human being:

- Consumed only what satisfies their genuine needs, prioritised housing, food and energy
- Satisfied their needs in most sustainable ways: their home would be sufficient (lagom) but not luxurious, their food would be local, seasonal and organic, their energy renewable
- Consumed only durable products

- Consumed products made from natural, renewable and biodegradable materials
- Practised frugal, voluntarily simple living and elements of zero-waste lifestyle
- Travelled locally
- Avoided cars and flying
- Did and made many things and objects themselves (cooked from scratch, made their own seasonal and home décor, clothing)
- Worked in professions that have at their heart care towards humans, non-humans and nature
- Shared, borrowed rather than bought something
- Organised tool libraries with local communities
- Participated in alternative organisations (repair cafes, swap shops, community gardens) consistently rather than as a novelty
- Foraged and shared their knowledge with others
- Was mindful when introducing new objects in their space
- Was slow to upgrade technology and used second-hand technology
- Took their time to learn about different parties' programmes and voted for those whose policies are pro-environmental and pro-social
- Was an activist in their everyday life and beyond

There are many more aspects that I could list. And yet, human beings are not perfect, and it is unreasonable to expect that every human being wants to or can live this way. I notice that many adopt at least a few of these practices (though not necessarily consistently), but I don't know anyone who practices all those things consistently and perfectly. I have certainly tried to live a "perfect" degrowth compatible living at different times in my life, but I failed to be perfect at it. Focusing too much on perfection is in itself unsustainable and not conducive to spiritual growth. It causes anxiety. This lifestyle is by nature discontinuous and ephemeral, and this is something I had to accept, live and work with. And I say this knowing that my circumstances in some parts of my journey were almost ideal for practising an alternative lifestyle on my own terms, as much as the system permitted. I had no dependents and no care responsibilities. My health was good but not perfect. Living with an autoimmune condition meant that at different times in my life I depended on conventional medicine that was produced by large businesses and that came in plastic packaging. I did not feel shame or guilt for that, as health is so important, but it immediately made me realise the limitations to perfection in my lifestyle. I realised that even with all the knowledge of ecological and social degradation, and all the care and gentleness that I genuinely feel towards the world, my practice is far from perfect. I did not always buy organic food. At least one apartment where I used to live was supplied with energy from a mix of sources, including renewable, fossil and nuclear energy sources. Even though I chose a profession that I was hoping would be of service, there are also many aspects of this profession that reproduce the status quo. I would grade students despite not believing in grading. I did not always go foraging, even when opportunities were abundant and near, and the weather was nice. There were times when I was working on a paper rather than went to pick mushrooms, herbs, roots, spruce tips, nuts, seeds, leaves and berries. In those moments, I realised that I prioritised one need (expressing myself through words) over a basic need (food). At times, I missed opportunities to borrow something, and I bought that something because it was a more convenient option. I did not participate much in community initiatives. I moved much in my life and unfortunately never became part of any community (e.g., eco-community). In other aspects I did perhaps more than some fellow humans in the Nordics, but I also realised that this lifestyle was not something that every human being would want to replicate. I lived without furniture for a long time and did not own a car or even a bike.

My hobbies have never been materially intensive. I enjoy walking, reading and writing. Other fellow humans are interested in crafts, mountain climbing, preserving food. All of these require many more possessions than my hobbies that require only a pair of shoes in cold seasons and a laptop. My path has been discontinuous and messy. There were periods of intense growth and intense anxiety, doing much and doing less, accumulating and shedding. Most of my life, I was lucky to live in very beautiful areas with nature – or nature transformed by humans – around. I took this proximity for granted, until I began to realise that access to nature is not a given. I did not take public transport to see nature because nature was so close to me.

Contemplating my own circumstances and privileges was eye-opening and humbling. I have been doing this exercise for many years. Can I judge fellow humans for their imperfect lifestyles? I could not. This does not mean avoiding criticising overconsumption and simply saying that a lifestyle is purely an individual's choice. The choice is personal and individual only on the surface. When I make a choice regarding how I live and consume, I, together with others, make this choice for humanity. But there must be a diversity of modes of living. It should be as acceptable to practise extreme minimalism as it should be acceptable to live self-sufficiently in the countryside, or as sustainably as possible in a city, or in an eco-community. I am thinking of fellow humans who live with much more than I do, and they keep those objects for many years. At times they donate or share, but above all they feel comfortable living with more. They do not necessarily overconsume, but they do accumulate objects for many decades. It is not my place to judge them.

At times, as much as I feel uncomfortable to acknowledge it, imperfect practice originated from my own agency. I felt I had to work constantly and thus had no time for some practice (e.g., to visit a farmers' market), or I felt idle, or I preferred a convenient option. At other times, there were constraints imposed by the system. For example, as there is no UBI (universal basic income), I could not simply move to a remote area to live self-sufficiently. I had to work to live. I rented apartments. Oftentimes, the only available options were supermarkets, conventional banks and ferries that looked more like hotels and shopping centres in the sea. Though I did not and do not own a car, on many occasions I was in a car with fellow humans. There are so many ways in which I took part in the system I criticise in my works and that I feel deep resentment towards. Businesspersons and businesses are likewise imperfect. Having practised extreme minimalism, voluntary simplicity and zero-waste for over 10 years and having studied my own practices since 2016, and having seen how challenging it is, I feel empathy towards businesspersons.

6 Reflections from Denmark

Being in Denmark

Studying businesses located far away from where I am based never made sense to me on my journey. In this case, if I were to study far-away businesses, as a researcher I would only be present in a location for a short period of time, or even worse, only speak to businesspersons with the help of technology. Very little can be understood in this research scenario. For this reason, I also embrace situations when my students want to study businesses or anything else in their own countries, in the contexts they are intimately familiar with. They often ask if they can study these contexts, and perhaps they intuitively feel that their deep knowledges of the context and languages will help, and this is beautiful.

Studying businesses where one lives is an interesting experience. You are familiar with, or are intensely learning about, the context, the constellations of natural and social structures and perhaps even the language. In one of the conversations that I had with a business employee in Sweden, they mentioned picking "berries and svamp [mushroom in Swedish]". If Swedish was a completely foreign language to me, I would not have paid attention to such words. Perhaps in my transcript I would mark this part of the sentence as unintelligible. Being familiar with a language allows richer and freer conversations. Many businesspersons I spoke to in English on my research journey used words from Swedish and Danish. It is such a rich way of expressing oneself. My partner and I use words from different languages in our home too, as it allows us to communicate our thoughts more precisely.

It is enriching for research to have one's own experiences and deeper connections with a place. Before I stepped on my PhD path, I learned at my first university that a researcher should not think about themselves and their own experiences when doing research. It took me some time to unlearn this nonsensical advice. A researcher is part of the same world we study. I am a human being in the same world as the businesspersons I talk with. Perhaps my own background and profession make me see things from a different standpoint. But my experiences with a place bring me and businesspersons together in beautiful spaces of intense and genuine exchange. I decided that I would never study businesses that are not in the place where I am, though I naturally talk to businesspersons in other locations, as their stories and journeys are equally interesting, and I learn much from them too.

DOI: 10.4324/ 9781003452300-6

The cases I used for my PhD research were British. Then I moved to Sweden and studied Swedish businesses there. Afterwards, I moved to Finland and got to know some local businesses. With Denmark my relationship was somewhat different. It was a country I had visited several times before I moved to the Nordics, but usually I would pass through it on my way to or from Sweden. I started working closely with a Danish researcher who later became my partner, and Denmark acquired a somewhat different meaning to me. Perhaps for this reason there are more Danish cases in this book. When I moved to Finland, I began to miss the Nordic countries where Germanic languages are spoken, and Denmark, though I do not speak Danish, felt almost like home.

I decided to write about Danish businesses, and my relationship with my Danish partner also pointed in the direction of me having a closer and deeper connection with that country. I contacted Aalborg University, and they welcomed me for a research visit. So did Roskilde University. My plan was to write this chapter on Danish cases in Denmark, intertwining my study of those businesses with my dwelling in that country and my experiences as a practitioner of voluntary simplicity and zero-waste. This chapter on Danish businesses is longer, fuller and richer than the chapters on Swedish and Finnish businesses. I started to write this book when I already left Sweden and was living in Finland. I was writing in Sweden only as a visiting researcher in Lund, but living in Denmark meant that I could dive much deeper into the study of Danish businesses. I was planning to stay in Finland longer but then I left the Finnish university.

Moments

As I work on my academic contributions, I very often try to capture moments in my personal journey that are relevant to either my explorations of the role of business in degrowth transformations or that reveal some nuances of trying to live more ecologically. Understanding these nuances of ecological living helps as oftentimes on my own journey I am a consumer of the products and services that the businesses I research produce and provide. As I am writing these words, I am in a hotel in Copenhagen. My partner and I left our very small home, a studio apartment in Frederiksberg, for some days to let a fellow human stay there. The decision was spontaneous, so we didn't have much time to think deeply about where to stay. I begin to wonder about degrowth and travelling. The hotel is a Danish chain. It's not a major chain, and they have many ecological initiatives. The most degrowth-compatible option would be to stay at a friend's home or in a very small independent hotel. This would require either close community, or knowledge of a small and independent hotel.

I walk around the centre of Copenhagen and there are hardly any degrowth businesses. At least, nothing stands out to me as an obviously degrowth compatible business. There are stores selling luxury goods, stores selling unnecessary souvenirs and expensive home décor. There are independent restaurants, perhaps family-owned, but they are expensive. Buying food in a supermarket is more affordable but it means shopping in a large business, and that food comes with much packaging. Oftentimes, we simply pick something up in a bakery. Since we are on holidays, we decide to get a drink. The drink is organic. As the fellow human makes drinks for us, I look around the bar. I wonder where all those beverages come from. They must be coming from so many places. I contemplate one of my new year's resolutions to consume more local teas. When I lived in Sweden and Finland, I would forage spruce tips, birch leaves and yarrow to make my own tea. In Copenhagen, there feels to be so little nature that I don't know where I could forage some leaves and herbs for a tea in spring and summer.

Møn

After staying in the hotel in Copenhagen, we went to Møn, to be with nature, non-humans, each other, the rural area, fields, stars and silence. We took a train, then a bus and then rented bikes to get to our destination. Train and bus companies, even when owned by the state, are not small and idyllic degrowth businesses. They are large businesses with enormous supply chains. Bike shops could be small and independent businesses, but the one we could rent the bikes from is part of Denmark's largest chain of bicycle shops. I was glad that there was an opportunity to rent a bike. At times, it feels like I am the only person in my social circle who does not own a bike. As a degrowth academic, I feel almost ashamed when I say that I don't own one. Neither do I own a car, but bikes, unlike walking, have never been my favourite mode of transportation. As my partner is talking to a fellow human at the bike shop, I am reflecting on rental services. In a degrowth society, it makes sense to rent rather than own. It would be even better to be able to use objects free of charge.

After we rented a bike, we went, or rather ran, to a supermarket. We had no time to research better alternatives. Days are still very short in Denmark at this time of year, and we wanted to get to our destination before it got too dark. We had no lights on the rented bikes, and no reflective clothing. Some roads in the countryside don't have pavements and bike lanes. It would feel unsafe to cycle in such a setting. The supermarket was part of a chain. There we got simple food, organic where possible, but certainly not zero-waste. In the same town, before we rented the bikes, we went to get lunch in a casual, independent restaurant. We had traditional Danish food called smørrebrød. It seems easy to make this food with local ingredients, but I do not know if the restaurant we went to used local ingredients or not.

It is certainly more affordable to live in a rural area, away from Copenhagen. The area instantly reminded me of many years of my childhood spent in a somewhat similar area. Though the area where I lived in my childhood had less roads and more nature. As we were cycling, I was taking mental notes for this book. I was contemplating that area, degrowth, business and my autoethnographic work. I was thinking about jobs in that area. The area feels somewhat like northern Sweden, though it is much more agricultural. Initially it comes across as nature, though one quickly realises that it is farmland. It is interesting how we came to call "nature" anything that is not a city, even farmland, parks and forestry estates. In northern Sweden where I used to live, there are artificial forests that fellow humans call "nature".

In the area through which we are cycling in Denmark, there are not many shops. In the town where we rented the bikes, there are independent cafes, some second-hand stores, some independent clothing shops and many shops selling yarn. On our way, we see several bed & breakfast accommodations. The area attracts many tourists due to its breathtakingly beautiful Møns Klint. I wonder if I lived in this area, what would I do, where would I work. Perhaps it would be possible to have a garden and be partly self-sufficient. It could be possible to work part-time at a university and commute there at times, to write books. I believe many fellow humans in this area do crafts, and perhaps they sell them online. I see some ceramic stores. I see local honey, local jams and pickled vegetables for sale.

We walked past a self-service shop, and I was taking notes for this book as I saw the shop. The shop was small, independently owned – a local business producing sweets. I say self-service shop because it has no sales assistant. The payment is made via the phone. Such shops are common in Sweden and Denmark, and perhaps in other places where I have not lived. The model is based on trust. It also makes financial sense, as the cost of the potentially stolen goods is lower than the cost of hiring a sales assistant. I've seen a similar shop in northern Sweden. Bread, local vegetables and chocolate were for sale in that shop in northern Sweden. In Copenhagen, I walked past a little stand selling plants and floral decorations. I had conflicted feelings about the shop selling sweets. On the one hand, it is a small, local, independent business, very much in line with what I am interested in. On the other hand, sweets are not a need, perhaps they are even bad for human health. Just by looking at the shop, it was hard to tell whether the ingredients were organic. The sweets were packaged in plastic too, which is not sustainable. At the same time, humans buy sweets anyway, and it is more in line with degrowth if we bought sweets from a local and small shop rather than a large corporation. I was contemplating the Swedish tradition of Lördagsgodis. It's when children get sweets on Saturdays (Lördag is Saturday in Swedish, and godis means sweets/candy). I like this tradition as it could (and perhaps does?) help with overconsumption of sugar. Often such sweets are in bulk bins, and one can mix and match. Though buying sweets this way looks like a zero-waste practice, I cannot know where the ingredients came from and how these sweets were packaged before they were transferred to the bulk bins. The small business selling sweets made me think about other businesses that I came across on my journey, such as wine and chocolate businesses. Wine and chocolate are not strictly speaking human needs, but they are very much part of tradition, ritual and culture more generally.

I was writing these words, transferring them from the mental notes I took in Møn into a Word document, on the first day of the new year, while I was slowly consuming a drink made with some gin produced by a small Swedish business. I was thinking about business and human needs again. A more serious conversation needs to happen on human needs within the degrowth discourse. Where is the line separating genuine human needs from wants? Do I have a right to outline genuine human needs while I consume food and beverages as part of ritual or tradition or culture?

As we were preparing to leave Møn, I became ill. We were going to go back to Copenhagen by bikes, a bus and a train. I could barely walk, so cycling back was not an option. My partner called a taxi to take us to the train station so we could take a train back to Copenhagen. I do not drive and do not own a car. In fact, I have not been in a car for many months. I do not advocate private car ownership, overuse of cars, car-centric city planning, car dependency in our societies, using cars as a status symbol. And there I was, a human being who avoids cars, in a car due to my health. There are many practices that fellow humans within the degrowth movement implement to use cars better. Some take part in car-sharing schemes, others use electric cars, for example. I do not know how cars could fit within a degrowth society, how cars and their components could be produced in a degrowth-compatible way.

Choosing Danish businesses

How did you or how will you select businesses for your study is a question I have heard many times before, and it is a question that often makes students feel stressed. The roots of stress appear to stem from an obsession with so-called objectivity (Buch-Hansen and Nielsen, 2024). As if one must prove that they are detached from those businesses and demonstrate that their choice is somehow impersonal. As if there is more value in detachment than in deep and intimate knowledge. As if fellow humans reading my works about small businesses will automatically and uncritically assume that the same findings apply to all other businesses and contexts.

I come from the perspective that all businesses are equally interesting. There are interesting, sometimes wonderful, sometimes ugly, dynamics unfolding in every business. It is also difficult to tell what one will find when talking to businesspersons, employees and when being on the premises of those businesses. During earlier stages of my research journey, at times I expected that some business would be less interesting than others, judging, wrongly, the surface or what I knew about the business after a brief conversation or after seeing some information about it online. Over time my understanding and position evolved, and I was humbled by the richness and depth of insights from every business I was in contact with.

I am a practitioner of an ecological mode of being that I call being of deep transformations. It constellates many elements of voluntary simplicity, extreme minimalism, zero-waste, deep ecology and other ecological movements. Inevitably, when one dwells within these spaces, learning about sustainable businesses is natural. Some businesses I have heard about and would not be able to trace in my mind the source where I heard or saw something about a business.

I decided to see my exploration as a journey where I meet fellow humans and not deny the fact of me being in the world with others (Heidegger, 2001). So, I asked others if they knew about businesses I could be interested in. Some businesses I learned about through my personal consumption of more ecological products. At times, I would simply walk somewhere in Copenhagen and become curious about a particular business. Such getting to know businesses is natural, organic, spontaneous and raw. And it led to interesting insights and learning.

Being at Aalborg University

I visited Aalborg University in the end of September 2023. That time of my life was very challenging. I did not feel safe in my work environment in Finland, and relocating to Denmark didn't go as planned emotionally. I felt unhappy in my relationship, though everything started to get better after a while.

The first day at Aalborg University was memorable. The work environment felt very similar to the work environment I experienced in Sweden. The space was peaceful and calm. There were no individual offices, and everyone sat together. Somehow it still felt cosy, and I felt welcome. It was the first time after many months when I could focus again and found inspiration to write this book. Being at Aalborg was a breath of fresh air after being in what felt to me a hierarchical and old-fashioned organisation. I decided that I would not be going back to my university in Finland. It was interesting to observe how my mental state and the feeling of (un)safety intertwined with my writing. When I felt safe, I immediately became more curious and again passionate about the topic I am writing about. New ideas visited my mind, and old thoughts crystallised into words. I found happiness at work again, though this work was being done amidst a challenging situation of relocating and intentionally leaving my previous job.

It is not often, if ever at all, that researchers disclose how they felt while writing a book or an article. In this sense, such works feel sterile, devoid of humanness. While I began to notice how my own emotional landscape shaped and directed my thought, I began to wonder if some works would have been written differently if the person felt differently while working on that scientific piece. In the social sciences, it is not hard to imagine that it could be the case. Oftentimes I have heard from fellow academics about their experiences of writing while feeling bad, sad, anxious, doubtful, even fearful. They read the same sentence multiple times and do not fully understand what they were reading. They write paragraphs they would be unhappy about later. They write much less, or less coherently. These are normal human experiences, but they are not revealed. It feels vulnerable to write this way. Yet somehow it feels to be crucial information. The setting in which one's research is done is not only, say, the socio-cultural, political and natural environment in which businesses are located, but it is also the researcher's own mental and emotional landscape, their own life experiences.

Being at Roskilde University

I visited Roskilde University right after visiting Aalborg University. The beginning of my visit coincided with my partner and I establishing our household together. I've lived my life in an extremely minimalist way, so I owned almost nothing. My partner left many objects to his ex-partner and donated much too, so we were buying some objects for our new home. I learned a lot about small, independent and sustainable Danish businesses during that time. We were buying objects from the kind of businesses I am interested in for my research. There was one business that specialised in only one product. It was reflected in the name of the business itself.

The product was for all genders and all sizes. I was thinking about that business for many days. Could it be part of a model of a business for a degrowth society? To focus on only one product and do it well.

As it was with Aalborg University, the first time I came to Roskilde University was memorable. The university is in an area that feels much calmer than Copenhagen. There is so much sky one can see. Just a few minutes' walk from the building where the office was could take me to meet sheep. From the office where I was, I could see a lake and beautiful willow trees. I immediately felt creative and productive in that office. I could write. My partner is based in this university, and the university invited me to be a guest researcher there until the end of 2024. Becoming a visiting researcher in the Nordic countries feels easy. One can simply write to a faculty member and ask if it's possible to visit. I believe most if not all would say yes. I wanted to be at Roskilde University for many reasons, apart from my partner being there. The university was established on alternative principles of organisation and teaching. I felt inspired by what they do. It felt more down-to-earth than more traditional universities.

I do not intend to romanticise the universities I visited. No university is perfect. Perhaps in contrast with the work environment I experienced before I moved to Denmark any other university would feel liberating. But somehow intuitively I knew that I would be able to write something good and useful in the spaces of the Danish universities I visited.

The questions I asked

I've been researching small, independent businesses since 2016. When I was working on the guiding questionnaire to use as part of my case studies in my PhD journey, I sketched 20 or 30 questions. Because it was a guide, during my conversations with businesses, many more questions would naturally arise. Those questions were generally based on my degrowth business framework, and I was also curious about the barriers businesses faced on their paths. Then I came to the realisation that 20 or 30 were too many questions, and I could do much better and give more space to businesspersons by asking far fewer questions. As my thinking was evolving and I was learning more and more, reflecting more deeply on degrowth business, five key questions were constantly coming to my mind. They are: (1) When did you start your business? (2) What does your business focus on in terms of sustainability? (3) Why are you on this path? (4) What hinders your path? (5) What empowers you?

The first question is about the general background of the business. Because these questions are guiding, and so the interviews are semi-structured, the first question usually leads to other ones about the background of the business and what the business does. Much of it I would know before the interview, but it is interesting to hear how businesspersons themselves frame their business, how they describe it, what they highlight.

The second question replaces multiple questions I had for businesspersons during my PhD journey. At that time, I felt that I had to ask them whether they used renewable energy, natural materials, designed their products for durability and so on. Later, I realised that it is much better to simply give space and listen. Unique constellations of sustainability practices arise in the answers. These constellations often depend on a product, but sometimes there are similarities between businesses. For example, natural materials can be used in both personal care and home textiles and clothing.

The third question is the key one I have for the businesspersons. There are many reasons why this question is so close to my heart. In my research journey I see causation between the worldviews of businesspersons and their business practices. As a critical realist, I am curious about causation. It is of course not always and necessarily so that a beautiful worldview results in perfectly sustainable practices. There are many barriers to the realisation in practice of such worldviews. But nevertheless, in the businesses I research, it is not an inconvenient pressure from customers or laws and regulations that make businesspersons pursue sustainability. They genuinely care about nature and others. And when there are no perfect practices, there are always ideas, desire to learn and awareness. Businesspersons often ask me questions about my area of expertise. They are curious about what other businesses and businesspersons, and even academics and movements, are doing in relation to sustainability. They want to understand what the most recent debates in sustainability are. Oftentimes they say that it is nice to speak to a researcher specialising in sustainability and business. Essentially, the third question is the why behind the "what" and the "how" of the second one.

Critical realism postulates that agents exist within structures that constrain and empower them (Collier, 1994). Hence, questions four and five arise. Initially in my PhD journey I focused more on various constraints and barriers. Much of earlier degrowth literature was focused on critiquing capitalism. While this is important, it emphasises critique so much that it becomes possible to present a very negative picture of sustainability journeys and forget to ask about what makes these journeys possible in society. I asked every businessperson I spoke with what the barriers to their sustainability practices were. One businessperson I spoke to brought my attention to both constraints and empowering structures. I am grateful for this because it resulted in a much more balanced and nuanced perspective. I tended to think that everything within the capitalist system was bad and constraining. Then I realised that in parallel with capitalism, there is so much that is beautiful, alternative and empowering. Gibson-Graham (2006) point out that capitalism in fact is sustained due to such alternative structures, organisations and attitudes. When I became more attentive to empowering factors and their importance, I became more familiar with them. I began to ask businesspersons about empowering factors and in my mind constellate them together with constraining structures, rather than solely emphasising constraints. Examples of empowering factors are working with likeminded suppliers and distributors, supportive family members and friends, customers who are also on sustainability journeys, academics who are interested in genuine sustainability, activists, and many others. Even more conventional organisations such as social media can be useful.

Asking far fewer questions and listening more feels better, results in slower paced interviews and less stress for me and the businesspersons I want to learn from. I remember an interview at my fellow human's office. Both of us had meetings right after the hour we dedicated to our conversation. The conversation was wonderful, we genuinely connected. After 30 minutes or so we checked the clock and were relieved to learn that we still had half an hour left. The interview was more akin to a discussion than something done as a research activity. Asking far fewer questions also results in deeper and longer answers. In the beginning of each interview or even beforehand I always tell businesspersons that I only have five main questions for them. They feel that not much of their time will be taken and feel they can answer my questions more fully and intentionally. I also notice that asking better questions means I can use more of the data I gather. Something I notice about qualitative research like this is that so few insights tend to be reported, so few quotes presented. Qualitative researchers like myself gather much data but much of it also remains unseen. And what remains unseen so often contains incredibly interesting insights. It has become my intention to use as much of the data as possible, to learn as much as possible from each interview.

Danish businesses

Being a researcher specialising in the connection between degrowth and business, I can't help but contemplate small businesses often when I see them, when I buy from them, when I visit their stores. In my area in Copenhagen (Frederiksberg, which is technically a separate city), I came across many businesses that seem very interesting from a degrowth perspective. These are both options for a degrowth society and examples of something that is currently only available to the materially wealthy which is incompatible with degrowth ideals. For example, there are plenty of stores specialising in bread and baked goods, salad, fish and seafood, wine and cheese. The pace of life feels slow in those stores. The staff and the owner-managers are knowledgeable and passionate about the (often expensive) products. There is a local store that is closed half of the week. There are some swap shops (byttestationer in Danish) too. Though these are not businesses, they are interesting places of exchange and need satisfaction. Anyone is free to bring there the objects they don't use or need any longer. They can take nothing or something they need in exchange. There is no money involved in this exchange. Swap shops feel aligned with degrowth ideas at least in some ways.

Organic homewares business

I came across this Danish business when I was looking for organic textiles for my own home when I moved in with my partner. There are many ways to be more sustainable when it comes to homewares than buying new things – making kitchen cloths from old bed sheets, buying second-hand towels, making old kitchen towels last long and embrace beautiful imperfections such as stains and small holes. Part of me wanted to live this kind of life, but the reality was that I had no homeware items of my own. The only bed sheet I had was still functional, beautiful and overall too good to cut up into cloths. Second-hand shopping, though sustainable, takes much time, and I feel anxiety when I go shopping. I avoid shopping as much as possible. The very few homewares I had in Finland I gave away to my fellow humans as I was going to carry everything that I owned to Denmark myself. When my partner and I walked into our temporary apartment, we had only a few bags.

I try to make things last, but when it comes to buying something new for my home, I try to pay particular attention to materials. I wonder where they come from, what impact they have on nature, what impact their production has on fellow humans. I try to use organic cotton, and this is how I came across this company. I reached out to them to see if they wanted to speak to me as a researcher. The owner invited me to visit their office. It was a beautiful and calm space in a diverse neighbourhood in Copenhagen. I said hi to several fellow humans who were working there and walked across the space. It felt like home. Perhaps it felt like home because the space was simple, even minimalist. It had a similar atmosphere to my own home. There were items that are durable, zero-waste, in calming colours. The owner and I went to one of the rooms to have tea and talk about the business and life.

Avoiding recording the conversation from the very beginning feels important to me. It is essential to remember that the person I am talking with is first and foremost a fellow human being, not merely a respondent. I always share something about myself too. With the owner, we felt like we were speaking the same language. She has a similar approach to being in the world as I do. We talked about the need for balance, to balance the masculine energy of competition and achievement with the feminine energy of cooperation and care. We talked about different paths in life, how a university education or having a highly paid job is not the epitome of success. We talked about giving up on something important in life to gain something better and more meaningful.

During our conversation I realised something that felt profound to me. It was not necessarily a new insight. It is something that I've been observing at least from 2016 when I started working on my PhD and that I knew intuitively. But there was something in that particular conversation that allowed my thoughts to crystallise. I came to the realisation that businesspersons are not awaiting for us, academics, for me, to tell them what business should look like for a genuinely sustainable society to be possible. They learn. They organise. They realise that one cannot be a "lone wolf" in society and also that one's own actions and efforts are not enough. They communicate and work together with other businesses, they take courses outside universities and at universities. They attend events, listen to scientists' talks. I realised that the range of sciences they are exposed to is often broader than what we tend to expose ourselves to in academic silos.

With this businessperson, we spoke about planetary boundaries, being an agent of change, ethics of care, love and gentleness towards nature and human and non-human beings. I learned about the production of cotton, the difference between conventional and organic cotton, what fellow humans can do to make objects last longer. We talked about business journey and life journey. The term this businessperson prefers to describe her business and her path is "regeneration". It felt more positive and hopeful to talk about this rather than about degrowth, though the values and practices aligned perfectly with what I called a degrowth business path.

Something that stood out to me is the businessperson saying that likeminded humans from different walks of life should unite. My mind took me to other conversations I had with businesspersons elsewhere, and they used to say something very similar. And not only did they say it but also behaved this way too. They united with fellow businesspersons, likeminded academics, likeminded politicians, activists, communities, religious organisations and many others.

The story

This businessperson started her business in 2007. The company produces homeware objects that are 100% certified organic. This means that the raw materials for their products are grown without pesticides and artificial fertilisers, and no GMOs (genetically modified organisms) are used. The processing itself is done in the least harmful way too. All aspects of the product are taken into account – the way humans are treated in the process of production, the agricultural aspects (e.g., the way land is treated), spinning, dyeing. This, according to the businessperson, should be the minimum in processing textiles. Their approach to business is not that of replacing conventional options with organic options, e.g., conventional cotton with organic cotton. They are acutely aware of multiple crises in the world. These not only include the climate and biodiversity crises but also resource crisis. For this reason, they are looking into replacing "a lot with one thing". They produce reusable items, items that allow consumers to reduce their impact and the quantity of items they consume and live with. They want to replace single-use items, poorly made items with long-lasting options, and make them better. They incorporate this thinking into their design principles. The product must be designed in such a way that it solves a problem, otherwise the product will not be launched. I am curious as to why. I ask the human being who runs this business why she is on this path. Using organic cotton is not a legal requirement. Neither is designing to help consumers to live with less.

She says that it is a matter of justice. She mentions that she has had a strong sense of justice since her childhood. She wants to manifest justice towards the soil via her business. She mentions again that going organic is the very minimum we can do for the soil. Agriculture should be regenerative and free from violence towards the soil. At the very least we can avoid polluting the soil with pesticides. She contemplates responsibilities and the need to do better. She feels that it is not responsible to be greedy and make poor choices on behalf of future generations, the soil and animals. Justice and responsibility and feeling them are the why behind doing business differently.

I wonder what hinders and what empowers her journey and the journey of her business. She mentions that what is hindering is being in the world, and trying to navigate the world that is "90% yang focussed". Because then you, she mentions, clash with this world, its systems and mindsets. But then you have to find your strength from "deep within". She says:

> it is my belief. You know in every cell of my body that we will have to do better than we do today. We'll just have to. […] You know that you can't throw knowledge out. You can just build on it. And my truth is based on knowledge and experiences and feelings.

She contemplates hindering factors such as being a change maker in this world. It entails convincing people, holding onto her truth, keeping moving forward to make sure that the business is running. She mentions that there are still rather few people working to change the world, considering how many fellow humans are on the planet. She views her business as being organic 2.0, a transformative business. We discuss empowering factors. What empowers her is

> networking with likeminded [humans], talking to the likeminded, reading about, listening to the likeminded. It empowers me when I meditate and when I focus on deeper things. It empowers me that I feel that I'm on the right path. […] You know, sometimes when you think of what you're doing, and you feel your purpose in life.

Learnings

While I was working on this chapter, some learnings began to constellate in my mind. I began to sketch the principles that matured in my consciousness when I was researching Danish businesses.

Empathy. I realised that it is important to come into conversations with businesspersons from a place of deeply felt empathy towards their journeys rather than scepticism. Businesspersons are fellow humans. They are more inclined, just like any other human being, to share about their struggles, worries, hopes, successes and aspirations in a safe space. Creating a safe space should be genuine and not utilitarian. Oftentimes, I talk to businesspersons merely with an intention to learn from them and share my learnings rather than to use their businesses in my research. I do not believe that there is a perfect number of cases for one's PhD or a paper, or that the more cases one studies the better. What counts is the quality and depth of conversations, not the number of businesses one researches. It took me a while to transcend worrying about the number of cases being too low, not sufficient.

Genuine interdisciplinarity. Embracing interdisciplinarity seriously is necessary to understand more holistically the journeys of businesses and to appreciate the knowledges that exist about businesses, human beings and places within other disciplines outside of business studies and economics. Some of most inspiring traditions for me have been, for example, humanism, new materialism and humanistic geography. Engaging with knowledges from other disciplines helps to appreciate what businesspersons are already doing on their deeply transformative paths, and better understand why they are not doing something.

Not waiting. One of the most profound learnings for me was realising that businesspersons are not waiting for the degrowth scholarship to tell them how to be genuinely sustainable. They are constantly searching, learning from fellow humans and nature and oftentimes working with others such as activists and likeminded businesses. I notice that often they learn from a much wider range of sources than we do within particular disciplines in academia.

Avoiding perfectionism. In the beginning of my research journey, like many fellow researchers, I was seeking perfect cases. Later I came to the realisation that every business is interesting, and it is important to understand diverse journeys of businesses in different places and industries. I found it most helpful to focus on the businesses in my local area, the Nordics, to be able to grasp the cultural, political and linguistic references and references to places, climate and nature more deeply and accurately. I am curious about businesses in other areas. When I am outside the Nordics, when I see small businesses somewhere, I wonder about their journeys. But I would study them only if I had an opportunity to live in those places.

Change. Being open to changing one's view has been an essential part of my journey. On my degrowth journey, perhaps similarly to many others, I developed a somewhat negative attitude towards growth. At least a sceptical attitude. The notion of growth has acquired a somewhat negative connotation within the degrowth discourse due to degrowth's critique of society's narrow focus on economic growth. Other types of growth have been overlooked (Buch-Hansen and Nesterova 2023; Nesterova and Buch-Hansen, 2023). Yet, growth, that is to say growth in our human capacities for care, concern, empathy, love and solidarity, is necessary for transformation to take place. Acknowledging this allowed me to ask better questions, including diving deeper into businesspersons' motivations, and to be more sensitive to different kinds of growth.

Skærsøgaard Vin

I have been interested in wine produced in the Nordics for several years, both as a business researcher and a practitioner of ecological living. As a practitioner, I try to consume food and drinks that are local and to support small and independent businesses. As a researcher, in my work on some occasions I spoke about Arctic winescapes, a phrase that came to my mind when I was living in northern Sweden. While grapes do not grow there, wine in northern Sweden is made from blueberries and lingonberries. As my colleague and I were driving to visit the business making wine from those berries, I was looking out of the car windows to see vast expanses of magical northern Swedish forests where the forest floor is covered by blueberries and lingonberries and moss. Those were Arctic winescapes.

There is something special about food and drinks production. First and foremost, it will exist in a degrowth society. But also, food and drinks are a beautiful space where human needs intertwine deeply with tradition, ritual, culture and celebration. When my colleagues and I contemplate food production in a genuinely sustainable society, we talk about localisation and consuming seasonal food, love towards the places where we are (Jungell-Michelsson and Nesterova, 2024; Nesterova,

2022a; Nesterova and Jungell-Michelsson, forthcoming). Food is something everyone consumes and has close relationship with. For me, as a practitioner, it is also a source of anxiety. This is one domain where my own sustainability practices are highly imperfect. I live in a city and don't grow my own food. For convenience reasons, I rely on supermarkets and visit farmers' and food markets only occasionally. While I try to buy organic, seasonal and local Danish food in supermarkets, supermarket shopping still feels impersonal. Partly, I also feel guilt and shame when I buy Danish wine. Even though I do it only rarely and buy it from a local wine shop or online, it is expensive. This act makes me contemplate living a life where local Danish wine can be part of it and identifying myself as a leftist. At the same time, apple wine is sentimental to me, as once I brought it for my partner as a gift from Sweden. Gift-giving is a challenging subject for those who practise minimalism and zero-waste. Food always feels acceptable.

Once I got to try Danish apple wine and I immediately became curious about the producer. I reached out to them, and this is how I got in touch with Sven. Here in my book, I refer to the name of Sven and his business that makes apple and grape wine openly. I asked Sven if he wants me to anonymise his business and he did not want that. Sven was so open to sharing as much as possible about his business. He sent me many materials about the business and articles where his business story was featured. He called me and we spoke for about 50 minutes on the phone. This was the only conversation for my book that I did not record. It felt inappropriate to record it, as I was standing on a windy balcony with my phone, looking over Copenhagen, at the sun and the sky.

I told Sven about my work, my book and a little bit about myself and my journey. I mentioned openly that I tried products from his company, and I genuinely liked them. We talked about wine production in the Nordics. Sven is very knowledgeable about this subject, and I asked him many questions about wine production out of curiosity and because something had been on my mind for a while, not because I wanted to use insights into the technical aspects of wine production for this book. For example, I asked him about orange wine, something that I saw in Denmark for the first time. He dived deep into the details of wine production. I was contemplating how beautiful such knowledge sharing is. Sven shares knowledge with many others and gives lectures on wine production too.

Sven, like many other fellow humans, feels sorrow about climate change. We share many of the same emotions about it. At the same time, he says, we have to work with the change and possibilities that unfold. I am reminded of similar discussions in England where I used to live. Climate change is a manifestation of ecological degradation, but it also brings new possibilities to some areas, like England and Denmark, to grow something that was impossible or more challenging to grow before, such as grapes. It is perhaps controversial to find opportunities and even joy in new possibilities when the environment is degrading. I was thinking, can I include this in my book?

Sven tells me that previously it was not possible to produce wine in Denmark due to regulations. Now it is, but to Sven possibility is not enough. He says that local wine also needs to be high in quality, comparable with or better than wines produced in other regions of the world.

He tells me more about grapevine. It is a temperate plant. For comparison, he gives me an example of bananas that cannot be grown in Denmark. But the Danish climate, as it is now, is highly suitable for grapevines, at least some varieties of them. Sven says that producing wine is art and also a skill. It takes generations to establish a winery, something that he will not see due to his age. We talk about his age and his path in life. He is currently in his 70s and he contemplates the journey of his vineyard. He is positive and hopeful about this journey and the future. He noticed that there is increased interest in the Nordic cuisine, local ingredients. It makes me think about many other conversations I have had with fellow humans in the Nordics, including fellow humans in the food industry. What they mentioned corresponded to what Sven was saying. I tell Sven about my own practice of consuming local, seasonal food. He shares much useful information with me and lets me know about some fellow humans in Danish academia who are interested in the same subject.

I mention in passing that I have researched another business, in northern Sweden, that makes blueberry wine. He tells me that he knows them. He has sophisticated laboratory equipment that the Swedish business did not have when I spoke to them. He performs quality tests for the Swedish business I researched. I find this moment rather beautiful, as I only knew that the Swedish business used a laboratory in Denmark to test their wine, but I didn't know who owned the laboratory and where exactly it was located.

Knowing my particular interest in kind and caring attitude towards the soil, Sven tells me that the wine they produce is organic. They do not use pesticides and fungicides in their vineyard. In fact, there are no such chemicals approved in Denmark for growing grapes, he tells me. He shares some information about different varieties of grape that can grow in Denmark. He mentions that they are resistant to fungus.

Sven tells me about other fellow humans who work with him. The winemakers are German, and they have lived here in Denmark for seven years. Sven speaks German, but he says the German winemakers learned Danish. They had children in Denmark too, who speak fluent Danish. We then discuss the motives behind his business. A strong belief that producing high-quality wine is possible in Denmark drives him. Passion for a high-quality product seems to be behind this business. Sven tells me that it is not about the money. We end the conversation by talking about my surroundings. It is a challenging topic for me, as I miss nature. I mention that I live in Copenhagen. Sven tells me about the landscapes that surround him. There is more nature than where I am standing. He says that I am welcome to visit them in May and June when nature and vineyards look magical.

Business specialising in renewable objects

Whenever possible, I try to buy local products and support small and local businesses, both retailers and producers. Moving to a new country always means discovering new businesses and learning about their paths. There is a small, independent store in Copenhagen selling zero-waste goods. As a practitioner of zero-waste living, I visit this store from time to time. They had some products made by a Danish family-owned business specialising in renewable objects such as water bottles and coffee cups. I wanted to learn more about this business and reached out to them. They were very open and willing to help me understand their journey.

We begin our conversation by contemplating what zero-waste lifestyles looked like around 2010–2011 when I developed interest in it. At that time, zero-waste options were limited. I remember niche products that did not work well or were much less effective than conventional products. Many zero-waste options were not beautiful. Perhaps to some the aesthetic element feels shallow, but in my own practice of minimalism I notice that living with a very small number of objects, all of which are beautiful to me, is helpful for the sustainability of my lifestyle and feeling joy in my everyday life. The businessperson I am talking with agrees. She tells me that sustainable products do not have to be less beautiful than conventional ones, and partly their business is finding success here in Denmark is because their products are aesthetically pleasing. At the heart of this business is making reusable products that are functional, beautiful, pleasant to use and eliminate the need for single-use products such as water bottles and coffee cups.

The company is careful to offer new products to the market because they do not want to make new products too often for sustainability reasons. They maintain a database of their customers whom they consult for help to understand in which direction the business should go. Once they asked their customers why they buy their products. The customers could choose any answer, including colour and design. The result of the survey was, above all, functionality. The businessperson tells me that if the product does not function well, humans might forget about it and not be inclined to use it in their everyday life. To offer functional products is very important, as their business essentially takes away convenience that comes with single-use products.

The businessperson tells me about their own family and children who use their reusable water bottles. The children enjoy having cold water during the day. The reusable water bottle keeps the water cold for 24 hours. She mentions that in summer this allows the business to compete with convenient plastic bottles that don't keep water cold. The topic of single-use plastic bottles is uncomfortable to both of us. We discuss the use of plastic bottles in Denmark. She mentions that even five or so years ago, there was no tradition in Denmark yet to bring your own water or beverage with you. When you were at school or on the road, you could simply buy water packaged in plastic. It was a matter of convenience. Then, suddenly humans began to care about the environment. People are "trying to do things in a new way", though convenience still remains important to the Danes, she reflects. As we are talking, I am thinking about water in Denmark. The tap water here is wonderful. It is safe and even delicious, which is such a privilege.

The businessperson tells me that it is oftentimes interior design shops that buy their products. She says that five or so years ago it was unimaginable that these shops would be interested in the products such as reusable water bottles and coffee cups. She sees that public attitudes are shifting towards environmental considerations. At the same time, she contemplates that design stores would not buy their reusable products if they didn't look beautiful.

We return to the question of engaging with customers to understand what is actually needed. The company has a day in January where they contemplate what will be unfolding with their product range in the current year. The businessperson says that they might have an intuition of what is needed or could be useful, what could be an interesting or fun product to create, but it might differ from what the customers need. As a company, they do not want to produce something that will not be useful to consumers. They want to create products that serve for many years, become part of humans' everyday life and eliminate the need for single-use plastic bottles, cups and other objects.

We talk about sales. She mentions that we have to be honest and economic sustainability matters to the business too. They have employees in the company, which comes with responsibility. As a business, they also want to afford donating to causes that matter much to them. They donate to UNICEF (United Nations Children's Fund), which is a cause very close to their heart. She realises that they are a small business, and their donations are not comparable to the donations made by large businesses, but they still decided to incorporate donation into their business model and sales. They do not donate only occasionally or in connection to a special event or a holiday such as Christmas. They "donate every day basically because we do it every time we sell a product". She is very proud of this and believes that if they managed to do it, big businesses should surely be able to incorporate donations into their business models.

We talk about business growth. She mentions that it is important that the business is "growing organically and that can be healthy enough to have employees". So, growth is important to them, but it is not the only important aspect of business. It is

> also having feedback from customers that they use our products every day, hearing from the stores that are selling our products that they get so much good feedback from the customers on our products, that the quality is high, that they look beautiful.

The businessperson mentions that they had a conversation with a business advisor once who asked them if they want to grow fast or organically. They contemplated it and decided that organic growth suits them well. They want to be in control of everything and avoid the company "blooming and then crashing afterwards".

She contemplates what empowers them as a business and mentions positive feedback from the customers who say that they use the products every day and running a business whose products make sense and that is economically sustainable.

We contemplate constrains such as convenience culture. She mentions that it is not possible to reach everyone, but it is "possible to slowly reach more and more people". She realises that they are playing a small part and do not want to see themselves and their business as "holy". They recognise that their products may not be for everyone, "which is fine".

She mentions that a serious constraint is not the end user of the product, but often it is the retailers and the retail system. Retailers expect new products and new colours, they want to do discount activities several times a year (e.g., Black Friday) and new collections. She says it is challenging to discuss this with retailers, especially those who could buy many of their products. She communicates to them that they as a company do not believe in activities such as Black Friday, they do not want to take part in the consumerist system. On Black Friday, she says, "we are double donating on water, instead of using discounts". She says they are still doing promotional activities, but perhaps once a year and on their own terms.

She reflects on how in Denmark the retail system relies on discounts. We talk about Black Friday. When I moved to Denmark, I was surprised that this event was so popular. There is Black Week and even Black Month. The businessperson says that Black Friday became popular 5–7 years ago when big retailers brought it to Denmark. Big retailers also started to send out offers and catalogues and offer discounts. She says that before Black Friday appeared, Denmark was not used to it. She contemplates the effect Black Friday has on small retailers in Denmark. Many humans in Denmark buy their Christmas presents during Black Friday sales, and small, independently owned retailers think that they will lose out if they do not participate in Black Friday sales. My conversation partner thinks a better strategy for small retailers would be to just wait until December when people are willing to buy Christmas presents at full price. She feels sorrow about big stores, chains and department stores directing the trends within the retail system and small stores struggling. We are contemplating possible differences between events such as Black Friday in the Nordics. The businessperson says that "in Sweden and Norway it's just not the same. I think we are much more price oriented in Denmark".

We then discuss affordability of ecological products, an uncomfortable subject that is close to my heart. The businessperson says that in Copenhagen (where I live) there are many stores, many highly educated humans who can afford to buy sustainable goods and are inclined to do so. She gives me an example of a store where she lives and says it is struggling while the same kinds of stores are thriving in Copenhagen. She mentions that some of their business customers are online stores with sustainable profiles and yoga shops. She says that as a business, they want their products to be part of everyday life of the Danes and not only of wealthy persons with sustainability-orientated worldviews and lifestyles. She feels that they are succeeding in it because people buy their products not only for sustainability reasons but also because of functionality and aesthetics.

As I am revising this case, I feel that I want to talk about it with my partner. I read out parts of this case to him, and he is reflecting on what he has observed around him living in Denmark. He mentions that a financial ability to buy sustainable products is not the only factor. There needs to be inclination to buy such products. He mentions fellow humans in the North Jutland region in Denmark who may be able to afford sustainable products but prefer to buy conventional ones.

The businessperson and I discuss affordability some more. She says it is a topic they discuss as a company, too. They want to reach people who do not usually shop in health shops and privately owned interior design shops with a green profile. To reach more people, they made an agreement with a large chain in Denmark. For them, a small company, it is a big deal. Their products are not currently sold in all the stores of the chain, but they are testing it out in a couple of stores to see how sales unfold. She contemplates the role of large chains in sustainability and says that now chains have health and wellbeing departments, and including sustainable products in their collection may help make sustainable living more accessible and affordable to more people. It may inspire humans to lead healthier lifestyles. She says that as a business they would never abandon working with small shops, and they are a large part of their success as a business. She notes that small, independent, ecological shops are not everywhere in Denmark, while the chain is.

The businessperson also shares with me that she noticed that large businesses that used to provide bottled water during meetings for their employees now buy reusable water bottles for them. They also buy reusable coffee cups as presents for their employees. She sees it is a positive development as it helps reach different audiences: "that's also a matter of getting our products out to all types of people". Towards the end of our conversation, we talk about production. She is reflecting on the fact that even though they are trying to make humans' everyday lives more sustainable, they are still putting a strain on the environment. Their products still contribute to carbon dioxide emissions. Recently they have done a report to evaluate their carbon footprint to improve it further. She thinks there are still things that can be improved on their journey: "as normal people, we are not perfect, but we're not perfect as companies either. We're just trying".

MagiCare

Whenever I don't make my own skincare, I always buy products such as bar soap and balm locally, from small, independent businesses. Personal care is one category of my consumption where I can practice zero-waste almost perfectly. I live with an autoimmune skin condition, which makes some form of skincare a necessity for me. When I moved to Denmark, I bought a balm in a health food store. The balm had very basic ingredients, was packaged in glass and had the Om symbol on it, one of the most important symbols in Hinduism. I was using the balm for some weeks as a lip balm, face cream, body lotion, hand cream and even on the ends of my hair. I was curious about the company that made it and reached out to them. Loui, the founder, responded to me and we decided to meet. Her company produces only three products (balm, lip balm, hair wax) from only three ingredients: shea butter, olive oil and beeswax.

Meeting Loui was a wonderful experience, as I felt we were on similar spiritual paths. Academically, Loui was a child of the university that was hosting me here in Denmark. We met at the office of another company she is heading. We begin with the story behind the business. MagiCare started back in 2010–2011 because Loui became a mother. She had her second child and was struggling to find suitable skincare products. She mentions that there was a lack of suitable products here in the Nordics for babies and children, and what was used commonly for children was also extremely damaging to the environment. The product Loui is thinking of was very sticky and would not flush properly in the drains. It was not very good for the skin either. She reflects:

> you know, you have these gorgeous babies. And you think they are so clean; I need to give them the absolute cleanest products I can. And so, I decided to search online and find a recipe to make it from organic, sustainable ingredients. And I found this recipe and I bought the ingredient. It was very simple. It was three ingredients. It was olive oil, shea butter and beeswax, and I mixed it in a bowl and heated it and put it in a marmalade jar and used it for my son. It worked really well. It's really weird because I don't have a background at all within the pharmaceutical industry. So, I had made a lot of this products, and you used a little only. So, I gave it to some of my friends who were also mothers and they all told me, 'this is amazing, what have you done?' And my husband is an entrepreneur. He loves setting up stuff. I'm not a big entrepreneurial type, but he said 'I think you're onto something here'. And somehow, a friend of mine had a friend who gave it to a blogger, and she wrote about it on the web, and it sort of spiralled from there. So, I bought more ingredients, and I went to the [large Danish chain] store and I bought 200 little jars and put the product in them and sent it out to my friends and said, 'you know, if you want to buy this, let me know'. It was sold out within a day. And I thought that's strange, and that was actually the start. It wasn't me looking for a project that I could create a business from it. It was more the other way around. I was actually not interested in starting a business, but everything kept pointing me in that direction.

We discuss skincare ingredients, something that has interested me since my childhood, as I have been allergic to so many ingredients. Loui mentions that when she started looking at the ingredients lists, she was wondering "why is there so much in it? It just doesn't make sense. I mean, I understand when you get to a certain age, you may prefer a perfume, but a baby doesn't need a perfume".

For a while, she was making the balms herself but after a while, she "couldn't keep up". She explains:

> so I had to find a factory to do it for me. And they thought I was crazy when I said I only want these three ingredients. And I am quite spiritual in my practise in daily life, and three is a very magic number for me. And they kept saying, let's put in some stabiliser. But it's stable, it's fine. Then they wanted to put in some vitamin E to make it durable. And I said, but it is durable, it's fine. It doesn't contain water. It's not necessary. And they agreed. And I don't even know that much about pharma. I didn't know anything about this market, I didn't have the network. I went to the [industry lobby organisation]'s website and had a look at their members because I thought, maybe one of them knows something. [A large French cosmetics company], for example, is a member, but there were hundreds. And I thought I need help, I need

> guidance if I'm supposed to do this. I closed my eyes and I just went scrolling until it said 'stop' and there was a name I didn't even know. I had never heard of them. I called and I said, can you help me produce this and bring it to market. And the person from the company said 'it is so weird that you're calling me because it's exactly what I want to do, and I don't do this for anyone. I've closed down my business. It's a mistake that I'm on the website'. So, you know, she was sort of an angel who helped me.

Loui shows me the label on the jar of one of the products and says,

> You need this bar code. I didn't know how to get a barcode. How do I get the Environmental Agency of the Government to approve the products so that I can put the product on the market? And all of that she could help me out with.

We discuss guidance we receive as individuals, as if from elsewhere. I can deeply relate to what Loui is saying. Then we talk about motivations. Loui says that she is not doing this for the money. She has a day job in another industry. She reflects: "I'm doing it because I think it's important that we have a clean alternative for the babies. I produce it in Denmark, which is extremely expensive. It's all in organic". She mentions how difficult it was to find organic beeswax because bees fly everywhere. But she was determined to find organic beeswax: "I said, it has to be organic. I will not accept anything if it is not organic".

She mentions fellow humans reaching out to her to share their stories about her products helping them and their children. We discuss glass packaging, as this is something that attracted me to the product in the first place as a practitioner of zero-waste. Loui says:

> It's in glass jars, which is also something I decided from the very day one. I don't want it in plastic containers because when there's oil, and plastic is oil, it interacts, and you don't want that. And a lot of our products unfortunately are in plastic because it's cheaper to produce. So, these [her products] are extremely expensive to produce. But they're clean.

We dive deeper into discussing the price. These balms are expensive in comparison to conventional options. As I use this product myself every day, I notice that I use very little of it because it doesn't contain any water. I also exclude other categories of products, such as makeup, to be able to afford locally made products such as the balm made by Loui's company. Loui agrees that there is a trade-off between quality and quantity.

Loui tells me more about the business, the connection between her children, her business and her spiritual practice. She has three children after whom the products are named.

> Our oldest daughter called Olivia, and the children have the last name of my husband and he's called [his surname starts with an M]. So, her initials

> are OM, which was very deliberate. I was pregnant with her when I went to India. I went to India to do yoga and ayurvedic treatments. I am very drawn to the Buddhist practice, so the Om sign has been with me for a long time for many years. And then he, August, when we had him, I created this whole company. And his name is August, and his last name is also [M], so his initials are AuM, which is also a way of writing Om. So, I just knew that the Om sign has to be part of this because my children are the reason I created this and they are very much part of this very, very enlightening and spiritual practise that I have. So that's why the Om sign was there from the beginning. I knew that it has to be in there, even though I thought some people might think that's a bit too religious or spiritual. I don't mind. They don't have to buy the product, but for me it was important to have it as part of the whole image.

The Om sign is on the packaging of Loui's products, and we talk more about the packaging, and how it could be possible to make the product less expensive. Much thought went into the packaging. The lid is made from aluminium. Loui tells me about the label:

> When you put this label on, it has glue, and the glue isn't environmentally very friendly, so we've been working on a new thing that has come out which is a film created from trees even though it looks like plastic. It is tree. And the glue is tree resin. So, it's resin that is the sticky part and it's the paper that comes from wood. I was so pleased. It's super expensive, but I was so pleased. I was like, that's a new way of optimising the packaging of this.

We discuss the question of money. Loui is saying that she wants MagiCare to be a sustainable business and make a profit. At the same time, she says

> I think we consume too much already, and the system of the way we consume and produce stuff in this world is a big problem. And I didn't want to contribute to that. So that was a thing I was thinking a lot about. Am I contributing to the overproduction in this world by setting out my products on the market? And decided no, I'm not because I produce it in a sustainable way. I package in a sustainable way. This is an alternative that is much cleaner. And so on and so on. I think it's important to mention this.

I can relate to such contemplations, being a degrowth researcher. I contemplate this topic as Loui shares her thoughts. Something that comes to my mind as a practitioner is how the products that her company makes replace so many products in my life. I ask Loui what she thinks about it. She mentions:

> When I started reaching out to distributors and interested people, they all said you need many more products. You need to make a line of products. You need to have 15 products, and I said, one covers the 15 products. I'm not

> going to just create 15 products. And it was actually a struggle and a lot of them said no, because they said, we can't market it.

We reflect on our experiences of being in a health shop here in Denmark with plenty of products on their shelves. Loui comments:

> there are tonnes of products, and this [her range] is tiny, and it's just there on a shelf, very quiet, and that's why they need 15–20 product. I do get it. I understand the marketing strategy behind it. It's just not sustainable. And I don't want to contribute to it.

Loui shares another story with me:

> I remember someone who called me and said, your recipe is being copied and people are doing it themselves and it's terrible. And I said no, it's not terrible. It's fine. I've made it so transparent. Of course, you have to write your ingredients, but I could have put in six, eight, 10 or more ingredients that no one understood, and you couldn't copy it. Mine is totally open and transparent. And it's a philosophy of mine: transparency. I want people, I want the consumer to understand. If people want to do it themselves, great for them. I don't mind. It is expensive on a relative scale, so if people can't afford it, by all means, make your own and then save the money. You still create a better alternative for your children or yourself or whoever you're going to use it for. People use it for their pets too. It's not about people stealing my recipe or copying it, but it was, of course, a different experience when I went on these links and it says, create your own Olivia's magic balm. And that's my brand. It's my daughter's name. It was different. If they said, create a great all round balm, it's ok.

Towards the end of our conversation, I ask Loui to reflect on empowering and constraining factors. She says:

> If we start with what empowers me, I think it was really from the very beginning I had these one-to-one testimonials from people. I have two very good girlfriends whose sons, by coincidence, had very, very sensitive skin. And when she was crying, she was saying, "this has changed our life because he is so tormented by having this sensitive skin." That really empowered me.

Loui continues:

> I can't believe I've just created something that actually helps. I could hardly believe it. So that was really empowering. And the other thing that really was empowering for me was also my husband's support. As I said in the beginning, I don't actually see myself as an entrepreneur, but he was just saying, "you should do this". I think I told you in the beginning, I was buying these

> jars of my own. And I was making these labels, and we were printing them on a A4 sheet paper on a printer, but we couldn't cut them because it doesn't look nice. So, he went into his garage, and he created a stick with a round knife. And then you could hold the stick, put that knife on the label, and you could do like this a lot of times. And then it would come off. It would look nice. And he would in that way support me. I still have that thing because it's an example and manifestation of how we were, during late nights, doing this together and he had a blister because he had done it so many times, and that was such a magical time for it because it was both tough and we were so in it together. And we had two small children. And we would be wrapping the balms in newspaper because it had to be sustainable. So, we were wrapping, we were creating them and then giving them as presents and selling them, and it was very empowering. And I remember I came home one day and I've sold another 150 balms. And he [Loui's husband] just looked at his hand and went, oh great. And here we go again. And it was really, really nice.

I ask Loui about constraints. She responds:

> I think my main constraint has been, which has been both the good and the bad thing, is that I have this job [her day job as a CEO] at the same time. In the beginning it went so fast, and it was so popular, and I remember I called [Danish chain of health stores]' supplier to decide whether they would take the product in. The individual stores buy everything from their website on standard terms. If they say no, which they do a lot, then you have to sell individually, go into every store and sell. And I asked them in the beginning because I heard that that's where you want to be. And they said, "absolutely no, we're not interested. We've never heard of it. There is no one asking for it, and we're not interested". And that's the standard response. I'm like, ok, that's fine. I just have to do it the hard way. So, every time I was out for meetings in this job, I would search which stores and baby stores are nearby and then I would go in. And in this job, I'm a CEO. I don't do those kinds of things. But here I was. It's a one man band. So, I would go in, "hello. This is a product. Let me know if you want to buy it. And I think a month went by. [Danish chain of health stores] called me and they said, "we need to do a deal. Because we have all these clients asking for the product that we're not able to give them." And it was such a turning point. It was like, now you're calling me. Things went really quickly there. And I got to the point where I was like, do I need to choose? Do I need to say goodbye to this, which is a great job. It's a secure job. It's well-paid. And you know, follow the dream, and explore this once in a lifetime opportunity. I decided not to. I decided that I want to keep both. It has its upsides and its downsides, of course. This becomes a bit of a guilty conscience. You know, I've been working here all day, taking care of the kids. I bring them to bed and then I need to start writing emails and stuff. And that is to this very day still something that I struggle with. From time to time I think I should sell this company so someone else

could do so much more for it. And that is still true. I wouldn't like selling it because it is my fourth child. But I do feel that it could have had a lot more growth, expansion, international record. It could be sold internationally. I'm sure. I just haven't had the time and the focus. So that's been a constraint of mine and it still is a unsolved headache. I'm sort of waiting for someone who walks into my life and says, I love your company, but you're not doing enough for it. Let me help you. I don't know. Let's see where the next journey takes it.

7 Reflections from Finland

Reflections

Before diving into the cases of businesses, there are several contemplations I want to share. It is somewhat easy to be in an office and create grand discourses. At times, I found myself and my fellow humans in academia sitting with cups of imported coffee, in a space that relies on multiple systems for its existence and sustenance and contemplating what a genuinely sustainable society would look like – local communities, flat hierarchies, alternative organisations, extremely short supply chains, local food. So many entities and systems would simply be gone. There would be no large corporations, no long supply chains, no fossil fuel industry, no fast fashion, no fast food, no fast furniture, no monoculture. Painting such pictures is often enough for us to sustain academic jobs.

It seems that whatever businesses try to do is not enough. Businesses and businesspersons are looked at by many fellow humans within degrowth academia with scepticism. I often have this attitude of scepticism towards large business and corporations myself. Many small businesses seem to try and step on sustainability paths, but their efforts always appear small. They are not often appreciated for the work they do. But I believe that the work that they do is oftentimes significant, though not perfect. I see much similarity between how small-scale and personal actions performed by individuals and actions performed by small businesses are downplayed. Oftentimes there is also a (rather unnecessary) opposition between change in our systems and changes in practices of individuals and small social entities. What small businesses do and why is my personal interest and I believe that it is important to celebrate spaces, practices, modes of being in, and relating with, the world that are different to the norms of the capitalist system. Relatively small-scale practices and worldviews are underestimated, while so much unfolds behind closed doors and in the depths of human psyche when businesspersons contemplate how they can participate in change.

Finland

Oftentimes, fellow researchers, including students, ask me which cases are the best ones to investigate. Many spend much time trying to find "perfect" cases. Of

DOI: 10.4324/9781003452300-7

course, perfect cases do not exist, and every business is interesting and worthy of attention. Everyone's journey, every business's constellation of practices and the setting they are embedded in, the constellation of supportive and constraining structures that they are exposed to, is unique. I believe that less attention should generally be paid to looking for perfect cases. Better cases, in my experience, are the ones a researcher can reach geographically and whose social, cultural, and linguistic environments they can understand deeply. Being already familiar with a business, with its products, owners and employees, is even better. It gives a richer understanding of what is unfolding. Pseudo-objectivity and detachment in doing case studies are detrimental, hierarchical, inhumane and may result in a shallow and tokenistic approach and misleading resulting knowledge. As I am revisiting this chapter, I am reminded of a case of a business that was featured in an academic article I read. The article was interesting, and the business appeared to do much in terms of sustainability on paper. I remember that on my sustainability journey, I invited into my life some objects made by that business. In my experience, they were of poor quality. I was thinking about this contrast between my experiences and that the business's sustainability strategy that was celebrated in academia.

My own exploration of the cases of businesses was based around several themes. They are the constellation of practices, the reasons for sustainability journeys, empowering and constraining factors. The reasons for those businesspersons to step on alternative paths embodied in their sustainability practices within the framework of both empowering and constraining structures was the focal point for me. While researching these businesses, I came into that space with an attitude of care, empathy towards their unique journeys and a desire to learn more and understand deeper, to think and learn together rather than to question or interrogate businesspersons with a forced and unnecessary scepticism that is not authentic to who I am as a person. From my previous research I understood that oftentimes practices are imperfect not because businesspersons are evil and want to destroy the planet and exploit human and non-human others. Often, businesspersons are very much aware of the imperfection of these practices and want to improve. They might not have the exact knowledge, resources or power to make changes, but the desire is not something that is lacking. The feeling of "they could have done more here and there" could inform contemplations of policies that might support this doing more. I believe that humanistic approach should also be exercised in research, as elsewhere. This quote resonates deeply with me: "A person can no more learn about humanism by reading about it than he can learn about music, painting, or teaching by intellectual efforts alone. They must all be experienced to be known" (Robinson, 1977, p. 636).

One might say that the businesspersons I interact with are an unusual group of people, that other businesspersons are not like this – not so caring, concerned and passionate. I did not choose to interact with these businesspersons because I somehow found out that they are self-actualised individuals, that they are somehow more self-actualised than other fellow humans. They are normal human beings. And if one comes across a businessperson who indeed says that profit is their only motive, and that destruction of nature and a utilitarian approach to non-humans and humans are justified, one must wonder what could be changed in society to alter these mindsets. I believe that no one is born with a desire to reproduce capitalism or to destroy nature. Some might even say we are born with a natural love towards places (Tuan, 1974) and nature (Wilson, 1984). Perhaps these people who have cynical and utilitarian approaches to human and non-human others and to life in general have become disenchanted. Our system of education too often offers tools for utilitarianism but not for growth and care, and this does not help.

I moved to Finland in the very end of 2022. I was going to stay there for two years, but I left Finland in September 2023 and resigned from the Finnish university in October 2023 from Denmark. My feelings about being there are mixed. On the one hand, I lived my dream extreme minimalist life without any furniture. I was close to some of my friends. I was close to nature. I met some wonderful humans and non-humans in that country. On the other hand, I did not have a good experience at the Finnish university, and I realised that I had to leave. I also missed being in a Germanic-language–speaking environment.

Second-hand clothing business

I was fascinated with the story of this business. The business was closed by the partners who were running it but when I heard the story, I knew I wanted to include it in this book. I feel good about including a business that no longer exists in this book. Perhaps keeping a business in operation is traditionally seen as a sign of success. But success comes in different forms. For the businessperson I spoke to, as I understood from our conversation, closing the business was the right thing to do. The person then moved on to achieve other meaningful things in life.

Buying second-hand is one of the best ways to meet the needs for clothing and perhaps also to experiment with different styles if one wants to. Second-hand market honours the objects that already exist in society. It also makes meeting these needs more affordable. Another sustainability practice, buying new clothing made from local and organic materials that are made in a way that is kind and caring towards nature, humans and non-humans, is expensive.

Personally, I have never bought second-hand clothing items because I generally avoid shopping as much as possible. When I invite something into my life, I look for particular fabrics that will not make my skin condition worse. Overall, I live with very few items of clothing and wear them even after beautiful imperfections such as holes and stains appear. Then I try to repair them to postpone buying more. But buying second-hand is, as I observe around me in the movements that I am part of (e.g., zero-waste, minimalism, voluntary simplicity), is now a standard practice. When it comes to this business, I do not have an intimate and personal connection with their business model, but I certainly see the benefits of such business and the role they could play in a degrowth society. In the movements I am part of, I am glad to see an overall positive attitude towards such businesses. When I was contemplating this case, an important learning for me was realising more clearly that every human being is different. Every businessperson is different.

Her story

The business started in 2013 by two persons. At the heart of the business was selling second-hand clothing on a consignment basis. The business started online but then also had a physical store. At that time in Finland, second-hand clothing was not yet a prominent part of sustainability discourse. Sustainability was built into the business model as the co-founders wanted to deal with the clothing that already exists in the world. The metric of success in business, the businessperson tells me, is the sales. Yet, due to their business model, the more they would sell, the more good they would do. This is because, she mentions, "buying second hand is the most sustainable option since you're not producing anything". In the case of second-hand, she says, you do not need to contemplate, e.g., organic cotton vs conventional cotton. But overall second-hand is the most sustainable option in terms of resources, job creation and "cultivating a change towards society that gets excited about reusing". The combination of these factors is something she loved about the business.

Something she recalls and finds interesting is that at the beginning of their journey, customers would ask them why they were selling second-hand clothing. At the very beginning, they felt that they needed to educate consumers about second-hand clothing, why it was important to consume it instead of buying new. Such education was part of running that business. The world in 2013, when it comes to sustainability, felt to the businessperson like a different kind of place. Opening a physical store at a large conventional shopping centre in the capital region in Finland was a big step and a space to educate fellow humans while talking to them in person. As time went on, and awareness of ecological degradation and of the need for action increased, customers started to tell them why their business was important. Currently, many brands deal with second-hand clothing, but it was not the case 10 years ago.

She mentions that the co-founder and she worked at the shop themselves. Usually the owner-managers, she says, do not work at the shopfloor, so it was interesting to hear from the customers what they thought about the business. She says that the customers would not "filter" their views thinking that she was a salesperson, and they would speak freely. It was "cool" to listen to the customers directly.

I ask her about how it all started, why she decided to step on that path. She recalls when her co-founder was explaining the idea to her and a group of friends. The co-founder had gone to flea markets her whole life, while the businesspersons I spoke to had not. The co-founder was wondering why they didn't engage in second-hand business, why they couldn't have an online fashion store where everything would be second-hand. My conversation partner reacted to it by saying that she didn't know why. She simply said, "let's do it". That idea in her mind immediately connected to how she observed the world around her with a "race to the bottom", with destruction and unsustainability. She saw an opportunity to use her power, her agency, to participate in shifting society towards a different path. It felt meaningful and purposeful to her. It felt better than going and getting a regular job. It felt compelling and empowering to step on that path with someone who was knowledgeable and skilful, someone who had experiences with flea markets her whole life. Her co-founder has not only "done it but was good at it". She felt there was something to start with, which was to take that idea, experience and skill and then build on it. It felt authentic. She observes that with many brands, it is unclear what they are based on. Perhaps it is something popular or has a potential. Their business idea felt different to her. She contemplates how she likes and admires those fellow humans who "produce a lot of good in the world and have a hard skill. They're really good at something, or they have a passion for something, and I admire that so much". She wanted this to be manifested in their business.

I am wondering about both constraining and empowering factors on her business journey. We start talking about what feels somewhat uncomfortable within a degrowth discourse. We talk about financing and money. She mentions that "money is a huge factor". She explains that "now in hindsight, I would say that if you want to grow to be really big and successful, you need money and you will most likely need external funding". Her co-founder and she never took any external funding because they had another company, so they had experiences with starting up a business. With the business I am interested in, they realised they did not want to take "easy money" and start the business with the resources they had. Eventually money did become an issue, especially towards the end. She always felt that they would need more "muscle" in their business. And now she could say that by "more muscle", she meant more money. Then they would have more power to explore different things and to grow. They grew only from their revenue. But, she notes, if a businessperson wants to "go fast", and she believes that it is important to go fast to establish yourself, then not having money would be the number one hindering factor. She contemplates that if you have money, then you can attract talent and hire whoever you want. So essentially, the money is number one constraint. I am thinking about growth and what we, at times, think within the degrowth discourse about growth in business. In degrowth society, businesses can still grow, and a business selling second-hand items seems to be a good example.

We discuss empowering factors. She says that

> you really need to be an exceptional individual, and because it's so difficult and you have so many obstacles and you just need to have so much fuel and you just you need to have a really strong fire inside of you. That makes you do it. And so, I think, me and my co-founder, we really had a lot of passion and we were so interested. It's just such a big reason to get up in the morning and get out there and do it and get things done and go after it. [...] Obviously it's a combination of many things, but the ideology and the values behind the company definitely were a big part of that and then who you do it with.

She had "so much respect and admiration towards my cofounder that it's really inspiring to work in such a company". Having this respect for each other allowed them to "build on each other". It was a dynamic that she described as each person giving 100%.

They closed the business in the spring 2022. She says she does not regret it, that it was a good decision. I am asking her if there is anything else she wants to share with me, an academic who does not have a business. She remembers that journey with fondness. For her, it was an "amazing journey". She mentions that "what doesn't get discussed enough is the long hours and the sacrifices you're making and the fact that it's socially very limiting". Around 10 years ago, she reflects, there was a "startup hype" and "we only talked about the benefits, but I didn't see a lot of discussion of the fact that, you know, 9 out of 10 fail or would do".

We discuss profit and the need to make it in a capitalist system, ways to survive in this system. My conversation partner is telling me that one of the ideas behind the business was to "change the system from within, and that was by far one of the greatest things about it". At the same time, she always wanted the business to be "very successful in terms of profit and conventional metrics because it honestly is the measurement of success, because the more people buy your product, the more popular you are". She contemplates that money has a bad reputation in our society and in sustainability circles. She says:

> if you have a business and you are selling something, and then people find your product or your service, whatever it is that you're selling, so valuable that they're willing to exchange our common metric for value, which is money, that they're willing to trade money for it, that's beautiful.

She mentions that she used to have many conversations with her co-founder and their friends about it. She says that some humans criticise money but at the same time want to get paid. They would not do their job if they were not paid: "you would not do it out of goodwill". She notes that "if you are in business, if you're not making money, you are out of business". She saw their relationship with money this way:

> the more turnover we would have, […] the more lives we're touching, the more people find it [second-hand shopping] something that they want to be part of. You know, that's something that they want to engage in. People find it exciting, and […] more people most likely means that you're touching more lives and you're engaging with a higher number of individuals.

We discuss capitalism, something that I am opposed to. I listen with interest and respect to her perspective. She is saying that "capitalism gets a lot of bad reputation". But she believes that "it's not the money that is the problem. It's the businesses". She says that goodness was built into their business model, and the more they were selling, the "more impact" they were having.

I asked her if she wanted to share why they decided to close the business. She mentions that there was a combination of internal and external factors. I will not disclose the internal ones that concerned the family life of the co-founder. But some factors that led to the decision to close the business were implementing expensive technology at a wrong time, and covid-19. They found a buyer for the business, but something unfolded in the due diligence process that led them to decide against selling.

After a few days, we continued our conversation via email. It made me reflect on both the content of our discussion with the businesspersons and on the fact that if you immerse yourself in research, it is hard to tell when the study of a business ends. She mentioned that it was good to talk about her business's values and purpose, something that occupied her mind for a very long time. She shared with me the origins of the word "company": "Btw I love the origin of the word 'company', originally from Latin but old French meaning 'society, friendship, intimacy; body of soldiers', it embodies a lot of what companies can be". What to call the social entities I refer to as "businesses" in my work has been on my mind since I started working on my PhD. Were these social entities enterprises, businesses, firms, companies? Oftentimes these terms are used interchangeably, and often humans in academia simply have preferences for some words over others.

We spoke about the nature of her business again and we discussed a large business that produces outdoor clothing and that is often favoured by humans interested in sustainability. My conversation partner agrees that their "items are definitely in the sustainability person's 'starter pack'". Both of us are critical about that business, using outdoor clothing as a fashion item, using human-made materials on a scale that the business we are talking about does.

Something that she says and that catches my attention is this:

> most people have an inner need for change and to renew themselves/wardrobes, and you can't change that, but you can change *how* to do that, into a more sustainable way. Which is what our business enabled people to do and why it made so much sense!

It is humbling to hear these words. Doing a long-term autoethnography at times made me focus too much on my personal consumption patterns and the ways of being. This focus on the self and own experiences is at the heart of autoethnography. In fact, the approach of autoethnography is to do just that, to dive into one's experiences. At the same time, it can distract from observing others with the same level of attentiveness. I've never had a strong desire to reinvent myself via clothing. As soon as I let myself wear a uniform, I felt liberated. It was a manifestation of simplicity, something that I value deeply. Wearing the same outfit every day made my life easier. I could spend much less time on shopping, I could make better choices and safer choices for nature, fellow humans and non-humans and for my own health. When I began to observe that many fellow humans in the same sustainability movements were advocating second-hand shopping without any limits, my initial reaction was thinking that such patterns represent eco-consumerism. While I was trying to normalise looking casual and wear the same items every day, I saw second-hand shopping as a replacement for excessive shopping within capitalism, just better for nature. Talking to my conversation partner made me yet again realise that there are diverse ways of being in the world, that to wear a uniform is just one way amongst many.

Consultancy business

This business is close to my heart. I have been wanting to include it in this book from the very beginning, and I am grateful that the founder told me her story. She is a fellow researcher and a businessperson. She started the business with her friend in the spring 2022. At the time of the interview, the business is around 1.5 years old.

At the heart of this business is consulting. They focus on sustainability strategy and planning for other businesses. They support other companies on their journeys and work primarily with small- and medium-sized businesses. They analyse how sustainability can be implemented in the context of those businesses, map it, plan and create a strategy of what could be done both in the near future and in the long term. I am curious about why they work with small- and medium-sized businesses, whether they intentionally exclude large companies. The businessperson tells me that they do not intend to exclude large companies, but they feel that the need is bigger among smaller companies

> who do not have the resources themselves to start learning about sustainability. I mean, sustainability is such a complex issue. So, to understand what it is and what to do about it requires probably one human resource or several, to really put a lot of time and maybe money also into engaging with that, and smaller companies perhaps do not have the possibility to do it.

In her view, smaller companies need outside expertise and support in the beginning of their sustainability journey. And if they receive this support in the beginning, perhaps they can continue it themselves.

I wonder about the motive behind the business, why she is on this path. She reflects on it and shares several reasons. One is career related. She has been researching sustainability, as an academic, for several years and she felt a need to "do something with that knowledge for others to turn it into practice in some way". Establishing this consultancy business felt like a convenient way to share her knowledge with others who might need what she knows. She contemplates another reason which she labels as "more or less selfish", related to the quality of life. Having her own business enables her to work the way she wants instead of being employed by someone else "who would then dictate how I work and when I work". Now she can "decide that myself and I value that very much, particularly in the life situation that I am right now with smaller kids". Having own business gave her the flexibility she needed. She shares her third reason with me: for many years already it has been very important for her to do "something that feels meaningful and to engage in sustainability both academically and on a more practical level". Further to this, being on this journey of running a business with a close friend gives meaning in many ways.

I begin to reflect on what she shared with me in terms of engaging with sustainability. She has done much wonderful research about strong sustainability, so I am curious how she handles strong sustainability specifically. She mentions that she feels that the distinction between strong sustainability and other sustainability discourses is "primarily theoretical". It "doesn't necessarily have to be directly translated into business practices. As such, it is perhaps the different ways of doing strong sustainability that can then be incorporated in different business". She shares further:

> I have been sort of maybe between the lines trying to apply perspectives of strong sustainability in my consultancy projects, but I've been feeling that it's a very sort of shaky ground to stand on and something that also requires at the moment a lot of courage, because it's very against the mainstream notion of what a business does and what sustainability in a business is. So, I've been perhaps trying some ground, but I've not been directly implementing it in the things we do.

I begin to wonder about empowering and constraining factors that influenced her journey. She shares that empowering for her have been "likeminded people, people who are gentle and caring in the ways of behaving towards other human beings and other beings in general, and towards doing business or doing some kind of work related tasks. That empowers me". She says further that what hinders her is everything that is

> very masculine, technocratic, growth minded, [...] a feeling that is still dominating in a lot of companies, which makes it very difficult to even suggest a different worldview, for example, based on the notion of strong sustainability, and you feel that you are directly under attack and you're very alone in that position of, and sort of arguing for, stronger sustainability. And that is itself a journey for me to have the courage and just throw yourself into those situations and have the courage to stand up for your thoughts in that sense, even though you are in the minority still.

The way we discuss these things feels candid to me and I share with my conversation partner that other businesspersons I met on my journey said very similar thing to me. She finds it empowering that other fellow humans feel the same way.

I wonder if there is anything else she wants to share with me. She has known about my plan to write this book for a while, and she knows what my interests are. It doesn't feel like an interview but more as one of many conversations we've had. She adds:

> Well, maybe that one thing that comes to mind is these contradictory feelings that are unavoidable when you work as an academic and as a practitioner of something. That is, you know, you find yourself saying something in theory when you write an academic paper, say, and then you find yourself saying something else and adapting when you do something in practice. And that is of course normal and human, but it creates a lot of challenging feelings which maybe could be hindering also in some sense for me to sort of continue on

> that path that I am on. That comes to mind, that it's difficult to wear both hats. Although I also find it very interesting and meaningful.

I share with her my experiences of being only in academia and how I try to navigate researching businesses. To me, it feels humbling to talk to the persons who are trying to manifest sustainability in practice, in the capitalist system to which destruction and degradation are central. It feels much easier to theorise degrowth business than to run a genuinely sustainable business and to navigate a path of, and towards, genuine sustainability. She agrees with me and contemplates further:

> It's navigation, really. What I found really encouraging was last week here in the [place] where I'm sitting, they organised the big event for the CEOs of, I think it was the 20 largest companies in Finland, stock exchange listed companies. Well, and it was a one day educational event for the CEOs around the topic of biodiversity, and the keynote speakers and teachers of that day were only professors from ecology. But not, you know, businesspeople, not something else. There were biologists and people who knew ecology and the dynamics and the dependencies of the ecosystems. I know it was a really a successful day and the CEOs have been super open to learning. You know, setting aside the whole business mindset and just trying to understand what nature is all about. And I think that was encouraging and super nice that there are these organisations that actually tried to bridge both worlds.

In a few seconds she adds, "I thought, wow, they're learning so much. That was so beautiful".

8 Reflections from Sweden

Being in Sweden

After living in England for around 10 years, towards the end of my PhD journey I started having internal dialogues, asking myself where I wanted to be and why, how I wanted my path to unfold in relation to both my research and my spiritual journey. I wanted to be close to nature, in a more equal society, and in a less hierarchical academic system. I chose Sweden and moved to the northern part of that country to join Umeå University. I felt instantly at home in northern Sweden. The city was relatively small, a drop of human activity in the sea of a forest or, rather, a forestry industrial estate. Nature's power felt profound there with large expanses of forest and cold winters. Nature's magic was present so prominently – northern lights, light pink sky in the middle of summer nights when the sun barely sets, beautiful cotton grass, spring unfolding extremely quickly before your eyes after a long winter, the Ornäs birch with its breathtakingly beautiful leaves.

I wanted to be in a department of geography because the importance of place for theorising degrowth business began to crystallise in my mind towards the end of my PhD journey, but it wasn't yet reflected in my writing fully. I began to think that my degrowth business framework was not place-sensitive. It was too general. And while this is what I intended it to be, it began to feel important to emphasise the place better (Nesterova, 2022b, 2022c). Businesses exist somewhere, within unique constellations of natural and social structures. Geography, and especially humanistic geography, was the science that would make me reflect much on this. It was humbling and enriching to be a business researcher in a geography department.

The small businesses I researched in northern Sweden emphasised nature a lot. Electric cars one business used would not work below minus 10 degrees. Greens such as lettuce and herbs needed to be grown indoors in vertical hydroponic agriculture settings (Nesterova, 2022a). Wine was produced using abundant blueberries and lingonberries that grow in Swedish forests. Many food and personal care businesses seemed inspired by the local nature, fruits and herbs – blueberries, lingonberries, rowan berries, aronia berries and nettles. Some may be sceptical about this use of nature and assume that businesses capitalise on nature's resources and sell what has come to be associated with the purity and magic of the remote and mysterious Arctic region. In my experiences with those businesses, the businesspersons were as in awe of, and

DOI: 10.4324/9781003452300-8

curious about, beautiful northern Swedish nature as many other fellow humans would be. As was I. These were some of the aspects of being a business in northern Sweden that made me reflect deeply about connections between a human being and a place.

While I lived in Finland, I missed being in Sweden. I felt comfortable with the Swedish language and, importantly, I found Swedish academia less hierarchical. When I moved from Finland to Denmark, I didn't have a plan for my future. I only had this book to write, and I didn't at all plan to stop working on it while I was contemplating a position that would replace my postdoctoral research position in Finland that I resigned from. Before the Finnish university closed my IT account, I decided to go through my emails. I emailed a fellow human at Lund University with whom we had a genuinely thought-provoking conversation to ask if we could stay in touch. I let them know that I resigned from the Finnish university. This fellow human asked me if I wanted to visit their department at Lund and in a few days they let me know that I was welcome to visit them for three months. I was happy about it not only because I had a feeling that I would have a good time at that place, but also because the opportunity to write this book in both Denmark and Sweden felt almost magical and in line with the place-based perspective that I emphasise in this book so strongly.

Looking for Swedish businesses

I notice that my starting point has often been my own consumption. This is where my research of businesses and my personal life intertwine. I imagine that it would make some of my teachers at the universities where I was educated disappointed. But at some point, I naturally grew out of the imposed on me desire to find businesses that would be representative of something and businesses from which I was detached. I began to see both myself as a researcher and the businesses differently as I freed myself from some of the teachings at the universities where I studied. Those businesspersons, the owner-managers of the businesses I was curious about and I are part of the same society. We are humans playing somewhat different roles in the research setting but overall playing the same role, that of human beings, agents in the social world.

As a practitioner of a lifestyle that includes various elements of voluntary simplicity, deep ecology, zero-waste and (extreme) minimalism, I consume products made by small, independent businesses that in some ways are on sustainability journeys. Personal care items, food, objects for my home, even alternative forms of transport are some of the domains of consumption where I try to be mindful of and explore which businesses engage in mindful and ecological production of these products. A critique I hear often with regard to both my consumption pattern and the businesses engaged in the production of local products such as berry wine, home textiles and soap made with Nordic ingredients is that these products are expensive. These products are expensive for me like for most fellow humans, and the only way for me to consume these products is to exclude many other categories of products from my consumption pattern. Items such as berry wine and a woollen throw made from Swedish wool I would buy only rarely.

Apart from being curious about businesses from which I acquired products personally, I also asked my fellow researchers who had lived in Sweden for a long time if they knew anything about local, sustainability-orientated businesses. Their recommendations were a mix of businesses they knew professionally and whose products they used personally. Oftentimes for them it was both: they would know those businesses professionally and consume their products. There are also contact persons within universities who specialise in improving interaction and collaboration between universities and local businesses. I reached out to those persons too. Some of those persons are customers of those small local businesses, too. They are acquainted with them personally and professionally. In the end, there was a large overlap between the businesses I identified and those I was recommended to contact.

It is not so that every business that I talk to becomes part of my paper or this book. This would be a utilitarian approach, in my view. When I was still studying, I was encouraged to identify a "representative" sample, reach out to those businesses, disclose how many of them responded and how many did not. Considering the philosophy of science perspective that I come from, critical realism, this feels unnecessary and old-fashioned. From a critical realist perspective, it is identifying the mechanisms behind various unfoldings in the universe that matters. How many businesspersons of the ones I reached out to responded is not important. Of course, it is interesting to contemplate why a fellow human responds or does not, but this is a topic for another discussion. With some businesspersons we simply had wonderful and inspiring human-to-human communications. With others, we would meet over tea and go for a walk. It is all part of learning simply via being naturally in the world with fellow humans.

Originally, I thought to include those businesses that are located in northern Sweden, as it is where I dwelled. Since then, I decided to expand my area of interest. This is especially because I relocated to Denmark, so what is local in terms of Sweden for me is the south rather than the north. There are many products that I started to either consume or become curious about that come from southern Sweden. Milder southern Swedish climate and nature, a flatter, more agricultural landscape, and the seaside so different to the North acquired meaning to me.

Cases

As I mentioned above, there are many businesses that I observed that I will not include in this book for various reasons. For example, while writing a book is a creative process, it still has a deadline, and unfortunately, I could not include some cases.

Generally, in every place where I lived, I immediately saw or heard about many small, independent businesses that incorporate ecological and social considerations, businesses on their own, unique sustainability paths. Some of those businesses collaborated or sold products of other small ecological businesses in the region. In or near the northern Swedish city I lived, I learned about a small producer of ecological, unpackaged soaps. They made soaps that could be used for personal care and also washing and dishwashing. In their store, they sold ecological products made by other creators too. They sold mugs, brushes, chocolate, condiments and even soaps made by other brands. There was a store that sold only locally produced food. There was a bakery where one could buy bread and other local products using a machine. There was a store where one could borrow sports equipment. A very small ecological shop where one could get everything from personal care to unpackaged food. That small shop sold the soaps by the small local business I just mentioned. Around the city, there were local farms.

There was also large-scale production unfolding. It was impossible to ignore it. Houses were being built, trees cut down and energy was produced. There was a large factory belonging to a large Swedish vehicle manufacturer. There was also a large factory making paper. I visited the paper mill as part of a trip my department organised, and it was a surreal experience for someone advocating small businesses and degrowth. As I was walking around the enormous premises of the paper mill, I was contemplating the question of whether large businesses could be part of degrowth. In fact, I was contemplating many questions that I haven't answered in my own research. Who would own these enormous businesses? Are their products necessary? Could such products be made by small businesses? What would happen to the employees if these factories closed? How can the employees manifest their ecological concerns in an organisation where everyone has their own role to play and where their agency is limited? I still don't have clear answers to these questions. In comparison to large businesses and their operations, the materials and energy they use, the scale of the businesses I am interested in seems so insignificant. But I do believe that if more humans consume less and for their consumption rely, where possible, on small local businesses, we would be closer to a degrowth society.

Company making objects from wool

The history of this family business goes back to the end of the 19th century. The premises are still the same and the company is now operated by the fifth generation of the same family that started the business. This business makes items from wool. They use Swedish wool, recycled and organic wool. The persons running the business currently are brother and sister. They took over from their father and started their role 20 years ago, in the spring 2003. For the first 10 years, their father was still involved in the business, and for the past 10 years he has been retired, though he still does a little bit of work in the business.

I was curious why the brother and sister decided to take over the business rather than sell it. The brother who I spoke to tells me that they decided to try and see how it goes, to see if they could work on the business, change it and develop it further. He tells me that their path has been successful, but at the same time, one never knows where that path leads. He says that if the ideas they had did not work out, they would have to think differently. He mentions that it is interesting to run one's own business. They had many good ideas and most of them worked out well.

I wonder about the sustainability aspects of the business. At the heart of their business operations are woollen products that are of high quality and made to last a long time. The brother highlights the fact that the quality can be insured because they own their factories in Europe, thus they are in control of the process of production. He also highlights that they do not own the sheep from whom the wool comes in the first place. They buy wool from different suppliers, and they are transparent about who they buy it from. He says that humans are becoming more interested in, and aware of, where the products come from, where and how they are made, how sustainable they are. So the owners try to develop the business in this direction. They have developed a range of products that uses Swedish wool. He mentions that there is not enough Swedish wool to satisfy production needs of this business. While they acknowledge the desire to source wool produced locally, they also recognise the need to buy wool from other countries than Sweden. The brother tells me about their investment in the efficient machinery for their factory to reduce carbon emissions and multiple certifications they have for their products that include animal welfare, the environment and quality. While they have these certifications, they also have their own standards for improving their business and products. One issue that he tells me about is that they as a company can control only the production side. They cannot limit the number of products a customer buys. He mentions that some fellow humans throw away things that are perfectly fine and then buy new things because there is something new available on the market. A figure came to my conversation partner's attention that he wanted to tell me about. Fifteen or so years ago humans in Sweden would throw away 8 kilograms of textiles. Now it is 14 kilograms or thereabout. Many people, he says, get rid of things that are still good, they buy a lot of things and do it more often.

The company sees value in recycling as a practice and thus uses recycled wool too. But when one uses a recycled material, energy still needs to be used in the process of production, and adding new material is also important to ensure the quality of the final product. Thus, he mentioned that buying something and keeping it for a very long time, taking care of it is the best practice. This is the most sustainable way. He mentions that what customers do after they bought the product, the business cannot control.

I am curious about what motivates them to do much more than what would be required to comply with laws and regulations. He mentions caring and a drive to improve the product they produce, to make it even better next year than it is this year. The team are always looking for ways to make this improvement reality. He believes that the product they make is of high quality, but they are always asking themselves how they can make it even more environment-friendly. He mentions there are businesses that produce low-quality and cheap products where one needs to "close their eyes and not care" about how the product was made, where and from what. They are not trying to compete with these companies, and producing lower quality and cheap products is not the space they want to dwell. They think about the design, the environment and the brand. He thinks that people who buy products from them also care and look closely at certifications. This is a way to attract these customers too. In a way, through the existing ecological practices and certifications, they try to "talk to the people who care".

I wonder what constrains and empowers them as a business on the path of sustainability. He contemplates that more and more businesses every year are trying to become more and more sustainable. But as a business, he says, you are dependent on others. You depend on what is available out there. One can have an idea of what a business can do or how a product can be improved, but it cannot be fulfilled due to a lack of availability. It helps when other businesses are on similar paths. For example, he notes that "some things that we wanted 10 years ago we couldn't get, but now we can get it [from other businesses]". He feels that even if some things are impossible now, they will become possible in a year or two. He believes that consumers are progressing as well. He notices how their customers are interested in what they as a business can provide, such as traceability, control of production, deep knowledge of their products. They have new ideas such as carbon-neutral production and transportation. He emphasises that some of the information they can provide, the consumers may not be able to compare it with anything, so it would be a standalone figure, especially if other businesses do not have the same level of disclosure.

As for empowering factors, he cites likeminded customers and fellow workers and designers who have great ideas. Consumers communicate with them directly at the factory store in southern Sweden and via social media. Communicating with consumers, who ask more and more, makes them move forward and develop further. The fact that "designers care, staff members care, consumers care" encourages them to improve. He contemplates that if he was alone in the factory, no one would ever ask, he perhaps would also not care as much.

He reflects on large companies and how they sell a lot in comparison to his business. Twenty or so years ago when he started, he was afraid that they would be outcompeted by large companies. But over time he realised that you can be a small company with a good product and can still compete. Social media makes it easier to communicate all the good qualities of the product. Before the widespread use of social media, it was expensive as communication was done via advertising. Now they communicate with customers in Denmark, Germany and other places. They receive feedback and ideas. And in comparison to 20 years ago, humans care about the product. Of course, the price is high in comparison to what large companies may be able to offer. But he tells me that this price arises from them avoiding doing the minimum and trying to do as much as possible instead.

He is reflecting on his own consumption and tells me about some furniture that he bought recently. He decided to spend more on those items to keep them as long as possible. He says that people can afford less expensive goods but in the long run they perhaps end up spending more on these goods as they have to re-purchase them. In the long run, it is cheaper to buy one good-quality item and take good care of it. The future way to consume, he notes, is to "consume a little bit higher quality and keep it longer".

He tells me about a large company that is one of their customers. I will not disclose much of this part of our conversation, but what attracted the large company was them wanting to develop a more expensive and sustainable product appealing to a different target audience who would care more about the environment and sustainability credentials of the product and where the item was produced. They came to this small company due to their knowledge, expertise and existing certifications.

The large company sells many other products. They don't have expertise in that particular product made by the small business or certifications that this product can receive. During that final part of our conversation, I was thinking about large and small companies and how deeply they are intertwined. It will probably be so in a degrowth society too. Even I, as a researcher of small businesses, too often thought about them as producers of goods that will be sold to final consumers on the market. I did not contemplate enough their role as suppliers to large businesses.

Finally, we discuss certification, and the information consumers get via reading the labels attached to products. He mentions that there is all the information that they want to share but it is getting more difficult to attach the labels due to their thickness. We discuss the future and different ideas the company has in terms on quality, design and sustainability.

Using recycled material, or rather, the impossibility to use 100% recycled materials (due to fibres getting shorter) to maintain the quality, comes up again. Creativity is mentioned as an important element of envisioning the future of the business. He says, "the day we don't have any ideas, we are screwed, you know". After I have asked all the questions, we talk about my experiences with their products as a practitioner of ecological living. We discuss how important it is to have all the information about the product. Something they are proud of as a company is full traceability and the information they hold about each product. They are thinking of using QR codes on the labels that can give the customers access to all this information. At the very end, he says it's nice talking to a researcher of sustainable business.

9 Degrowth and consumption

It is interesting that oftentimes in business schools, production and consumption are studied separately. Researchers identify themselves as either business, organisation and management scholars or consumption scholars. But production and consumption go hand in hand. In my view, we need to understand both well, and every business researcher needs to understand consumption as deeply as they understand business. If they do not wish to study consumption in depth, then it would be helpful to be curious about it or be a practitioner of sustainable consumption themselves. Dialogues between scholars of production and consumption within degrowth are unfortunately scarce.

Genuinely sustainable business is only possible if consumption is also genuinely sustainable. This is something businesspersons always share with me. I do not think that they do it to push responsibility upon consumers. Rather, it is common sense. There is only so much a business can do. Businesspersons can engage in dialogues with consumers and share their knowledges and worldviews, but this is not enough. Alternative organisations such as swap shops depend fully on consumers' participation. Well-made, durable products are sustainable only when they are consumed in moderation and looked after for a long time rather than treated as fast-fashion goods for the materially wealthy.

I have learned much about sustainable consumption from businesspersons when they share with me what it is that they require from consumers. Many businesspersons I spoke to throughout my academic journey are themselves practitioners of sustainable consumption. I also learned much from reading different literatures about consumption or about relating differently with the world that has implications for consumption. Deep ecology (e.g., Sessions, 1995) and voluntary simplicity (e.g., Elgin, 2010) literatures come to mind. But perhaps most of my knowledge and contemplations come from my own consumption and my autoethnographic study thereof.

Many fellow humans warn me against studying my own consumption for several reasons. Some worry that it is not sufficient to study one person's consumption in depth, as it is not representative of how fellow humans might live. Others consider autoethnography narcissistic. Yet others believe that I put myself in a vulnerable position by self-disclosing to this degree that I believe autoethnography necessitates. Autoethnography indeed makes one feel vulnerable and a subject to public

DOI: 10.4324/ 9781003452300-9

judgement. It also reveals the patterns of one person, while there are so many different ways of being and consuming. But to this date, I have not found a method that is able to offer the same depth of insight as autoethnography has done. In many conversations with fellow humans who are also part of the same movements as I am, such as minimalism, voluntary simplicity and zero-waste, I realise that the issues I have faced and that I deal with routinely as a practitioner are not so unique. In fact, they are very common. Everyone who, like myself, lives in a capitalist system faces very similar challenges with genuinely sustainable consumption. And while at some points in my life I experienced privileges such as earning enough to afford more expensive sustainable goods, at other points in my life I experienced the need to be very careful with my spendings.

Far from trying to simply show what an ideal pattern of consumption for a degrowth society should be, what I have been trying to do via my autoethnography is to reveal multiple challenges and nuances. My consumption pattern is not perfect or ideal. But it has always been a starting point to contemplate consumption that is counterpart to degrowth business.

Just like degrowth in business is a journey, genuinely sustainable consumption is also a journey. When my fellow humans see how I live, I always want them to know that this way of living did not manifest overnight, and neither is my consumption pattern totally stable. I was thinking about this when I was in Finland, in a small rented studio apartment, without any furniture and with very few possessions that could fit in a tote bag and a backpack. Many of the objects I lived with were borrowed from friends. I slept of a yoga mat. I feel that it's important to say that I was absolutely happy with this arrangement. I did not feel deprived or as if I sacrificed something for sustainability. I was genuinely content, and this way of living was my choice entirely. The empty space gave me immense aesthetic pleasure. Even though I use the word *empty*, it was full of light. Looking after that space and the objects I lived with was humbling and very easy. It took very little time to clean my apartment and the objects I lived with. The amount of possessions I had at that time was perfect for me. But I knew that this lifestyle would not last forever.

When my partner and I started talking about moving in together, I knew that my consumption pattern would change. Both him and I practise sustainable living, but in different ways. We agreed that our common consumption pattern will be minimalist, organic, natural, zero-waste wherever and whenever possible. We would not own a car, not fly, live in a small space and use ethical banking. We would not dedicate our lives to chasing career and status and try to support one another in the case of voluntary unemployment. Something that I gave up on was furniture-free living. When we moved in together, we acquired some furniture. Though our home looked more home-like, and perhaps our guests felt more comfortable than my guest felt when they visited my Finnish apartment, I felt like I was stepping away from the mode of living that was ideal for me. Though all the furniture came from small, independent Danish companies or was brought in by my partner from his previous apartment, I would have preferred to live without furniture. I also gave up, at least for the time being, on my dream to live closer to nature. When I moved from a beautiful island in Helsinki where I spent countless hours with the sea, the stars, rocks, trees and animals, to busy Copenhagen, I felt that I was moving away rather than towards my ideal mode of living.

Some of our sustainability practices aligned and some of my previous practices diminished. Other practices of mine improved. We would shop more in food markets and would buy organic food more often. We would give away our objects via a *byttestation* (swap shop) in our local area. I noticed that even though it is more difficult or even impossible to practise sustainable living exactly the way I wanted it when I was in a relationship, it was also easier in some ways. Very often in our household we had discussions on how we can improve our practice even further. These discussions are very helpful and allow us to think deeply about sustainability and our own practice thereof. They also bring our attention to our existing deep dependence on capitalist structures. Both of us being degrowth scholars, this causes sorrow.

Example

Living sustainability and doing autoethnography about it means that I can share examples of my own lived and imperfect practices. I can share feelings and emotions that accompany these practices. I have made all of my practices and accompanying challenges, feelings and emotions, public. I did it so that fellow humans can see how exactly one person tries to consume less than what is the norm in our society, to figure out how to consume what is *lagom* ("just right" in Swedish) to them. Too often such discussions take shape of abstract theorising. We say that we need to consume less. Such abstract theorising is helpful, but at some point, it needs to be taken to the level of actual lived and felt transformations. This is because change happens through these lived and felt transformations in reality, rather than in theory.

Before I started sharing examples of my own consumption, I had many conflicting thoughts in my mind. Mostly they relate to self-disclosure. In autoethnography, the level of self-disclosure can be profound. And I believe that this is exactly what makes autoethnography valuable, raw and beautiful. I was wondering about sharing information about feminine hygiene products and socks. Will I talk about this in my autoethnography? Will I pretend that such objects do not exist or that I do not use them? Will fellow humans reading my work feel repulsed by this? Will my students feel repulsed? We seem to be used to sterile academia. Somehow it feels more comfortable to say that I own a reusable water bottle than to say that I have feminine hygiene products. There are not many industries whose products I consume, so I realised that sooner rather than later I will talk about clothing and personal care too. It is also important to talk about these, even if just for the reason that in a degrowth society production will be focused on human needs. Clothes and personal hygiene items are human needs.

In what follows I will go through my own consumption. I would like my fellow humans to not see it as anything extreme, though many have referred to it as such. There are still many conventional systems and practices that I participate in. I do not own land. I buy my food in supermarkets, farmers' markets and food markets. I use public transport. I rent my apartment.

I will start with my sufficiency list. This is a playful list of objects that I sketched many years ago when I stepped on a minimalist and ecological path more intentionally. I simply asked myself, what would be sufficient for a good life, considering my circumstances? What was a playful and personal exercise in the beginning became a method, part of my autoethnographic study (Nesterova, 2023a). I made this list public. I have maintained this list for many years. What I noticed over the years was that the content of the list has not changed much at all. Most changes related to the climate of places where I lived. For example, as I moved from England to northern Sweden, I had to add mittens and a scarf to my list. My ownership of some of the items on the list changed. Though I found some items to be necessary for me, oftentimes I did not actually own them. For example, in northern Sweden I borrowed most of my kitchen items from the geography department in Umeå University where I worked. In southern Finland, I borrowed most of my kitchen items from a friend. In Denmark, my partner and I shared the kitchen items, and many other items. As I came to Denmark with only a few possessions, my partner brought some from his previous apartment, and we started using them together. Otherwise, the sufficiency list reflects to a large extent the contents of the tote bag and the backpack I travel and relocate with and also includes them. When I first sketched this list, I wrote the items down as they came to mind, so there is no particular logic behind the order.

Here is my sufficiency list from August 2022:

- Laptop
- Phone
- Headphones
- Passport and other documents
- Notebook and pen
- Shoes
- Backpack
- Bank card
- Personal care items
- Towels
- Sweatshirts/T-shirts
- Trousers/shorts
- Bowl
- Fork
- Spoon
- Knife
- Stockpot
- Dish brush
- Tote bag
- Jacket
- Handkerchief

- Scissors
- Blanket
- Lunch box
- Mug
- Scarf
- Mittens

Here is my sufficiency list true as of January 2024:

- Laptop
- Phone
- Headphones
- Passport and other documents
- Shoes
- Backpack
- Bank card
- Personal care items
- Towels
- T-shirts
- Trousers/shorts
- Bowl
- Fork
- Spoon
- Knife
- Stockpot
- Dish brush
- Tote bag
- Jacket
- Handkerchief
- Scissors
- Blanket
- Reusable water bottle
- Reusable mug
- Scarf
- Hat

As one can see, the list is almost the same. The difference is that the one from 2022 I wrote in northern Sweden where I needed mittens and sweatshirts. I wrote the one from 2024 in Denmark where it is warmer. Most of the objects in the list are sustainable, though in different ways. My electronics are very old. Most documents are digital. My bank is socially and environmentally responsible. Most personal care items are zero-waste. Most of the textiles are made from organic cotton. None of the kitchen items are my own.

There are many categories of products that I exclude from my consumption. Jewellery, makeup, home décor, car, tv and many other electronics are some examples that fellow humans usually consume. I do not require any extra objects for my hobbies, as my hobbies either require only nature and my laptop. As for the categories of products that I do consume, I will explicate them below in more detail. I will structure them around my basic human needs.

Shelter

In the past several years, I have lived in rented apartments. These rented apartments have been very small studio apartments. My apartment in northern Sweden was around 20 square metres. The one in Finland was 29 square metres. The one in Denmark is around 40, but it is a place I share with my partner. While my apartment in Sweden I got access to via the university, the one in Finland was not owned by the university. When I moved to Finland, I tried to rent an apartment via the university, but it took a long time for them to get back to me. They distribute apartments based on their own criteria, and by the time they got back to me, I already signed a rental agreement, and the apartment I could rent via the university would be too big for me, though it was also several hundred euros a month cheaper than the one I ended up renting. I was renting from a for-profit business. Before my partner and I moved in together in Denmark, we wanted to buy a home. But it was very difficult, and I also resigned from my position in Finland. It felt uncomfortable to buy an apartment, so we decided to rent. We rent from a for-profit business. The rent in the area where we live is very high, but we didn't have a choice due to my partner's childcare responsibilities.

I have conflicted feelings about my relationship to my home. On the one hand, the size has always been lagom for me. Perhaps it is too small for society's standards, but practising extreme minimalism means that I do not live with many possessions and do not need spaces for storage. I have enjoyed living in small homes. The one in northern Sweden was my favourite. It was also affordable. There are many aspects that I do not like and do not find sustainable about my current consumption of shelter. Renting from a for-profit business goes against my values. So does living in a large city in an expensive area. A much better option would be, for instance, living in an eco-community. But I have not lived anywhere long enough to step meaningfully into a community. And at this stage of my life, it is also impossible due to my relationship.

Warmth

I buy electricity. In northern Sweden, much electricity comes from renewable sources, and it was also cheap when I lived there. In southern Finland, my electricity came from a mix of sources (nuclear, fossil and renewable). I did everything I could to minimise energy use when I lived there. My energy bill was 13 euros a month on average. But to achieve that, I lived with very few light sources, without a washing machine, vacuum cleaner and other electronic devices, apart from my laptop and phone. In Denmark, our household's energy comes from renewable sources. While this feels good, it is far from living off-the-grid.

Food and water

I do not grow my own food. Whenever possible, I forage. I pick spruce tips, berries, mushrooms and herbs. I used to do that in northern Sweden and southern Finland, but I don't know if it will be possible in Denmark. Living in Copenhagen means that I am far from nature. Still, even when I have opportunities to forage, foraged food accounts for next to nothing of my daily nutrition needs, and I would only do it in late spring, summer and early autumn. At times, my partner and I regrow some herbs and greens at home, but it also does not satisfy our need for food. In the autumn, my partner brought many apples from his cottage. Yet even these apples satisfy almost none of our needs. We buy most of our food. Most of our food we buy in a supermarket for convenience reasons. Some we buy in food and farmers' markets, but we do this only when we have enough time. I often say that living zero-waste in a city is a full-time job. When one has a full-time job, shopping zero-waste becomes almost impossible within existing structures. When we buy food, we try to buy organic, unpackaged, local and seasonal food. Both of us are vegetarian. Our practice is imperfect. At times, we buy food packaged in plastic. At other times, we buy food that is not local. Occasionally we eat out. We prefer independent cafes and casual restaurants rather than something popular or something that could serve as a status symbol. Oftentimes, we buy bread and *fikabröd* from local, independent bakeries. In such bakeries, one can get their bread unpackaged. One issue with the bread from bakeries is its price. It is rather expensive. Water in the Nordics is affordable if used carefully. Tap water is safe to drink too, so I never buy water in plastic bottles. I feel privileged to have access to clean and safe water every day.

Clothing

For many years, since approximately 2011, I've maintained an extremely minimalist wardrobe. My reasons are ecological, aesthetic and spiritual. As for ecological reasons, as a degrowth researcher, I believe that overconsumption takes place. I want to play a small role in addressing this issue. I do not think that me living with a lot less than what is the norm in the Nordics makes an enormous ecological difference. But I do try to change culture in a small way, by normalising wearing the same outfit every day. I acknowledge that in many ways my privileged position enables me to wear the same outfit every day. I've never had to wear a uniform, and generally there is no dress code in academia in the Nordics. But I have heard it many times from my fellow humans in academia that I need to dress differently to claim power and even to "be attractive". None of these phrases sounded convincing to me, and oftentimes they went against my values. So, I stayed on the path of living with very few clothing items. I do not have clothes for different occasions. I wear the same outfit for resting, walking, travelling, teaching, formal and informal meetings, formal and informal events. If an event has a strict dress code, I will not attend it. For example, I skipped all graduation ceremonies, weddings and funerals. This is not to say that my fellow humans should do this. There are other options such as borrowing or renting appropriate clothing. Aesthetics is very important to me. From my personal experience, I notice that living with very few objects that look beautiful to me is easy. This includes clothing. I also believe that highlighting the aesthetic sides of sustainability makes fellow humans more interested in it. By beautiful I do not mean perfect or new. Spiritual reasons relate, for example, to letting go. Letting go of expectations, societal norms (e.g., how women should look), the rhythms of the fashion industry and even thinking in terms of nature's seasons. Focusing on myself, the kind of human I want to be, on nature by taking from nature only what I genuinely need. I believe that partly my extreme minimalist practice in relation to clothing comes from the fact that as an individual, I have never been interested in fashion. I have always felt drawn to certain colours and fabrics. In addition to that, I live with an autoimmune skin condition, and many fabrics feel unpleasant and uncomfortable to me. In the worst case, I would get severe skin irritation. I've always tried to avoid synthetic materials. Oftentimes, my fellow humans notice that I wear the same outfit every day and they ask me how many items of clothing I own. I do not count my clothes. At times, there is a little bit more, at other times there is less. Mostly it depends on the climate. For example, I've lived in England and northern Sweden. It's much colder in northern Sweden, so I had to invite mittens and a scarf into my life. At times, I borrow my partner's clothes. It's not because I don't have enough but it's a habit I've developed. At times, I donate clothing when it's no longer a suitable size for me. When my clothes wear out, I turn them into cloths. But I do not stop wearing something if it has a hole or a stain. I find holes and stains beautiful. Whenever possible, I repair my clothes. I'm not very good at it but repairing in imperfect ways also works.

Here are all the clothing items I live with:

- Two off-white linen shirts
- Three pairs of sweatpants
- One long sleeve top
- One pair of shorts
- Two white T-shirts
- A few basic tops
- One jacket
- One scarf
- Two unisex hats (to share with my partner)
- Three pairs of shoes (two pairs of sandals and running shoes)
- Arm warmers
- Socks and underwear (I have not counted)

All my clothing items are made from either organic cotton or linen. A couple of items are made from organic bamboo viscose. I'm unsure about bamboo viscose, it is a semi-synthetic material. The jacket is the only item that is made from polyester. I wish it was made from another material, but it gets cold and wet in the

Nordics, and wool takes a long time to dry and is heavy. Everything I wear is either off-white, beige or grey. I mentioned aesthetics above, and these are the colours I personally like. They are calming to me and remind me of nature. Having very few colours in my wardrobe makes laundry very easy too. I own nothing with patterns, writing or explicit logos on it. I wish none of my clothing were dyed, as I am in awe of the natural colours of cotton and linen.

There are some downsides of living with very few clothing items. Living with so few items means that clothes wear out quicker. If something happens to an item of which I only have one, I will have to replace it. It can be expensive to replace objects that are certified organic and sustainably made. But it is necessary that clothes are well-made if one wants to have an extremely minimalist wardrobe. It is impossible to maintain a well-functioning extremely minimalist wardrobe with fast-fashion items. At times, perhaps living with a bit more objects would work better. For example, it rains a lot in Copenhagen, and as I walk everywhere and don't own rain clothes or an umbrella, some days I have many wet objects in my home and much less to wear.

My fellow humans often ask me why I do not buy second-hand, as it is a popular sustainability practice. I do not shop second-hand because I do not like shopping and I have very particular characteristics that I seek for in clothing, such as organic material, certain colour and certain size. I believe it would be time-consuming to find exactly the items that I would enjoy living with for many years.

There are better ways to approach clothing than mine. For example, it would be more sustainable to make my own clothing or buy handmade clothing.

Personal care

When I was writing my first autoethnographic article, I included a category "personal care items" in my sufficiency list. At that time, I did not yet feel comfortable to write openly about personal care. After all, it is such an intimate topic. As years have passed, I have grown as a human being and a researcher. I do not feel ashamed of discussing personal care in my academic works. Yet, the topic is personal care feels vulnerable. I think about the enormous "beauty" industry that equates consumption of its products with self-care and even self-love and puts pressure on humans to wear makeup and dye their hair. I think about the chemicals that are being both absorbed into, and washed off, our bodies when we use various products made by that industry. I also think about my own health. My skin reacts negatively to many ingredients such as perfumes and preservatives in skin and body care. From my childhood, I came to associate skin and body care products with discomfort and even pain rather than with self-care or self-love.

Just as is the case with fashion, I never liked makeup. I am of course referring to my personal preference for myself. At times I used to wear makeup, but I always preferred the way I looked without it. Before I moved to Sweden, I used to live in England. In England it rains often, and I loved the feeling of rainwater on my skin. I didn't want any makeup products to stand between me and the rain. I stopped wearing makeup completely in my early 20s. I'm 34 as I am writing these words.

Due to my autoimmune skin condition, at times I need prescription medication, so my consumption of skin and body care products is not perfectly plastic-free. But I have also noticed that using extremely minimalist skincare has been very beneficial for my skin. At times I make my own simple skin and body care products from natural ingredients such as shea butter, almond oil and argan oil. Sometimes I add lavender or tea tree essential oils, but I do it rarely. Essential oils require much raw material for their production. I don't necessarily buy from the same companies, as I try to buy local products whenever I can. The products I currently use are the following:

- Toothpaste packaged in aluminium
- Wooden toothbrush
- Solid shampoo
- Crystal deodorant, unpackaged
- Unscented balm in a glass jar from a small Danish company
- Bar soap
- Lip balm from a small Swedish company, packaged in paper

I like multi-purpose products. For example, the balm I can use for my face and body. There are some items that my loved one owns that are also part of our household. In general, we do not separate my items from his. There is one object that is more sustainable but that I discontinued using due to self-harm: some time ago I replaced a plastic razor with a reusable one. I found the reusable razor easy to use but my mental health was more important to me. I borrowed a plastic razor from my partner and then purchased one myself. For a while, I felt bad about this, as a plastic razor is certainly something that stands out among more sustainable products. At the same time, sustainability practice cannot be perfect, and using plastic razors was something that I was prepared to accept.

Medicine

There is insufficient conversation about what medicine production will look like in a degrowth society, especially if a degrowth society is highly localised. Supply chains for medicines are long, and production, not to mention research and development, requires high technology. Personally, I have never researched a business producing medication. So, from this perspective, I cannot say much. But I can reflect on medication as a consumer. I live with an autoimmune condition. Most of the time, I do not require medication. But at times I do. On occasions, conventional medications saved my life. Consuming medication is certainly not a zero-waste practice. Medicines come in plastic packaging. And then I know very little about the supply chains and what happens with these chemicals as they leave my body. Apart from the ecological side of medication consumption, there is the social side. I believe that high quality, modern medical care should be available to all free of charge. I have been fortunate in the sense that I have lived only in the countries with free healthcare. It is not perfect or immediately accessible in many cases, but I never had to borrow to pay for my healthcare. I would never move to a country where healthcare is not free.

Transportation

Walking is my preferred mode of transportation. It is free and brings me joy. I walk in all kinds of weather. Rain, snow and hail do not prevent me from walking. At the same time, preferring walking means that I am very restricted geographically. When I lived in a small city in northern Sweden, I could walk to all the places I needed. When I moved from there to Helsinki, I realised that walking everywhere would take much time. I lived in westernmost Helsinki, and walking into the city centre took 1.5 hours. I could not do it when I felt ill or was in pain. So, I began to rely much more on public transport. Unlike many of my fellow humans in the field of sustainability, I do not own a bike. When I cannot reach my destination on foot, I use public transport. I do not own a car and do not drive. I do not fly either. Since 2013, I have taken only one return flight from England to Finland. Before taking that flight, I had done the same journey by trains and ferries, and the journey was long and very expensive. Public transport in the Nordics is expensive, so I try to be careful about the days when I visit my university in Denmark.

Holidays

I almost never go away on holidays. Because I do not fly, I am restricted geographically. But there is another reason for avoiding travelling far away. I love the region where I live. I feel deeply connected with Nordic nature and feel safe here. I know what to forage, I have my favourite places. If I have a choice to go anywhere I want, I choose another destination in the Nordics. Travelling in the Nordics is expensive, so I do it very rarely. It has not always been like this. When I was younger, I used to travel more around Europe, but over time I realised that what I genuinely wanted was being in my local area. Perhaps partly this is because I have lived in five countries and countless places within them.

Like many fellow humans, I observe holidays such as Christmas, but I do not own or ever buy decorations. I also ask my fellow humans not to buy gifts for me. The gifts I give are either food or drink or zero-waste items.

Other consumption practices

There are other consumption practices that I implement. One is learning from my fellow humans. I like discussing sustainability not only as something I and others study, but something I and many others are living. I am curious about their experiences, lived practices and feelings that accompany them. I try to buy certified products whenever possible. Some certification labels that the objects I own or use are Krav and GOTS. I buy from small, local, independent businesses whenever possible. It is not always possible. Many of the businesses I have researched are the ones I have products from. Looking for joy in simple activities is something that makes my life not only more sustainable but also very pleasant. I walk, swim, read and write. These are things that require very minimal financial investment. I do not feel ashamed of relying on others or asking for help before I buy something. For example, on numerous occasions I borrowed objects from fellow humans. I share many objects with my partner. At the same time, I try to give away whenever I have such possibility. There are whole categories of products that I exclude from my consumption. But there are also categories of products that include wants rather than needs. I do not feel bad about consuming those products, but in this case, I try to consume *lagom* rather than consume such things often. Examples are chocolate and Danish apple wine.

I notice that practising minimalism and extreme minimalism necessitates consuming durable, well-made, high-quality goods. Oftentimes, these goods are expensive. I could certainly not afford them if I consumed in line with what is the norm in my society. But I can afford them most of the time because I consume very little overall. Below I want to give a concrete example of how expensive ecological goods can be. I take my personal care list from above as an example. The prices are in Danish crowns (DKK) as I live in Denmark.

- Toothpaste (DKK 69)
- Toothbrush (DKK 20)
- Solid shampoo (DKK 80)
- Crystal deodorant (DKK 70)
- Balm (DKK 149)
- Bar soap (DKK 58)
- Lip balm (DKK 57)

Whenever possible, I choose the most casual option. For example, I do not own handbags. I use reusable cotton bags instead. I do not have wooden or plastic storage. For storage, I also use cotton bags. For a long time, until my partner gave me a reusable mug as a gift, I used a glass jar that came with pasta sauce for water and tea.

Electronic files are invisible, but they have ecological impact. I try to minimise the amount of e-waste I produce. I rarely keep old emails and store almost no photographs.

Principles of consumption

There are certain principles that guide the practices I mention in this chapter. Gentleness and care are the very basic principles that guide me in life. Gentleness and care manifest in more concrete ways in consumption via, for example, sufficiency and simplicity. I emphasise sufficiency more than "less" in my conversations with fellow humans because I try to consume what is lagom for me. This way, I do not feel deprived or that I am sacrificing something. For example, above I mentioned that I live with three pairs of shoes. Perhaps one could also work, but three pairs of shoes make my life comfortable. If my shoes get wet in the rain, I can wear another pair. In summer, I can wear sandals and in winter I wear my running shoes. As for simplicity, it manifests via, for example, my preference towards simple designs, neutral colours, easy to use objects, simple ingredients and simple packaging. I cook simple food. I dress very simply. Using natural materials (organic cotton, certified wood) is another more concrete principle. Yet another principle is buying local whenever possible. For example, I prefer to buy Danish apple wine, made locally from Danish apples. I also embrace imperfection, both in acknowledging that my sustainability practice is far from perfect, and in more concrete ways, such as living with holes and stains on my clothes. Apart from imperfection, I embrace change. While my practice is settled, every now and then there are changes that I welcome. For example, it allowed me to avoid feeling bad or guilty for using public transport more in Helsinki.

What could be improved?

There are countless things that could be improved about my consumption pattern. Growing all or at least some of my own food would be a big improvement. Living in my own or community-owned property would be better than living in an expensive rented accommodation. Perhaps living outside a big city, Copenhagen, would be better too. Making my own objects such as clothing and shoes would be better. I could participate more in zero-waste practices, such as always shopping in farmers' markets. I used to live more in line with zero-waste principles, but it became too time-consuming. I could retain some of my previous practices such as cleaning the floor and clothing by hand. When I moved in with my partner, we started using a vacuum cleaner and shared washing machines in our building. I could preserve more of the food that I forage. I forage food to consume it in the days to come rather than preserve it to consume it in the following year, for example. Often, I could prepare better. When I travel, I often buy my food and drink (apart from water), on the go. I could prepare my food and bring it with me. I could live even with a lot less than what I live with currently. At different times in my life, I have tried this and did not feel less happy. In fact, I felt free and joyful.

Other possible ways to consume more sustainably

There are some practices that I am aware of and that fellow humans are doing and that I am not doing for various reasons. In conversations with my fellow humans, I often mention these practices to show that my way of living and consuming is not a benchmark and not the only way that is in line with degrowth. As we can see above, in many ways it is not in line with degrowth at all. Moreover, not every human being wants to live the way I do. Many fellow humans' circumstances differ from my own. For example, I do not have my own children. Neither do I have pets and other care responsibilities currently. Buying second-hand is a very common practice within various sustainability movements. It allows humans to consume more or less normally rather than minimally and at the same time have a lower environmental impact. It can help humans decorate homes for holidays or experiment with different clothing. Personally, I do not shop second-hand because I dislike shopping and I buy things very rarely. The ones I buy need to satisfy my criteria and I believe that it would take a long time to find exactly what I would need. Living in an eco-community is likewise something practised by many fellow humans I've met on my sustainability journey. I have not had an opportunity to explore this option as I've moved much in my life. As I am writing this book, my Danish residence permit is temporary. Some fellow humans prefer to live self-sufficiently (fully or partly) and off-the-grid. Community-based initiatives such as community gardens, tool libraries, clothing swaps and many others are good ways to participate in sustainable consumption with fellow humans. For those who rely on cars, car-sharing schemes could be useful. This is certainly not something I have explored as I do not drive. Rescuing food, such as via engaging in dumpster diving, is a common practice within sustainability movements.

Consumption across the four planes or being

Sustainable practices that I described above, and many other ones too, can be thought about in terms of the four planes of being framework that I have used extensively in this book and in my other works. The four planes of being allow us to capture a wide variety of practices, from inner growth to material practices such as careful use of energy. I find it useful to combine the four planes of being framework with the "less and more" framework that my co-author and I developed to think about degrowth in a more nuanced way (Buch-Hansen and Nesterova, 2023). Less and more allows us to see that degrowth practice is not about reduction but rather it is a dialectic of less and more. I believe that most of the practices I outline in the table 9.1 below are self-explanatory, and I am sure that fellow humans could supplement this table by practices from their own lives or something they observe around them. So, I do not intend this table to be final, but rather indicative. Most of the practices I include in the table are the ones my partner and I practise ourselves. We wrote some of them down as they came to mind, so the order does not matter much. We wrote down the practices that are both more impactful and less impactful, more and less concrete, more and less specific to our country (Denmark) and our climate. The practices I captured in my autoethnographic study are as follows:

- Walking and using public transport (no car)
- Ethical banking
- Local, seasonal and unpackaged food
- Local holidays (no flying)
- Natural, local home décor (shells, stones)

- Organic, natural textiles (cotton, linen, wool)
- Reusable cotton bags
- Reusable water bottle
- Natural cleaning solutions (biodegradable sponges, baking soda, vinegar)
- Soap bars (natural, locally made, package-free)
- Solid shampoo
- Safety razor
- Wood/bamboo toothbrush
- Natural toothpaste
- Natural, locally made, basic skincare
- Second-hand or old electronics
- No food waste
- Mindful, careful recycling
- Supporting small, local, independent businesses
- Certified products (e.g., GOTS, Krav)
- farmers'/food markets when we can
- Giving away (via a swap shop/byttestation)
- No makeup
- No fancy clothing/occasion wear/fast fashion
- Naturism whenever possible
- Regrowing food
- Zero-waste gifts
- Joy in simple activities (walking, reading, writing, contemplating)
- Using inherited items
- Very few electric appliances
- Durable, simple, minimal furniture
- Minimising electricity use
- Sharing as many items as possible in our household
- Natural exercise (e.g., walking)
- No curtains
- Reusable, organic cotton tea bags
- Avoiding plastic whenever possible
- Doing nothing
- Cooking at home most of the time
- Danish wine
- Foraging whenever possible (e.g., herbs, spruce tips, berries)
- Upcycling
- Borrowing (e.g. books from a library)
- Working from home whenever possible
- Buying bread from local bakeries
- Wearing simple, casual clothing always
- Repairing and fixing things
- Embracing small imperfections (e.g., stains and holes in home textiles)
- Do not express love via gifts

- Donating money when we can
- Talking about ecological living with others
- Using cotton bags for storage
- Minimising e-waste
- No pets
- Embracing all kinds of weather
- Jars as glasses and storage for cutlery
- No paper tickets/using apps
- No meat
- Natural remedies whenever possible
- Renewable energy supplier
- No own washing machine
- Small/lagom space/flat
- Using the same item for multiple purposes

The list above, just like the sufficiency list earlier in the chapter, should not be seen as some universal list of practices. These practices should be seen in context. For example, buying Danish wine from small, local businesses only makes sense because this wine is local to us. It is made from apples grown in the country where we live. Some of these practices are better than conventional but still could be improved. For example, we could make our own bread rather than buy it from bakeries, even if the bread we buy is organic. Avoiding cars may not be possible for fellow humans who live in a very different area to where we live. Practising naturism may not even be legal in other spaces. Some of these practices are something we tend to do rather than do absolutely perfectly. For example, we almost never produce food waste, but very occasionally we throw food away. In Denmark, there are bins specifically dedicated to food waste (madaffald). I will comment on each of the four planes individually below.

Material transactions with nature

Perhaps no one will be surprised if I say that to live, individually and collectively, in harmony with nature we need to reduce our environmental footprint. We need to live in smaller spaces that are well-constructed and do not require too much energy to keep warm or cool. Keeping homes warm for a large proportion of the year is important not only in the Nordics where I live but also in many other areas in the world. We need to avoid flying and private car ownership and reliance on cars as a society. I believe that there are many categories of products that we could avoid too. While personally I avoid store-bought home décor and use stones and shells I find in nature instead, I do not think that every other human being must live the same way. Home décor can be part of our living, but we can also approach it in a more degrowth-compatible way. For example, better ways than buying unsustainably made single-use home décor is making it oneself, buying it second-hand, keeping it for a long time. I find it difficult to name exact categories of products that should probably not exist in a degrowth society, as something that seems unnecessary and even wasteful to me could be useful and important to someone else.

Dwelling on the Earth in a caring manner means taking from the Earth what is lagom. This can manifest in, for example, living in a space that is sufficiently sized rather than too big. I notice that partly the perception of what is lagom is mediated by culture. But partly space is perceived via the lens of one's lifestyle. My extremely minimalist living means that I simply do not have many possessions, so I do not need much space. I would have nothing to put in extra rooms if I had any. A small studio apartment is lagom for me. My partner and I live with so few objects in our studio apartment that when his child came to stay with us, there was more than enough space for all of us and for the child's possessions.

We need to consume goods that are durable and repairable and see each object as a life companion rather than something temporary. Whenever I invite something into my life, I ask myself whether this is something I want to live with for the rest of my life. Very likely some of those objects will not be with me this long. For example, even well-made clothes wear our. But buying with an intention to keep and honour the objects for many years to come is helpful. It helps me to see objects as embodied nature, beings (such as cotton plants) and embodied labour of my fellow humans.

Durable and repairable goods are often expensive. What helps me consume these products is consuming very little and excluding many categories of products from my consumption. Affordability is an important issue that could perhaps be addressed by eco-social policies such as universal basic income, subsidising consumption of high-quality goods and regulations that encourage businesses to produce durable and well-made goods. As a consumer, I notice that at times businesses emphasise only one aspect or several sustainability-related aspects of their products. Organic material can be an example of this. At the same time, the product can be poorly made and not last long. This inconsistency makes it difficult for consumers to choose goods that will genuinely last.

If we are to use cars less and fly less, public transport needs to become much more affordable. It needs to be subsidised or made free. Cycling is popular here in Denmark, but in places the infrastructure for bicycles is not sufficient. For example, in rural areas in some places there are no bicycle lanes, which makes one feel unsafe. Affordability of public transport relates closely to local travelling. Oftentimes it is more expensive to take a train and a holiday in Denmark than to fly to some far-away destination.

I believe that sufficiency is a helpful principle to contemplate in relation to degrowth-compatible consumption. I find it easier to have engaging and beautiful dialogues with fellow humans from different walks of life about sufficient consumption and what it may mean than about consuming as small amount as possible. Though there need to be spaces for those who want to practise extreme minimalism and experiment with living with only a small number of possessions, explicitly less than what is the norm. I have practised extreme minimalism for many years. Many fellow humans found my lifestyle too radical, while it should be accepted as one way of living among many.

Natural, biodegradable materials that do not release microplastics into nature should become the norm. As a consumer, I experience the benefits of synthetic fabrics such as polyester. But the occasions on which I benefitted from wearing or using such fabrics were very rare. Regulations, for instance, of the fashion industry, should be stricter.

When I was younger, I felt that my family used energy mindlessly. They would encourage my brother and me to switch off the lights when we left the room, but oftentimes in winter our home was heated to +25 degrees and our windows were open. This is incredibly wasteful. When I grew up, I decided to use energy in a way that manifested respect towards nature's resources. My partner and I use renewable energy, do not own a car and avoid electronic devices apart from the ones we consider necessary currently (laptops, phones, cooker, lamps, vacuum cleaner).

Social relations

In our society, many social interactions seem to revolve around consumption. Going to restaurants, shopping centres, resorts and theme parks is commonplace. Consumption often mediates relationships. I notice this, for instance, in gifts being used as a manifestation of love. The jewellery industry makes use of this narrative effectively. Instead, humans could interact in and with nature. This may require consumption of public transportation, but it is more in line with degrowth than driving to a shopping centre to spend the day there. Non-capitalist spaces such as community gardens and repair cafes could become spaces for human interactions. They exist currently in our society, but they are still marginal.

Human interactions can revolve less around monetary exchange and more around non-monetary exchange, care, volunteering and help. Borrowing and sharing tools, giving time to share knowledge freely are examples. When I was much younger, I would often go to a forest with a fellow human. I learned about mushrooms, berries and herbs that one can forage in a forest. At that time, I took receiving knowledge from the fellow human for granted, and only later I realised what value such knowledges had in my life. Not only could I get food from nature, but it also allowed me to feel safe in nature, see nature as abundant rather than bare and hostile.

Consumer activism, such as boycotting, can be a personal practice, but in my own life and participation in social movements such as zero-waste and voluntary simplicity, I notice that this practice is collective and is facilitated by social relationships that empower one to act. Consuming less and living an extremely minimalist lifestyle may feel lonely in a society where excess, accumulation and status-based consumption are normalised. I find much encouragement in my fellow humans who are on similar paths and who are also trying to understand how to live more in harmony with the self, others (humans and non-humans) and nature.

I remember that moving to Finland where many of my friends practise sustainability in different ways was comforting. We spent much time discussing the topics I am discussing in this book and in particular in this chapter. In such conversations, I realised how fellow humans' circumstances are different. I also realised that exposure to the same social structures has very similar effect on us. For example, many struggled with the issue of having no access to land. Most needed to sell their labour to have enough money to live. They had barely any time left for personal growth and engaging in alternative organisations and sustainability initiatives. I have learned much about sustainability practices, successes and struggles in conversations with fellow humans who are not in my social circle. I have spoken to countless humans in trains, hospitals, universities and so many other places. It was very helpful, liberating and reassuring to speak to fellow humans who engage in certain movements and activist consumption patterns such as extreme minimalism and zero-waste.

Social structures

The topic of social structures is difficult. This is not only because so much needs to change in the current social structures so that our societies become genuinely sustainable. It is also because social structures have a real and felt constraining effect. I can feel and experience it just as any other fellow human in sustainability movements who tries to practise, for example, zero-waste, self-sufficiency, minimalism and voluntary simplicity. In the very beginning of my minimalist journey, I was very young. I was in my teens and early 20s. At that time, I was thinking much about my personal actions, my personal possessions. I quickly began to see that everything I did was either made possible, or was constrained, by social structures. Even something that I thought was completely my own, i.e., my personal growth and spiritual journey, were at least to some extent results of my upbringing, education and opportunities that I experienced as a child and continued to have access to in my life.

To outline a list of perfect practices that combines various elements of simple living, zero-waste and minimalism is not difficult. Let us imagine a perfectly sustainable lifestyle. Perhaps it would entail growing and foraging one's own food, making one's own clothing from home-made undyed or naturally dyed fibres. It would entail buying from small, local, independent businesses. At times participating in alternative organisations such as repair cafes and swap shop. At times, travelling by train. It would also entail not caring at all about status, power, social norms such as what to wear for special occasions. Countless learning opportunities would be available, and much time would be available to learn new skills. I genuinely tried to adopt some sustainability practices, and I did succeed in some. But immediately when a picture of a perfectly sustainable lifestyle is painted, one cannot help but think about possibilities of bringing this lifestyle into being. This lifestyle requires access to land, skills and knowledge about making one's own clothing, growing food, raising animals, foraging and preserving food. It requires easy access to alternative organisations or time to organise with one's local community. It requires so much time for organising, learning and unlearning. As things stand, at least initially this lifestyle is expensive. Buying from small, local businesses is expensive. Train travel is time-consuming and expensive. Immense personal growth required to care less about status, power and social norms is time-consuming and can be expensive. That is to say, perhaps the easiest way to grow as a person is to take much time off work to dedicate to spiritual growth, learning and unlearning. This is not possible for many humans. There is much discussion of reduced work hours and a shorter work week, but while I am writing these words, I am not seeing these changes rolled out of a large scale around me. Moreover, reductions such as these need to happen alongside stepping away from competition, so that humans do not end up working as much as we do now, but for free. I believe that many fellow humans in academia who research transformations as part of their job take learning and growth for granted. During my academic journey, I have tried as much as possible to learn what fellow humans outside academia think about degrowth and transformations we, degrowth academics, talk about. Something that these fellow humans tend to highlight is a lack of time as well as a lack of resources, not a lack of desire.

There need to be policies such as universal basic income and universal basic services to free up time, to provide free education. There needs to be much heavier regulation of advertising that encourages trend-based and status-based consumption. There needs to be ethical financing for alternative organisations.

Inner being

Having briefly discussed social structures, I cannot avoid discussing inner being too. Changes need to unfold in both, our inner being and social structures at the same time. In addition to that, there is a relationship between our inner being and social structures apart from the one I mentioned above, that social structures constrain (or empower) us. We either reproduce or transform social structures. For example, we can vote for one party or another. We can bring what we do not need to a swap shop or throw it away. We can buy an object we need or ask our friends if we could borrow it from them. If we have free time, what do we do with it? Do we go shopping or do we read or reach out to fellow humans to organise a tool library or learn together? While capitalist structures are incredibly powerful and persistent, oftentimes we have a choice. I always feel inspired and humbled by fellow humans from all walks of life who try to reproduce sustainable structures and try to transform unsustainable ones.

It is not my intention to outline a perfect worldview. I certainly do not want to moralise or take the moral high ground. I am not a perfect person myself. But being imperfect does not prevent me from trying to live in harmony with nature and fellow beings. I do believe that it is important to deviate from possessiveness, having and ownership. I find it challenging to engage in conversations about this topic because within me, I have always found a strong desire to not have, to shed, to let go. I have found this attitude helpful on my sustainability journey. But I also recognise that others may have other desires. For instance, one of my previous partners described his relationship with objects as follows. To him, living with many objects provided a sense of comfort, safety and home. Perhaps for those fellow humans who do not find within them a desire to *not have*, exploring values such as sufficiency and simplicity could be a good starting point.

Table 9.1 Consumption across the four planes of being

Planes	*Less*	*More*
Material transactions with nature	Large spaces Fast (fashion, furniture, food) Single-use items Food that is not seasonal Food waste Long-distance travelling Flying Cars Categories of products (mass produced seasonal décor) Human-made fabrics E-waste Fossil-fuel–derived energy Excessive energy consumption	Lagom spaces Sufficiency Efficiency (e.g., energy use) Renewable energy Careful energy consumption Durable, reusable and repairable goods Public transport, walking and cycling Local travelling Local holidays Local, seasonal and unpackaged food Natural, handmade objects (e.g., natural decorations) Natural, organic textiles Upcycling Recycling
Social relations	Interactions based on consumption Gifts as a love language	Co-living/sharing space Experiences in nature Interactions in non-capitalist spaces Borrowing Sharing objects Sharing knowledge Giving Homemade gifts Consumer activism, boycotting Activist consumption patterns (zero-waste, self-sufficiency, minimalism/extreme minimalism)
Social structures	Consuming products produced by large corporations Status-based/conspicuous consumption Occasion-based consumption Conventional banking Buying as the solution	Local food, farmers markets Foraging Ethical banking and financing Making, creating Alternative and not-for-profit organisations and initiatives (swap shops, clothing swaps, second-hand shops, flea markets, charity shops) Growing food Supporting small, independent businesses Education for genuine sustainability Consumption based on comfort and genuine needs
Inner being	Having Ownership	Simplicity Inner growth Embracing imperfection Embracing idleness, doing nothing

10 Conclusions and steps forward

Learnings on this journey

While writing this book, the first thing I noticed was how over the years the concepts I feel comfortable with and the words I use and feel comfortable using have changed. The old paradigm based on hierarchies, binary thinking, pretentious vocabularies feels outdated. I wanted to write in a way that is imperfect and natural, coming back to the same points over and over again. When I look back on my education path and think about where I am now in terms of my research and how I relate with it, I realise that I had to unlearn so much. Sample, response rate, interviewer, respondent, scientific language, objectivity – these words do not apply to my research. The word sample does not apply because I do not come from a positivist perspective. I select businesses in a biased manner. These are businesses whose products I consume, businesses that are near, businesses that catch my attention as I walk through the streets of Copenhagen, businesses that fellow humans recommend to me. I do not keep track of how many businesses I speak to on my journey. Every interaction and story is unique. Some of the stories I want to tell, while others I simply learn from. I do not see myself as an interviewer and businesspersons as respondents. We are all human beings. We play slightly different roles in this research setting but in the end of the day, we all play the most important role we can, that of a human being, trying to make the world a better place while also making mistakes on the way. The businesspersons I speak to are my conversation partners rather than respondents. The language I intentionally used in this book is, I hope, not pretentious. While I am a social scientist and engage with various concepts, theories and ideas from the social sciences, I see no need in employing language to obscure. I am not chasing objectivity in my work. I do not believe that research can be objective.

I have learned not to have unrealistic expectations. I have learned to expect imperfection, repetition, something new in what feels old, see old ideas in seemingly new things, and messiness. When I talk to businesspersons, which I have been doing since 2016, it feels humbling. It is so easy to imagine an ideal "degrowth business". None of the businesses match this ideal picture. "Degrowth business" is not a model. It is simply a framework, a sketch, an outline of a constellation of what should potentially be thought of. When telling the businesses' stories that I have

DOI: 10.4324/ 9781003452300-10

shared in this book, my hope was that the readers will see the complexity, imperfection and nuance in them, witness how different, and at times conflicting views co-exist. I did not want to over-interpret these stories and jump to conclusions.

I have learned to look for beauty and hope in what exists right now. We want a better society, co-existing harmoniously with nature and within itself. This society will not manifest itself out of nowhere. It will not be completely new. Whatever will unfold will unfold organically from what *is* right now, from the structures that are already in place, from the minds of humans who act in the world, in different places (Buch-Hansen and Carstensen, 2024).

I felt that the words I was previously using in my research on degrowth transformations were restrictive. There is still felt anxiety, probably arising from years of mainstream education, that prevents me and fellow others from using the words that feel too soft, unscientific and casual. And yet I want to use these words freely. They are, for example, empathy, hope, self-transcendence and awe, depth, nuance, ephemerality, non-binary thinking and imperfection. I'll say more about why these words matter to me and why they feel important.

Empathy. I shed an expectation I had as a first-year PhD student that businesses somehow can and need to comply to some model to be truly transformative. It is when I stepped more intentionally on my path of living differently, manifested in a constellation of zero-waste, deep ecology, voluntary simplicity and extreme minimalism, I understood how hard and even impossible it is to be perfect in one's practice, whether it is business or consumption practice. I could not be a perfect consumer, a perfect practitioner of zero-waste, a perfect practitioner of extreme minimalism, whatever it might mean. I could not expect businesses I research to be perfect.

Hope. Ecological degradation makes us feel hopeless. There are plenty of ideas of what a "better" society would look like, but not enough recognition of where it will arise from and the messiness of this "where". Many of my fellow scholars in the field of degrowth seem pessimistic about change – if not in classrooms, then oftentimes in private conversations. Alternative spaces are marginal, alternative organisations are too small or dependent on capitalism. Promising eco-social policies are not taken up sufficiently. Many humans are consuming too much. And yet, there are discourses, events, social entities, modes of being and social movements that provide hope. Humanism is a stance that gives me hope. Humanism brings to light our potential and capacities for so many things that can only be described as beautiful – empathy, compassion, love, gratitude, creativity, self-transcendence, awe and wonder. Witnessing that so many humans' ways of being correspond to humanist ideals in many ways gives me hope. Diverse economies is a field that offers hope too, as it acknowledges that the good co-exists alongside the bad.

Self-transcendence and awe. Self-transcendence is one of those capacities that humanism claims we have. Before I started to engage with humanism, I learned about self-transcendence from deep ecology. Deep ecology, in its pursuit of being in the world differently, encourages humans to expand each individual self to a larger Self, to see the rest of existence as at one with oneself. This allows us to feel deeply towards others. I highlight awe amongst various self-transcending emotions because it returns a sense of wonder and enchantment to reality, including our everyday life.

Depth. For any change to be possible, we need to understand and honour the depth of reality. It adds, I believe, to the sense wonder. I use critical realism to capture the depth of reality. The four planes of social being (material transactions with nature, social relations, social structures, inner being) help us appreciate that everything happens in so many domains at once. Originally degrowth was concerned with material transactions with nature and social structures. Social, inter-personal relations and human psyche (or the soul) were overlooked for a long time, and my hope is that these matters will be discussed more.

Ephemerality. Everything is always in becoming and nothing lasts, at least not in the same form. Practices change over time, their constellations change. We age. Ownership changes. Even if we capture a business's practices in some moment, they will look different the next month. The following year they will look different still.

Nuance. The journey of every human being and of every business is different. Originally my degrowth business framework was an idea of what every business should be like for a genuinely sustainable society to be possible. As my thinking was evolving, I became more sensitive to nuance. How sustainability manifested in business looked very different in different businesses, in different places. Relocating to northern Sweden and a geography department from a business school in England was humbling. I began to see how climate matters. Every businessperson deals with their own unique circumstances. Even though it goes without saying that everyone is exposed to the same violent capitalist system, experiences differ a lot. Some businesses find small niches where they operate. They have customers who love them. They work with activists, or those businesspersons are activists themselves. They carve out within the capitalist system their own spaces where they try to make a difference. One may say that this doesn't change much if a small business finds a niche. But it is indeed often on the minds of those businesspersons what else they can do, how they can do more. So, they try and seek new connections and dialogues. Nuance can be learned in long conversations and stories, not so much in brief interviews.

Non-binary thinking. Those contemplating change at times tend to think in binaries. Capitalism is bad, an alternative is good. Business is bad, cooperatives are good. This results in a situation where the current system feels hopeless, and we begin to see fellow humans who are engaged in something *conventional* as enemies. But things are much more complex than that. I feel that complexity is often not taken seriously enough. Businesses are not either this or that. Businesses are not either degrowth or not degrowth, sustainable or not sustainable, low-tech or high-tech, circular or not circular, sufficient or not sufficient. There are always constellations of various practices. This does not mean that there should be no goals, aspirations, ideals and that anything goes. But presenting only perfect models – which are not achievable or achievable only in certain industries under certain circumstances – is disempowering. Labelling a business as "not degrowth" excludes them from participating in the degrowth discourse and robs businesspersons of hope that they can also be part of a genuinely sustainable society. Oftentimes businesspersons want to change their constellation of business practices. Adopting a more empathetic, non-binary approach and avoiding labelling businesses as "bad" is helpful. It is of course not difficult to find examples of businesses that are obviously not in line with degrowth thinking. Oil and gas corporations, fast-fashion companies, online retailers selling cheap goods come to mind. Yet, most businesses are not like this. And those "bad" businesses are still made possible by humans, the workers. While the business model may be bad, the humans are not. They might have had no other opportunities but to work for that business. Mechanisms need to be in place for workers to be able to step on a different path and for existing "bad" businesses to change their operations.

Imperfection. Seeing everything in the shades of grey, in a non-binary way means being more comfortable with existing imperfection. Every business is messy. It is established and is made possible by imperfect humans. Its practices are always going to be imperfect. Perfect practices exist only in academic papers. Imperfection is not necessarily a negative word. Humanism recognises and even celebrates imperfection. Maslow (1970, p. xxii) notes that "if the imperfect is defined as evil, then everything becomes evil, since everything is imperfect". I like this quote very much. The imperfect does not have to be defined as evil. It is simply a condition of existence. Accepting it allows us to avoid stagnation and instead become curious about the nature of real businesses and their practices as they exist and unfold.

What helps

I feel that it is important to not only give the words above some thought, but to also develop a different attitude, that of helping each other. This applies to humans within academia and in business. To be able to help businesses, we, humans in academia, need to come into conversations with a desire to learn from businesspersons and with **empathy towards others' journeys**. In science, we are taught to approach everything with scepticism. If a businessperson says that they operate their business not with a profit motive in mind, but to make a difference in the world, a researcher is often sceptical. It is not even so that the researcher doesn't want to believe a fellow human (a businessperson in this case). Rather, they were taught to approach interviews with suspicion. A better approach seems to be curiosity and adventurous exploration via genuine conversations. In such spaces, businesspersons are also more likely and willing to share their own struggles, doubts, worries, dreams and hopes. They do not feel that they are being judged by someone who, in their eyes, is just a fellow human.

Adopting a growth orientation helps. Merely criticising social systems and social entities is not enough. Elsewhere, my co-author and I go as far as to note that growth (most often non-material growth) is at the heart of degrowth (Buch-Hansen and Nesterova, 2023). This creates a more hopeful, positive and honest message. It inspires humans to act rather than become hopeless and pessimistic. It encourages humans to recognise that there is so much potential in our species for care, empathy, solidarity, love and gentleness.

Spaces need to be either nurtured or created for human goodness to be manifested, for growth to occur and for hope to grow. Eco-social policies should be there not to limit, but to encourage growth. Here, I refer to growth in alternatives (e.g., alternative organisations, alternative modes of being in the world) and in human capacities. Eco-social policies are not unknown. Much research has been done on them (Buch-Hansen et al., 2024). Apart from eco-social policies, wherever possible, individual humans and communities need to take responsibility for creating spaces. Oftentimes when I mention individuals, my fellow degrowth scholars are sceptical. And yet there is so much that individuals can do. It goes without saying that individuals exist and act within social structures that constrain and empower, and that some experience more constraints than others. But often there is some freedom or scope to act, and there are choices to make. I will mention the space where I work, i.e., academia. A person, say, a teacher, can be unsupportive, hierarchical and lack passion or have more passion for power than for empowering fellow humans. These teachers are highly educated and often privileged humans. Those working in the field of sustainability know that gentleness and care are central. Some choose to act contrary to these principles. Others choose to create spaces where mutual learning, kindness, support, respect, care and many other beautiful things can thrive.

Here in the Nordics, but also in England, I noticed that it is possible to create new courses and to moderate existing ones. It is puzzling that many courses on business and sustainability still do not include philosophy – deep ecology, humanism and philosophy of science. While questions of ethics and business ethics are discussed, conversations and contemplations of ethics in business should go far deeper. It should be less about business and more about being in the world.

Recognising privilege helps. This book was written in the context of materially wealthy Nordic nations. At least parts of it were written in a safe and peaceful atmosphere conducive to hope. Other parts of it were written in a psychologically unsafe work environment. It is indeed so that other contexts need to be understood and voices from other areas of the world heard. However, everyone needs to participate in transformations, including humans in the Nordic countries. Oftentimes, such participation amounts to creating spaces for others. Apart from being a practitioner of voluntary simplicity, I am a researcher, and I teach. Though I believe that development of a worldview to which gentleness and care towards nature and human and non-human others starts much earlier than when one goes to school or a university, within higher education spaces my aim has always been to give my fellow humans who happened to be my students scientific and philosophical tools so they can take them into the world and make a difference. Having access to these tools should not remain a privilege of academics.

I believe that **being humble** helps. For me, being humble manifests in a deep respect towards others, having a genuine interest in their views and knowledge. I am in awe of how talented students are, and how deep and nuanced practitioners' insights are. It is so important to come with an attitude of learning, empathy and care into classrooms and when talking to businesspersons.

Academia

I say it very often, but business education needs to change substantially. It is interesting to observe that courses in business and sustainability, though they may include more radical strands of sustainability thinking such as degrowth, are still rooted in the old paradigm. For instance, deep ecology, new materialisms, humanism, pantheism (Levine, 1994) and other useful and interesting fields are not taught. And even when they are mentioned, it is often superficial. Questions of human nature are not often discussed within business schools. Personal growth is not emphasised enough. In addition to that, there still exists grading which is a tool for comparison that promotes competition. A student's relationship with a subject is reduced to a number. No wonder some students pursue a certain grade rather than growth. Overall, higher education feels mechanistic, with start and end dates. It feels planned and inflexible. It normalises stress and facilitates anxiety. I have heard countless times from my students, especially those coming from mainstream economics and business backgrounds, that they often had to unlearn what they learned at universities. This should not be acceptable as those humans spend their precious time in universities. What they learn needs to be useful for their personal growth and bringing about a genuinely sustainable society. Naturally, education starts much earlier than when a human being goes to a university. Education for stepping on degrowth paths needs to start in kindergartens where young humans can begin to develop ecological ethics, love and respect towards the self, human and non-human others and nature. It needs to continue at schools. Education needs to allow time for contemplation and have a balance of teamwork and solitary reflections: "in the solitude to which every man is always returning, he has a sanity and revelations which in his passage into new worlds he will carry with him" (Emerson, 2009b, p. 76).

I believe that teaching needs to change substantially and become much less hierarchical. Without exception, students, my fellow humans, are perceptive and talented. Many came into researching business from other academic backgrounds. It is always humbling to hear their perspectives. Some would, like me, weave together their research and own life experiences. When I was an undergraduate student and then a master's student in England, I was discouraged from weaving my personal life experiences with research. These days, as a teacher, I advise my students to do just that, to connect as much as possible their research and their own experiences, observations, feelings, emotions and intuition. Naturally, some would disagree with this. But in my experience, doing this gave me new insights, something I would not have gotten if I were on a different path, that of separating my life and my research.

Shedding hierarchical relationships is necessary. Such hierarchies include, for example, teacher-student, manager-employee. Shedding these hierarchical structures allows one to recognise one's own limits and imperfections, see opportunities to learn from others, including from students. In my field, many students are activists. Many are involved with social movements, alternative organisations or practise sustainability in their everyday lives. They already know and experience a lot of what I discuss with them. They have lived experiences of the theories and concepts I teach. Teaching should not be about transferring knowledge or forcing fellow humans to read certain books, do certain tasks and tests. It is about care, learning together, personal growth. A classroom, especially a traditional lecture hall, seems outdated. Being with nature is a much better setting. Honouring diversity is incredibly important. Group tasks are easier to grade, but they are not suitable for everyone. There is such a variety of personalities that "one task fits all" is not a good approach.

To me, checking what the students have learned does not feel useful. I do not offer quizzes to my students to check if they have memorised something I said during a lecture. I ask them how they feel. If they feel tired, they will not contemplate as much. I ask them how they feel about a particular topic. I do not believe that grading is at all useful. Too often when the students are graded, the task itself turns into an enterprise to fulfil certain criteria and getting a certain grade. The point of doing a task should be learning and growth.

To avoid presenting myself as an expert and taking a higher position in the teacher-student hierarchy, I rely on examples from my own research and from my autoethnography. It helps me highlight how learning is a process, to bring attention to the mistakes I've made, what I've learned and how my thinking is ever evolving. My autoethnography helps me demonstrate how I am, like my students, businesspersons and everyone else in society, on a journey. It shows how practices are raw, ephemeral, changing and sometimes disorienting.

I try to avoid overloading my lectures with information. I prioritise slower pace, deeper and more engaged feedback, talking, contemplating and reflecting. It may feel like a luxury to teach this way. Oftentimes teaching this way resulted in me needing to complete my other tasks in the evenings. This is not something that should be asked from others, so the structures of academic need to be organised in such a way as to support a slower pace, teaching smaller groups, supervising less students per person.

Meaning

Modern business, economics, organisation and management education often misleads humans into seeing the meaning of life in so-called success (material success), career, outcompeting others, in profit, growth in possessions. It does not provide sufficient tools for acquiring and constructing meaning. Changing education, including business education, requires offering sufficient tools in finding meaning elsewhere: in nature, in love towards the world, in simple living, caring for human and non-human others. This should become the core rather than a token or an afterthought. Tools for seeking meaning need to be provided throughout a human being's life. Education has become about getting degrees and stepping into employment rather than constant becoming of a human. I tend to think that meaning can be contemplated more deeply when one has time. Universal basic income is needed to provide people with space for contemplation. Within the current system, it is assumed that to learn something new, one needs to go to a university and take classes. Over the years, students have reached out to me asking which courses and classes to take. Tools for reflection and contemplation need to be already shared before one goes to a university. Personally, I have experienced immense growth in the periods of my life when I could be alone. I was doing my PhD from home. Some evenings and weekends in northern Sweden and southern Finland, especially in long winters, were conducive to reflection, learning and growth. The days when my partner in Denmark had childcare responsibilities, I also could be alone. When I was reading Rogers (1995, p. 15), I felt great affinity with his words:

> I have come to value highly the privilege of getting away, of being alone. It has seemed to me that my most fruitful periods of work are the times when I have been able to get completely away from what others think, from professional expectations and daily demands, and gain perspective on what I was doing.

Such privilege should not be a privilege. It should be available to every human being to facilitate growth.

What humans can do

Genuine sustainability journeys. More businesspersons need to step on genuine sustainability paths.

Walking the path. Deep spiritual transformation comes from "actually walking the path: putting the values and theories into practice, bringing them to life" (Salzberg, 2008, p. 6). Salzberg (2008, p. 6) continues: "The path begins with cultivating appreciation of our oneness with others through generosity, nonharming, right speech, and right action".

More businesses. This may sound controversial in the degrowth discourse, but there need to be more businesses that are based on craft, skill, passions and deep knowledge and small-scale, ecological production. When I contemplate my own consumption, I realise that so many of the objects I live with can be, and are, produced by small, local, independent businesses. Similar products are made by large corporations too. Oftentimes it is easy to buy items that are produced by large corporations. Having small, local and independent businesses nearby makes it easier to practise more sustainable living. Small businesses can also provide a sense of independence and flexibility to humans.

Consumer activism. Pushing all responsibility onto consumers is wrong. As a long-term practitioner of simple living, zero-waste and various practices common within these movements, I understand how difficult it is to practise alternative modes of living. Constraining structures are everywhere, and these structures are something that pre-exists me and my fellow humans. However, I also believe in agency and our capacity to (collectively) transform social structures. I have been writing my autoethnographic notes for some years now. One day, as I was writing my autoethnography, I decided to write down my practices as a simple list. I wrote them down in one go, and initially I had a list with more than 60 practices that I do as a human being, a consumer, in society. I do not expect that everyone else should adopt the same mode of living. Indeed, so many fellow humans live more sustainably than I do in Denmark. And yet, many of those practices could be taken up by even more humans and contribute to transforming various social structures.

When it comes to consumer activism, small, independent, local businesses are not enemies, they are allies. Oftentimes, businesspersons running these businesses themselves are also participants in movements such as zero-waste and voluntary simplicity. These small businesses are often the ones that make various sustainable practices possible. Businesspersons often communicate closely with the customers and have more freedom to adjust their offer or offer something that solves problems.

Business activism. Businesses participate in consumption. That is to say, they source ingredients and materials for their own production. Their approach should be activist, directed at transformation of the structures of production, supporting those producers who care about humans, non-humans and nature and whose care manifests in concrete ways in their practices. Many years ago, I would be sceptical if someone told me that businesspersons can be activists. That was before I actually started to research businesses and having deep conversations with businesspersons. Some explicitly work with activists, call themselves activists. Others do it more gently, but in no less important ways. For example, many talk about gentleness. To me, practising gentleness is a form of everyday activism, though more subtle and nuanced.

Small businesses that are necessary in a degrowth society, are, for example, zero-waste shops, small local farms, businesses specialising in repair (of clothing, electronics, music instruments, bikes), organic textile businesses, small and independent bakeries and cafes.

The way we do science

Better business education. Equating big with successful feels old-fashioned. There are generally so many ideas that persist in business schools and that feel old-fashioned. We know so much more and so much better these days. Ethics should be taught widely and deeply in business schools.

Research. It is essential that we research actual businesses and not simply make assumptions about them and about businesspersons. After my PhD, I wanted to spend as much time as possible doing research and engaging in deep conversations with businesspersons. This meant going down a postdoctoral path, not associated with any project and working on my own most of the time and seeking mentorship in various spaces myself. From a conventional career perspective, it was not the best move, and this is something I understood when I intentionally chose this path and not that of trying to get a lectureship position as soon as possible. A lectureship position would perhaps offer more security, but it would also mean I would not have enough time for research.

Something that helped me to make this choice and feel comfortable with it is seeing my career in a somewhat different way. There is one lifelong career that

I have, that is of spiritual growth. What I do in academia is not a career, it is a space where I can manifest the result of that growth and growing further together with my fellow humans, including my students. Once a businessperson I spoke to in England told me that he saw profit as a byproduct of all other things being right. His words affected me deeply. At that time, I just finished my master's degree in international (conventional) business and finance. I have been thinking about his approach for many years afterwards, and it keeps revisiting my mind every now and again. Over the years, I realised that so-called success was not the goal for me. It was a byproduct. By success, I do not mean jobs, publications or citations per se. What I mean is reaching my fellow humans through my work. And it feels easier to reach businesspersons, students and activists and other fellow humans more generally when my work is based in reality and is easy to understand, rather than abstract, inapplicable to the real world and otherwise unrealistic.

Down-to-Earth environmentalism. Our environmentalism needs to become more down-to-Earth. It is not difficult to imagine perfect degrowth business. After a brief explanation of what degrowth is, businesspersons are no less able to outline a picture of degrowth business than academics in this field. But in reality, no business is a perfect degrowth one and businesspersons are aware of it. Degrowth business is a journey ridden with conflicts.

Learning from each other and one's own experiences. Scholars can learn from businesspersons and vice versa. One can learn from one's own engagement with structures. Researching my own everyday practices is one of the most helpful things that I have done in my academic journey. It is conducive to understanding nuance and constraining and empowering structures within we, humans, exist. The same structures often empower and constrain businesspersons too.

Interdisciplinarity. It is not new or radical to suggest that our efforts in researching the relationship between degrowth and business need to be interdisciplinary. No single science or discipline or even a field such as degrowth can provide all the answers. Interdisciplinarity needs to be adventurous and curious. I notice that it has become almost the norm to see one's own field as radical and truly conducive to human and non-human emancipation, while other fields are seen as not trying hard enough, if not actually working against emancipation. This has often been the case with, for example, circular economy and corporate social responsibility. Many scholars in these fields are genuinely curious about degrowth, so spaces can be created to think together and bring to the surface issues associated with each field. Our attitude to teamwork needs to change. Naturally, there are fields such as mainstream economics, that are not in line with what degrowth is trying to achieve (Buch-Hansen et al., 2023). Yet understanding the arguments of this school of thought can help us understand why, for instance, some policies are in place, why some humans hold beliefs stemming from mainstream economics or honour the unfolding and evolution of economic thought. There are multiple fields that hold and develop useful knowledges. New materialism and deep ecology are such fields.

What is at the heart of scientific pursuits. Apart from interdisciplinarity, the way we do science needs to change in researching degrowth business. Apart from concrete practices, I contemplate principles very often. At times, I think about the principles I live by that make my personal sustainability practices more sustainable. At other times I think about the principles that guide my research. Overall, it feels to me that there is just one principle for everything, and it is love. Love, at the same time, for the self, human and non-human others, and nature. I am aware that it is strange to some to use words such as love in relation to research. With my co-author, we use the word "gentleness" to signify that kind of love, as the word love is associated with love towards human individuals or is used in a casual way to say we love, say, chocolate or an artwork. We placed gentleness and care at the heart of the pursuit of a genuinely sustainable society. It equally applies to how we do science as it applies to all other pursuits. With enormous pressure to publish, oftentimes science is not performed with gentleness and care. Overly broad and dismissive statements are made about seemingly opposing schools of thought, empirical research is often rushed or replaced by merely conceptual research. Research projects are driven by wondering what is most likely to result in granted funding rather than what is most interesting to investigate. Perhaps the responsibility for it should not be placed only on the shoulders of researchers but on the system that nurtures competition and speed and encourages overwork, rather than nurturing gentleness and care. Scientific efforts need to be slow paced and deep, underpinned by contemplations of philosophy of science.

Slowing down. One important learning that Rogers (1995) shares in his book "On becoming a person" is the need he felt not to rush or fix things, to instead listen to one's own and others' experiences. This made me reflect yet again on a processual character of degrowth business and businesses' journeys. The practices, or what businesses need to do, are very well known and clear. It is the process of implementing them and the desire to be present in this process that we need to focus on.

References

Becker, C. (2006) The human actor in ecological economics: Philosophical approach and research perspectives. *Ecological Economics*, 60(1), pp. 17–23.

Bhaskar, R. (1989) *Reclaiming reality: A critical introduction to contemporary philosophy*. London: Verso.

Bhaskar, R. (1998) *The possibility of naturalism: A philosophical critique of the contemporary human sciences*. 3rd ed. London: Routledge.

Bhaskar, R. (2000) *From East to West: Odyssey of a soul*. London: Routledge.

Bhaskar, R. (2008) *Dialectic: The pulse of freedom*. London: Routledge.

Bhaskar, R. (2012) *The philosophy of MetaReality: Creativity, love and freedom*. London: Routledge.

Bonner, E.T. and Friedman, H.L. (2011) A conceptual clarification of the experience of awe: An interpretative phenomenological analysis. *The Humanistic Psychologist*, 39, pp. 222–235.

Bookchin, M. (1982) *The ecology of freedom: The emergence and dissolution of hierarchy*. Palo Alto: Cheshire Books.

Buch-Hansen, H. (2021) Modvækst som paradigme, politisk projekt og bevægelse. *Nyt fokus: Fra økonomisk vækst til bæredygtig udvikling*, 17, pp. 6–9.

Buch-Hansen, H. and Carstensen, M.B. (2024) What kind of political agency can foster radical transformation towards ecological sustainability? *Policy & Politics*, https://doi.org/10.1332/03055736Y2023D000000025

Buch-Hansen, H., Koch, M., and Nesterova, I. (2024) *Deep transformations: A theory of degrowth*. Manchester: Manchester University Press.

Buch-Hansen, H. and Nesterova, I. (2021) Towards a science of deep transformations: Initiating a dialogue between degrowth and critical realism. *Ecological Economics*, 190, p. 107188.

Buch-Hansen, H. and Nesterova, I. (2023) Less and more: Conceptualising degrowth transformations. *Ecological Economics*, 205, p. 107731.

Buch-Hansen, H., Nesterova, I., and Koch, M. (2023) An economics of deep transformations. *Real-World Economics Review*, 106, pp. 42–46.

Buch-Hansen, H. and Nielsen, P. (2020) *Critical realism: Basics and beyond*. London: Macmillan.

Buch-Hansen, H. and Nielsen, P. (2024) *Videnskabsteori i praksis*. Frederiksberg: Samfundslitteratur.

Burkhart, C., Schmelzer, M., and Treu, N. (eds.) (2020) *Degrowth in movement(s): Exploring pathways for transformation*. Winchester: Zero Books.

Camus, A. (2005) *The myth of Sisyphus*. London: Penguin Books.

Collier, A. (1994) *Critical realism: An introduction to Roy Bhaskar's philosophy*. London: Verso.

Coplan, R.J. and Bowker, J.C. (eds.) (2014) *The handbook of solitude: Psychological perspectives on social isolation, social withdrawal, and being alone*. 1st ed. Hoboken: Wiley-Blackwell.

Dufourmantelle, A. (2018) *Power of gentleness: Meditations on the risk of living*. New York: Fordham University Press.

Elgin, D. (2010) *Voluntary simplicity: Toward a way of life that is outwardly simple, inwardly rich*. New York: Harper.

Emerson, R.W. (2009a) *Essays: First series*. Auckland: Floating Press.

Emerson, R.W. (2009b) *Essays: Second series*. Auckland: Floating Press.

Fritz, M. and Lee, J. (2023) Introduction to the special issue: Tackling inequality and providing sustainable welfare through eco-social policies. *European Journal of Social Security*, 25(4), pp. 315–327. https://doi.org/10.1177/13882627231213796.

Fromm, E. (2013) *To have or to be?* London: Bloomsbury.

Gibson-Graham, J.K. (2006) *The end of capitalism (as we knew it): A feminist critique of political economy*. Minneapolis: University of Minnesota Press.

Gibson-Graham, J.K. and Dombroski, K. (2020) Introduction to *The handbook of diverse economies: Inventory as ethical intervention*. Edward Elgar Publishing: Cheltenham.

Gowdy, J. (ed.) (1998) *Limited wants, unlimited means: A reader on hunter-gatherer economics and the environment*. Washington: Island Press.

Gowdy, J. (2020) Our hunter-gatherer future: Climate change, agriculture and uncivilization. *Futures*, 115, p. 102488.

Hankammer, S., Kleer, R., Mühl, L., and Euler, J. (2021) Principles for organizations striving for sustainable degrowth: Framework development and application to four B Corps. *Journal of Cleaner Production*, 300, p. 126818.

Heidegger, M. (2001) *Being and time*. Oxford: Blackwell.

Heikkurinen, P. and Ruuska, T. (eds.) (2021) *Sustainability beyond technology: Philosophy, critique, and implications for human organization*. Oxford: Oxford University Press.

Helin, J., Kostera, M., and Srednicka, J. (2023) Vertical ethnography: Writing the poetics of materiality. *Management Learning*, 0(0). https://doi-org.libproxy.aalto.fi/10.1177/13505076231207940

Jungell-Michelsson, J. and Nesterova, I. (2024) Digging for roots of sufficiency in the food industry: Exploring how ecological embeddedness supports sufficiency in business. pp. 135–154.

Khan, J., Emilsson, K., Fritz, M., Koch, M., Hildingsson, R., and Johansson, H. (2023) Ecological ceiling and social floor: Public support for eco-social policies in Sweden. *Sustainability Science*, 18(3), pp. 1519–1532.

Koch, M. (2012) *Capitalism and climate change*. London: Palgrave Macmillan.

Lawson, T. (2015) The nature of the firm and peculiarities of the corporation. *Cambridge Journal of Economics*, 39(1), pp. 1–32.

Levine, M.P. (1994) Pantheism, ethics and ecology. *Environmental Values*, 3(2), pp. 121–138.

Maslow, A.H. (1943) A theory of human motivation. *Psychological Review*, 50(4), pp. 370–396.

Maslow, A.H. (1970) *Motivation and personality*. New York: Harper & Row Publishers.

Max-Neef, M. (1991) *Human scale development: Conception, application and further reflections*. London: The Apex Press.

Mendham, M. (2010) Enlightened gentleness as soft indifference: Rousseau's critique of cultural modernization. *History of Political Thought*, 31(4), pp. 605–637.

Mumford, C., Holman, D., McCann, L., Nagington, M., and Dunn, L. (2022) Enacting care amid power relations: The role of 'Veiled Care' in organisational life. *Organization*, 29(4), pp. 577–595.

Naess, A. (1995) Deep ecology for the twenty-second century. In G. Sessions (ed.) *Deep ecology for the 21st century*. Boston: Shambhala, pp. 463–467.

Nesterova, I. (2020a) Degrowth business framework: Implications for sustainable development. *Journal of Cleaner Production*, 262, p. 121382.

Nesterova, I. (2020b) *Small business transition towards degrowth*. Derby: University of Derby.

Nesterova, I. (2021a) Small firms as agents of sustainable change. *Futures*, 127, p. 102705.

Nesterova, I. (2021b) Small, local, and low-tech firms as agents of sustainable change. In P. Heikkurinen and T. Ruuska (eds.) *Sustainability beyond technology: Philosophy, critique, and implications for human organization*. Oxford: Oxford University Press, pp. 230–253.

Nesterova, I. (2021c) Addressing the obscurity of change in values in degrowth business. *Journal of Cleaner Production*, 315, p. 128152.

Nesterova, I. (2022a) Being in the world locally: Degrowth business, critical realism, and humanistic geography. *Frontiers in Sustainability*, 3, p. 829848.

Nesterova, I. (2022b) Business of deep transformations: How can geography contribute to understanding degrowth business? *Geography and Sustainability*, 3(2), pp. 105–113.

Nesterova, I. (2022c) Degrowth perspective for sustainability in built environments. *Encyclopedia*, 2, pp. 466–472.

Nesterova, I. (2023a) Being of deep transformations: A personal journey inspired by Clive L. Spash. *Environmental Values*, 0(0). https://doi.org/10.1177/09632719231184615

Nesterova, I. (2023b) Responsibilities towards places in a degrowth society: How firms can become more responsible via embracing deep ecology. *Society Register*, 7(1), pp. 53–74.

Nesterova, I. (2023c) The nuanced practice of degrowth in organisations. *Ephemera*, forthcoming.

Nesterova, I. and Buch-Hansen, H. (2023) Degrowth and the circular economy: Reflecting on the depth of business circularity. *Journal of Cleaner Production*, https://doi.org/10.1016/j.jclepro.2023.137639

Nesterova, I. and Buch-Hansen, H. (2024) Depths of sufficiency in business: Diving through the planes of social being. In M. Gossen and L. Niessen (eds.) *Sufficiency in business*. Transcript: Bielefeld, pp. 83–97.

Nesterova, I. and Jungell-Michelsson (forthcoming) A business of deep transformations is a business of sufficiency. In D. Skrbina, T. Nyfors, and T. Ruuska (eds.) *Sufficiency in nature*. Brill: Leiden.

Nesterova, I. and Robra, B. (2022) Business in a strongly sustainable society? In D. D'Amato, A. Toppinen, and R. Kozak (eds.) *The role of business in global sustainability transformations*. London: Routledge, pp. 201–216.

Page, T. (2020) *Placemaking: A new materialist theory of pedagogy*. Edinburgh: Edinburgh University Press.

Perlman, F. (1983) *Against his-story, against Leviathan*. Detroit: Black & Red.

Phillips, M. (2016) Embodied care and planet Earth: Ecofeminism, maternalism and postmaternalism. *Australian Feminist Studies*, 31(90), pp. 468–485.

Porter, M.E. and Kramer, M.R. (2011) Creating shared value. *Harvard Business Review*, 89(1/2), pp. 62–77.

Robinson, D.W. (1977) The human potential movement. *The Phi Delta Kappan*, 58(8), pp. 636–638.

Robra, B. and Nesterova, I. (2023) The need to align research on economic organisations with degrowth. In S. Russell and R. Padfield (eds.) *A research agenda for sustainability and business*. Edward Elgar: Cheltenham. pp. 217–231.

Rogers, C. (1951) *Client-centered therapy: Its current practice, implications and theory*. London: Constable.

Rogers, C.R. (1995 [1961]) *On becoming a person: A therapist's view of psychotherapy*. Boston: Houghton Mifflin Company.

Salzberg, S. (2008) *Lovingkindness: The revolutionary art of happiness*. Boston: Shambhala.

Schmid, B. and Nesterova, I. (2023) Unearthing intentionality: Building transformative capacity by reclaiming consciousness. *Environmental Values*, 0(0). https://doi.org/10.1177/09632719231175245

Schneider, K.J. (2009) *Awakening to awe: Personal stories of profound transformation*. Lanham: Jason Aronson.

Schneider, K.J., Pierson, J.F., and Bugental, J.F.T. (eds.) (2014) *The handbook of humanistic psychology: Theory, research, and practice*. Thousand Oaks: Sage.

Schumacher, E.F. (1993) *Small is beautiful: A study of economics as if people mattered*. London: Vintage Random House.

Schweizer, H. (2022) On gentleness: Rilke's hands. *Journal of Modern Literature*, 45(4), pp. 77–92.

Sessions, G. (ed.) (1995) *Deep ecology for the 21st century*. Boston: Shambhala.

Spash, C.L. (2011) Social ecological economics: Understanding the past to see the future. *American Journal of Economics and Sociology*, 70(2), pp. 340–375.

Spash, C.L. (2012) New foundations for ecological economics. *Ecological Economics*, 77, pp. 36–47.

Steiner, R. (2011) *The philosophy of freedom: The basis for a modern world conception*. Forest Row: Rudolf Steiner Press.

Stone, D. (1978a) The human potential movement. *Society*, 15, pp. 66–68.

Stone, D. (1978b) New religious consciousness and personal religious experience. *Sociological Analysis*, 39(2), pp. 123–134.

Trainer, T. (2012) De-growth: Do you realise what it means? *Futures*, 44, pp. 590–599.

Tuan, Y.-F. (1974) *Topophilia: A study of environmental perception, attitudes, and values*. New York: Columbia University Press.

Tuan, Y.-F. (1976) Humanistic geography. *Annals of the Association of American Geographers*, 66(2), pp. 266–276.

Tuan, Y.-F. (2008) *Human goodness*. Madison: The University of Wisconsin Press.

van Deurzen, E. and Adams, M. (2016) *Skills in existential counselling & psychotherapy*. 2nd ed. London: Sage.

Wilson, E.O. (1984) *Biophilia*. Cambridge: Harvard University Press.

Index